Tungsten John

for The Harrisons — (if you actually want to use the book, let me know first)

TUNGSTEN
JOHN

*Being an Account of Some Inconclusive
but nonetheless Informative*

ATTEMPTS

to Reach the

SOUTH NAHANNI RIVER

by Foot and Bicycle

*Interspersed with Stories of Research
into a number of startling new FACTS
concerning the dramatic HISTORY of NAHANNI*

by John Harris *"Tungsten"*

(author of SMALL RAIN *and* OTHER ART)

with Maps and Directions *for the Dedicated ADVENTURER by*

Vivien Lougheed *V. Lougheed*

(author of CENTRAL AMERICA BY CHICKENBUS,
FORBIDDEN MOUNTAINS, *and*
THE KLUANE NATIONAL PARK HIKING GUIDE)

New Star Books
Vancouver
2000

New Star Books Ltd.
107 · 3477 Commercial Street
Vancouver, BC V5N 4E8
www.NewStarBooks.com

Design by Cardigan Industries
Printed and bound in Canada by Transcontinental Printing and Graphics

1 2 3 4 5   04 03 02 01 00

*Publication of this work is made possible by grants from the Canada Council, the British
Columbia Arts Council, and the Department of Canadian Heritage
Book Publishing Industry Development Program.*

THE CANADA COUNCIL | LE CONSEIL DES ARTS
FOR THE ARTS | DU CANADA
SINCE 1957 | DEPUIS 1957

CANADIAN CATALOGUING IN PUBLICATION DATA
Harris, John, 1942–
Tungsten John

ISBN 0-921586-70-1

Harris, John, 1942- – Journeys – Northwest Territories – South Nahanni River Valley.
2. South Nahanni River Valley (NWT) – Description and travel.
I. Lougheed, Vivien. II. Title.
FC4195.S6H37 2000   917.1983   C99-910870-0
FI100.S6H37 2000

Dedicated to

the Pitt family – Terri, Gerald,
Natasha, and Alex – the caretakers of Tungsten
and to Alfred Lewis and Bernie Richardson,
last of the old guys

The Ballad of Tungsten John

Boys, it's true I was once like you,
    and many another buck.
I came down here to drink some beer
    and bitch about my luck.
And the amber glowed, and the bullshit flowed,
    'til I fed some to my wife,
And she ran off with half our stuff
    to get herself a life.
Then the kids grew old and the house got sold
    and I was all alone
'Til Viv came by and winked her eye;
    then, brother, I was gone.

Since then, our packs strapped to our backs,
    we've spanned the hemispheres,
From Kazakhstan to Saskatchewan,
    Cote d'Azure to the Azores.
Yes I've pushed my tush through the Hindu Kush
    where Elphinstone met his fate,
I've hauled my ass up the Chilkoot Pass
    on the Trail of '98,
I've dragged my tail down the Inca Trail
    – now there's one thing I know:
I'll hoist my bum to Kingdom Come
    'ere Vivien hollers "Whoa!"

For hers is the code of the open road,
    and the will of wind and tide.
The end of the trail is her Holy Grail,
    and that pass to the other side
She seeks like a knight in armour bright,
    she seeks like a soul denied,

She fights any tether of wind or weather
   that keeps her bound and tied,
and she'll cross that sand to the Promised Land
   – I just go along for the ride.

You'll ask, I know, what makes me go,
   but I'm no philosopher.
I've thought it through, but I'm dumb like you,
   so all I can say for sure
Is there's things that'll shake a man awake,
   and things that'll soothe him to sloth,
For he knows when he goes to a thing that glows
   he'll fall in flames like a moth,
But of all the things that a lifetime brings,
   I swear by the stars above
There's only one that could make me run,
   And, brother, that thing is Love.

Introduction

WHEN VIVIEN LOUGHEED and I shifted our summer wilderness treks from Kluane Park in the Yukon to the Tungsten area of the Northwest Territories, we discovered the best hiking ever. "Ever" includes walks in the Simiens in Ethiopia; the Himalayas in Tibet, Pakistan, and Nepal; the Swiss Alps; the Bolivian and Peruvian Andes; and the Rockies not far from our own doorstep.

For me, the mining roads are the major factor, about 200 kilometres of all-season roads with culverts and bridges. Though many of the culverts and bridges are in rough shape, the roads can still be cycled for great distances. It is possible to cycle to a trailhead with plenty of supplies and then work your way by various passages through the mountains to the legendary Nahanni River.

Then there's another 200 kilometres, roughly, of winter road. These stretches, ploughed through bush, swamp, and creek and originally used only when earth and water are hard as rock, can ease passage and indicate direction.

This book could be dedicated to the bulldozer, the hiker's best friend. Nature, for all her merits, abhors a flat spot, but "Where the bulldozer goes, there go I," I recite to myself, striding along at up to two kilometres per hour or pitching my tent on a beautifully flat piece of ground. The all-season roads go into Tungsten and also touch places like the Flat Lakes, where there are four comfortable cabins. One of these roads sweeps along the cliffs and impenetrable forests along the Flat Lakes, down the Little Nahanni, up Steel Creek and Placer Creek, to the ruined airstrip and mine at Howard's Pass. There it turns into a winter road and meanders beyond Howard's Pass, halfway to Macmillan Pass on the Canol Road.

For me, the way to the Nahanni River is up the all-season road to where Steel Creek flows into the Little Nahanni, then east along the winter road to the Union Carbide exploration site above Lened Creek where (you will learn) the over-zealous prospectors burned all the cabins. I admit my heart failed me when I saw that, and I dragged Viv out, even though we were only a day's walk, much of it treeless alpine, from the river.

For Viv, the way in is straight off Highway 10 (the Nahanni Range Road) above Tungsten, across the Flat River to Mirror Lake, up the valley behind and over to the Rabbitkettle River. From there she'd carry on to Rabbitkettle Hot Springs, where George Dalziel had a trapline, worked in 1937 by Alfred Lewis and Harry Vandaele. Or she'd go over to Glacier Lake, where in 1936 Bill Eppler and Joe Mulholland worked another of Dalziel's lines – and never came out the following spring.

For Viv, given that she must hike, roads or not, the legends evoked by any hike are the major factor in estimating the quality of the hike. In 1984 the river drew her to do a float. After that she could not put down the books and articles that describe earlier voyagers. Raymond Patterson and Albert Faille became her saints, in the shadow of whom I have to live – and believe me, it's not easy. She led me on my historical researches just as she led me through the mountains, and in research as in the mountains, one intriguing view always leads to another.

If we write more about the Nahanni, her focus will be on the enigmatic bush pilot and famed "flying trapper" George Dalziel, who in the thirties traversed the area on foot and then flew many men in to trap or prospect. Some who went in with Dal – like Eppler and Mulholland and too many others as far as the RCMP are concerned – never came out. My focus will be on two, Lewis and Vandaele, who did come out with notable inefficiency, élan, and good humour. Surprising Dal and many others, they became famous (or notorious) as the only men to raft the lower Nahanni at high water and live to tell about it.

Roads, mountains, and legends are always attractive. More mysteriously, both of us love Tungsten too, even if it is only a town. It sits abandoned at the head of the Flat River and near the Flat Lakes (the source of the Little Nahanni River), and is full of the relics of an enviable social life. We have discovered that it is mourned by many of its previous inhabitants, and we know that most people who see the town want it to live again.

For Viv and me, this has become a political cause. We would like to get the boundaries of Nahanni Park expanded to the north and east, thus incorporating the Little Nahanni and Flat Rivers. Tungsten would be the way in. We have sent pleading letters to the wardens and to the Yellowstone-to-Yukon (Y2Y) park corridor people. We're thinking of writing to Canada's prime minister and to the secretary general of the United Nations as well.

We know that such an expansion of Nahanni Park would somewhat adulterate the experience of hiking in the Tungsten area. We know that if Viv were elected mayor and I got the concession for a cappuccino stand at the junction of Highway 10 and the Flat Lakes Road, we'd be grounded all summer. The Tungsten hot springs would be full of tourists; trailers would line up in front of the Recreation Centre. Worse, the park wardens (desk-bound bureaucrats that they are) would have all those useful and interesting cabins, bridges, and pieces of mining equipment removed.

But we can live with all that. What we can't live with is the encroaching inaccessibility of the area as the roads grow over and the town disintegrates. Nahanni Park has always been a "water park," as R.M. Patterson put it. It exists, as he complained, "for the benefit of the few people who can pay five or six hundred dollars for a ten days rush up the river and back down again." Patterson described how hikers who want to see the country must fly in and float down, hiking as they go.

Enough! Faille perceived the answer that Patterson couldn't find. "Tungsten Road is already in at the head of the Flat River," he said near the end of his life. "A road to Virginia Falls would come in from there."

Meanwhile, and even better, there could be a trail. So *vive* Tungsten! Viv for mayor! It's time for us hikers to claim the Nahanni.

Introduction to the Trails

by Vivien Lougheed

THIS AREA IS NOT A PARK, so if you want groomed trails, designated campsites, and available rescue services, these routes are not for you. In this book we suggest that you travel on partially overgrown mining exploration roads that lead to places like the fabled Nahanni River or the abandoned mining town of Tungsten. If you have an explorer's heart and a blockage in your brain against fear, then the Tungsten/Nahanni region offers a ragged range of untrodden mountains and historical sites where the spirits of Canadian heroes still wander.

Although some of this region could be explored with an all-terrain vehicle, I suggest keeping it pristine by either walking or riding a bicycle. Once past the Kilometre 146 washout on Highway 10, where most motorized vehicles cannot or should not pass, there are habitable cabins in which to stay, scenic campsites where you can pitch a tent, and hundreds of alpine passes to explore.

Tungsten itself is out of bounds, but you can enjoy its hot springs, where thirteen individual springs were funnelled through an A-frame by the miners while the mine was in operation between 1961 and 1986. And if, like Tungsten John himself, you like a roof over your head, there is the Canada Day shelter near the springs where you can spend a night or two. Cabins both north and south of the town are waiting for new explorers, and the accommodations at the Flat Lakes are luxurious by any standards.

The surrounding mountains are rugged, forbidding in bad weather but beckoning under the sun. There are abundant berries to pick, and clean water to drink everywhere (except the settling pond at Tungsten).

We have never used purification tablets or a filter for the water and we have never had ill effects. The animals you will see are truly wild because most have never had contact with humans, so they are spooked by our presence. This includes bears, all of whom moved away when we came into their vicinity. However, this does not mean that you should be without an easily accessible and fresh can of pepper spray. And remember: No sex in the wilderness! The resulting smells attract bears.

You must be totally self-reliant and skilled in back-country travel when going into this region. If you have an accident or run out of food, there is no rescue service available nor are there other people close by to give you a hand. Being on your own is part of the adventure but it is also a risk. Note that the trail descriptions often lack distances because we can never tell exactly where we are either on the map or on the terrain.

Good equipment is essential. Rain gear that will keep you dry is a must because hypothermia is always possible. This area has rain almost every day and sometimes all day, with winds to boot. A leak-free tent is another essential to keep yourself warm and dry. You should pack healthy food like dehydrated yogurt (rich in calcium) and bananas (phosphorus) and have huge carbo meals at the beginning and end of every day so that your body will produce the energy you may need in a stressful situation – like crossing the Little Nahanni River. A three- to four-minute glacial crossing can be dreadfully painful for your feet, so you will also need creek-crossing shoes.

Pick your challenge and enjoy. I've written my guide to accompany John's hiking stories. The descriptions of routes and landscapes in those stories are accurate, so the trail descriptions and stories complement one another. I imagine you climbing into your tent each night with this book to read about what happened in the distant and recent past in the place you are at. Usually I read Dickens when I hike, but *Tungsten John* could be almost as interesting.

However, if you feel that this area is beyond your abilities, travel with Tungsten John on the page and leave the landscape to people like Albert Faille, Vandaele and Dalziel, or Lougheed and Harris.

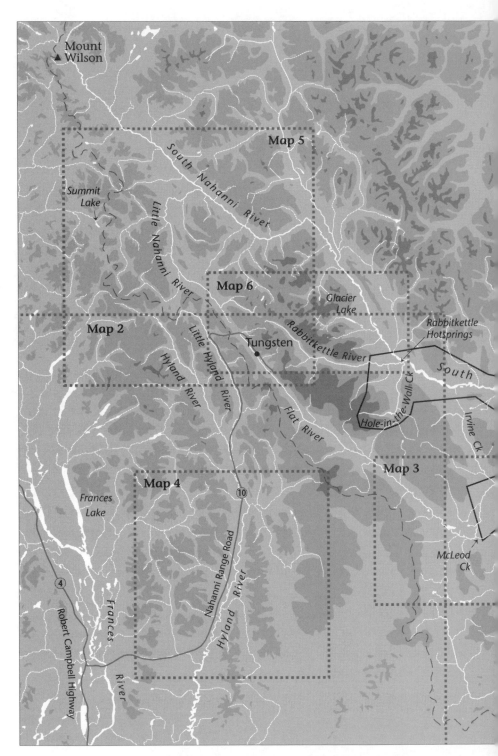

MAP I: THE SOUTH NAHANNI RIVER AND SURROUNDING AREA

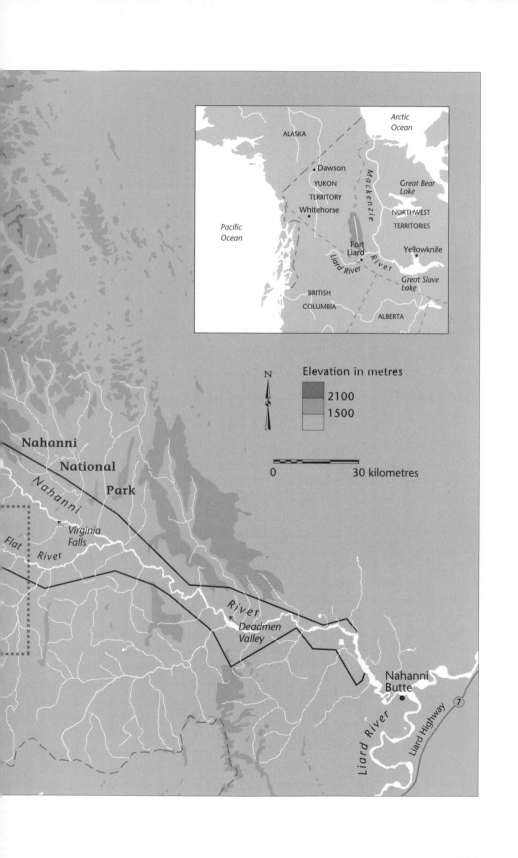

Arctic
Ocean

ALASKA

• Dawson

YUKON

TERRITORY

Whitehorse
•

Mackenzie

Great Bear
Lake

NORTHWEST

TERRITORIES

Pacific
Ocean

Fort
Liard
•

River

Yellowknife
•

Liard River

Great Slave
Lake

BRITISH

COLUMBIA

ALBERTA

N

Elevation in metres

2100

1500

0   30 kilometres

Nahanni

National

Park

Nahanni

Nahanni

Flat

Virginia
Falls

River

River

Deadmen
Valley

Nahanni
Butte
•

Liard River

Liard Highway

⑦

I

The McLeod Mine and Other Mysteries

IN THE SUMMER OF 1995, Vivien and I got the idea of hiking into the South Nahanni River, often referred to more simply as the Nahanni River, as if to indicate that it is not really important to distinguish this mighty flow of water from its much smaller namesakes, the Little Nahanni (a tributary) and the North Nahanni. The Nahanni drains one of Canada's remotest wilderness areas.

We were looking for adventure and a subject for another guidebook, and our idea didn't come out of thin air. Like hundreds, by now maybe thousands, of serious adventurers, among them one of Canada's prime ministers, Pierre Trudeau, Vivien had flown in to the upper reaches of the Nahanni and canoed down the Nahanni to the Liard, and down the Liard to its confluence at Fort Simpson with the Mackenzie. But that was over a decade ago, and though she would often state, vaguely, that the country had "potential," the trip was one she never wrote about and that she would have preferred to forget. She had been, as she demurely put it, "out of her element" on that trip. She had become interested in river canoeing solely for the purpose of doing the Nahanni and, with her friend Joanne, had taken only a few weekend lessons on local rivers before they set out. They had deliberately kept their plans secret from their instructor, a personal friend who would have flung himself in front of their car rather than let them test their limited skills on the Nahanni.

Of course this is the sort of haphazard preparation that Vivien decries in all of her books. And for good reason, as I found out after some probing when Vivien and Joanne returned. They had come very close to dying on the Nahanni. Within two or three minutes of dying. Within a kilometre. They had almost slipped into the chute, from which there is no exit, that sweeps down into Virginia Falls, at 315 feet (twice the height of Niagara) one of the highest and biggest falls in North America. Only the chance glimpse of a piece of coloured board flashing from the trees far across the river, and a resulting flash of paranoia – easy to deny when it's late in the day and you are tired yet determined to put in another hour – made Vivien shout to Joanne at the prow. They backferried across the river to the flagging board and made it, but only just, with Joanne pausing halfway across and shouting, in exasperation, "Why are we *doing* this?" On the other side they found themselves on a small landing-dock at the head of a trail. They followed the trail past a campsite and up a bluff until the shaking of the ground indicated their exact location, and then they returned to the campsite.

They didn't, at that point, want to hazard a look at the falls. Their imaginations were already active enough. In a state of shock, all they could do was light a fire and sit at it, Joanne systematically and silently working her way through half of their remaining supply of scotch, and Vivien desperately throwing more and more wood on the fire in an attempt to get warm. She was also trying to keep herself from breaking into tears whenever she realized what had just about happened and, worse, in terms of her self-esteem, how far out she had been in her estimation of where they were.

The bits and pieces of this story, as I got them, were supplemented by books that Vivien pushed at me, books like R.M. Patterson's *Dangerous River* and Dick Turner's *Nahanni*. She had also, during her preparatory research for the canoe trip, acquired a stack of photocopied materials from the Northwest Territories Division of Tourism. These materials included a copy of an article from the RCMP *Quarterly* entitled "Valley of No Return," which provided a summary of various investigations into the large number of deaths and disappearances that occurred between about 1900 and 1939 on the Nahanni and its largest tributary, the Flat. I went on to read some popular and easily available histories, among them Pierre

Berton's *The Mysterious North,* T.W. Paterson's *Ghost Towns of the Yukon,* Philip H. Godsell's *Pilots of the Purple Twilight,* and Heather Robertson's *Nobody Here But Us.*

It was R.M. Patterson in particular who inspired me, mainly through his descriptions of the Selwyn Mountain country adjacent to the Flat River and through his commonsensical description of, and humourous commentary on, what he calls the "Nahanni legend."

The legend starts with the three McLeod brothers, Willie, Frank, and Charlie. They were the Métis descendants of Alexander McLeod who, in 1823, under orders from Hudson's Bay Company governor George Simpson to expand the fur trade, made the first recorded expedition up the Nahanni. The brothers' father was Murdoch McLeod, factor at Fort Liard, a settlement located up the Liard from the mouth of the Nahanni. As Patterson tells it, the brothers were fascinated by Indian reports of gold on the upper Flat River, close to the Yukon divide. In 1904 they made an impressive and, it seems, deliberately circuitous journey to get that gold. They set out from Edmonton (Patterson suggests they may have sold some furs there or been "working for good wages in order to finance the trip") and took the train to Vancouver. From there they embarked on a coastal steamer, getting it to put them ashore at Wrangell Island, where they bought dogs and supplies, chartered a boat, and got themselves dumped on the frozen Stikine River. They went up the Stikine to a trail that led to Telegraph Creek and through the wilderness of northern B.C. to the Liard River. They crossed the Liard not far from Fort Liard, went up the Hyland and Little Hyland Rivers, and then turned east through the mountains that separate the Yukon from the Northwest Territories. They came to the headwaters of the Flat River, near the present-day mining town of Tungsten, and then they travelled down the Flat to the Nahanni and so on out to the Liard.

On that journey, somewhere on the Flat or possibly on the Nahanni itself, they discovered a rich deposit of gold. They took some of this gold with them, but it was lost in the river.

The following year, Willie, Frank, and a young Scottish engineer named Robert Weir returned to find and work the deposit. Weir ran a riverboat on Slave Lake and had heard about the McLeod find from another McLeod brother, Fred. Fred was the Hudson's Bay Company factor in Fort Providence, NWT. Weir went to Fort Simpson and contacted Willie and Frank, arranging to provide the financing if he could accompany them on the return trip to their mine.

The three men disappeared. The remains of Willie and Frank were found a couple of years later by Charlie, near their cabin on the Nahanni at Meilleur Creek, just below the mouth of the Flat. There was no sign of Weir. Inside the cabin was a note that said, "We have found a fine prospect."

The area where the bodies were found came to be known as "Dead Man's Valley" or (and this is official) "Deadmen Valley." For a time, sensationalist reporters referred to it as "Headless Valley." This is because when Charlie McLeod informed the RCMP of his brothers' deaths, he reported that Willie and Frank's bodies were missing their heads. He also said he was convinced the Nahanni Indians had murdered them.

Here the McLeod legend mixes with another, older legend that goes back to times long before whites arrived in the area. The Slavey Indians spoke of a warlike "people of the west," the Nah'aa, who regularly descended from the mountains to raid Slavey settlements along the Liard and Mackenzie rivers. These people had metal weapons and large hide-boats. The Nah'aa were eventually wiped out by the Slaveys, but stories persisted that their spirits still roamed the mountains, killing any and all intruders. White explorers picked up the idea that these Indians were headhunters, had a lighter pigmentation, and were ruled by a female chief.

Patterson says he first read about these headhunters in *The Arctic Forests,* a book that he picked up on a visit back to England in the winter of 1926–27. This was the book that inspired him to go to the Nahanni; it showed him a water route from the Peace River area where he lived.

According to *The Arctic Forests,* the homeland of the headhunters was a tropical valley, heated by hot springs, where monkeys cavorted in the trees. Stories of this valley are now thought to be the first hints of the existence of the magnificent and extensive hot springs accessible today from the Alaska Highway where it crosses the Liard River. But many people thought the valley was farther north. Among them was Hudson's Bay Company explorer Robert Campbell, whose journal is undoubtedly the source of some of the embellishments that so entertained Patterson when he was reading *The Arctic Forests.* From 1840 to 1852, Campbell traced the sources of the Liard and Pelly rivers. In his journal he mentions actually meeting the dangerous Indians and their female chief. He states that she was about thirty-five years of age when he met her, tall and fine looking, with eyes that flashed like fire. She rescued Campbell's party from a massacre. "She was truly a born leader whose mandate none dare dispute," a grateful Campbell reported.

So the legend grew, impervious to mere fact. In 1906 a party of Indians found another body upstream from where the bodies of Willie and Frank had been found. Police felt these Indians, the Little Nahannis, were "of good repute" and deduced that the third body was Weir's. In 1909 a Corporal Mellor took Fred McLeod in to investigate, and the two men reported that there was no doubt that Willie, Frank, and Weir had starved to death. Their bodies were then scattered by animals. Fred informed Corporal Mellor that his brother Charlie was "given to exaggeration." Case closed.

But Charlie McLeod was not convinced. He decided it was Weir, rather than the headhunting Indians, who had killed his brothers and escaped with the gold. A few years after the murder, Charlie claimed to have tracked Weir to a saloon in Vancouver where Weir was spending large amounts of money. Weir escaped from this encounter, only to be brought again to bay by Charlie at a lonely homestead in Alberta. Confronted by Charlie, Weir confessed to the murder of Willie and Frank. He told Charlie that, since the murder, he had lived a life of remorse, worse torture than anything Charlie could inflict as revenge for his brothers' deaths. He had worked on the railway for awhile and then located a homestead where he could live in wretched isolation.

After telling all this to Charlie, Weir climbed onto a haystack, lit it on fire, and shot himself in the head. Strangely, the contents of Weir's confession did not seem to include the location of the "fine prospect." At least, the prospect was never found by Charlie.

Charlie harassed the RCMP for years with these and other stories. As late as 1929, the RCMP *Quarterly* reports, he dragged some officers to Edmonton's Corona Hotel to confront a man who "couldn't possibly have been Weir in view of his present age and make-up." Another brother (would it have been Fred?) wrote the chief justice of Canada in 1922 to report Weir's return to Fort Providence. It turned out to be a different man.

Charlie also led many expeditions in search of the lost McLeod mine. Independently, dozens of others, some of them McLeod descendents, took up the search too. Many died mysteriously, some possibly due to losing their heads, adding to the Nahanni legend and attracting more adventurers to the area. A dozen men and one woman are reported to have died on the Nahanni in the vicinity of Deadmen Valley. Another half dozen died on the Flat. The list of the dead has become a litany, the mere recitation of which evokes the legend: the McLeods, Eppler, Mulholland, Powers, Hall, Jorgenson, Holmberg, Shebbach.

Patterson came to the area in 1927, bored by post-war London and even by his homestead and horses in the Peace River. The McLeod legend was, he thought, "gorgeous invention," but still it drew him in. Basically, he "liked the life," as he put it, but he also admits that he "hoped to find, buried at the far end of the rainbow, the crock of gold." He also, evidently to the end of his life, according to T.W. Patterson, believed that the McLeod brothers *had* been murdered – and this despite the fact that it was Patterson who first thought to obtain and publish the RCMP report on the deaths (which stated, unequivocally, "death by starvation").

The legend also drew in Albert Faille, the most famous of the Nahanni trappers and gold seekers. Faille was made famous by Patterson and Turner, and then by popular historians like Heather Robertson. It is clearly Faille's personality, as much as his history, that endeared him to people. He was a delightful man. He also exhibited a single-minded determination to find the McLeod Mine, spending the entire last half of his life in a fruitless search. His determination is illustrated in a National Film Board documentary, titled *Nahanni,* of one of Faille's later journeys up the Nahanni.

Faille also exhibited, like Patterson, considerable skepticism as to whether the mine existed. Turner and Patterson believed that their friend merely needed a simple excuse to go up the Nahanni every year. "I'm looking for the lost mine," he would say, just as I often say, when explaining my yearly hikes to my wondering colleagues at the college where I work, "I'm trying to keep in shape so I can collect my pension."

Faille's history suggests that he really was in love with the bush. Raised by harsh foster parents in Pennsylvania, Faille ran away from home at age nine and learned wilderness survival (including trapping) from a tramp.

In his wanderings he drifted ever farther north, into Michigan and then across the border into the Canadian Shield country north of Lake Superior. When the United States entered World War I he returned home to enlist, spending the war in France with the U.S. Forestry Engineers. After the war he returned to Pennsylvania and married a banker's daughter named Marion. However, he seldom lived with her. He drifted to the Canadian bush again, even farther north this time to the Beaver River near Fort Providence in the Northwest Territories. There he felt fully at home. He asked his wife to join him but she refused, and he made his choice: he stayed in the Territories alone. In his thirty-ninth year, Faille moved from Fort Providence to Fort Simpson. In 1927 he made his first trip up the Nahanni, meeting Patterson on the way.

The meeting of Faille and Patterson was a meeting between a hero and his publicist-to-be. Patterson had made his way down the Peace and the Slave rivers, along the south shore of Great Slave Lake to Fort Providence and the Mackenzie River, and down the Mackenzie to Fort Simpson and the mouth of the Liard. He was poling his canoe up the Liard towards Nahanni Butte when Faille picked him up in his motorized canoe. The two must have made an odd pair. Faille was short and stocky and wore pants made out of red wool. Over his years in the area, the local Indians took to calling him "Red Pants." Patterson was thin and well over six feet tall. There are pictures of him in his books. In the pictures he's wearing wire-rim glasses, drill trousers, and dress shirts. A silk scarf is knotted around his neck. He looks like what he was, a banker. But he is a banker carrying a rifle or wearing a backpack, a Stetson, or a holstered pistol.

Despite their differences in background and experience, the two men became instant friends and spent their first two nights on the Nahanni together, sharing their respective stories as well as some laughs over the various elaborate twists of the McLeod mystery. Charlie McLeod, they agreed, certainly could spin a yarn. Faille then showed Patterson how to track his canoe upstream with a double line (a trick that saved Patterson countless hours), and they made their way separately, but encountering and assisting one another at times, up the river.

Faille spent the rest of his life exploring the Nahanni and the Flat. Patterson spent the following winter of 1927–28 in Deadmen Valley, exploring and trapping with his friend Gordon Matthews. Patterson sketched a detailed map that was so accurate in its compass bearings that it was copied over and over by travellers going into the Nahanni. Later the map, along with some notes that Patterson wrote to accompany it, was adapted by the Topographical Survey of Canada as the primary source of information on the area.

In the spring, Matthews and Patterson emerged, rosy-cheeked and loaded with furs. It was a challenge to the ghosts and to the legend-spinners in Fort Simpson. Then Patterson moved on, seeking more rivers to conquer.

Dick Turner and his brother Stan came to the area in 1930 from their father's Alberta farm, victims (or, as it would turn out, beneficiaries) of the Depression. On their way through Fort Simpson they met Bill Eppler, a trapper established up the Liard near Nahanni Butte. From him they picked up their first information about the country. Ultimately they decided to cut short their trip up the Liard into B.C. and stayed in the Nahanni area. They learned how to canoe, trap, and prospect, mostly by trial and error. Their first adventure, described by Turner in *Nahanni*, occurred in 1934. In that year, Dick Turner went into the Flat River country in search of the McLeod mine. His party included Faille and Eppler. They were part of a small gold rush that fizzled two years later, an "episode of romantic buffoonery" that Patterson alludes to at the beginning of *Dangerous River*.

As Turner describes it, the rush was started in the fall of 1933 by Jack Stanier and Bill Clark, a prospector from Fort Simpson. Stanier, in his seventies at the time, was one of the Klondikers who passed through the area en route to Dawson City in 1898. Stanier and Clark claimed they had found, on McLeod Creek, a couple of rotting sluiceboxes, which could have belonged to the Indians or to the Klondikers. Even better, the sluiceboxes could have belonged to the McLeods themselves. Word went like spring virus along the river, around Fort Simpson, and into Edmonton, where the story appeared in the *Edmonton Journal*. A party of local prospectors, including Stanier and Clark, flew in from Fort Simpson in the winter, staked more claims, and flew out again.

In January 1934, twenty trappers from the Liard area went in by dog team, 120 miles one way from Nahanni Butte. Among this group were Stan Turner, Faille, and Eppler. They visited Gus Kraus, a trapper who had flown in and pitched a tent at MacMillan Lake, just above McLeod Creek, so named because it was suspected to be the location of the lost mine. Kraus provided Faille, Eppler, and their partners with some badly needed food. They staked claims and came out.

In the summer, some of them returned by boat. Eppler, Dick Turner, and Ole Lindberg were in one of the boats; Eppler had gotten hold of Patterson's map and description of the river. Turner, Eppler, and Lindberg picked up Faille at Irvine Creek. Faille had been far up the Flat in May, checking out some of the creeks. Somewhere above McLeod Creek the four men had a minor disagreement: Eppler and Lindberg were disappointed with the results of the trip and upset at running out of fine cut tobacco. They wanted out. Turner and Faille, figuring they had come a long way and might not soon be back, wanted to dig more holes. As Turner reports it, he and Faille gave in, knowing that after weeks of isolation, men in small groups can get into serious disputes. Turner bore a grudge though, saying of Eppler that his one problem was a tendency to argue.

Despite his experience in 1934, Turner, like Faille, never gave up the search for McLeod gold. In fact, more than anyone, Turner promoted the legend, adding his own extensive speculations to it. He may have done this because buffoonery loves company or because he was one of the few prospectors smart enough to learn how to make money from the legend. For example, he says in his book that in 1934, at the height of the excitement, he sold two of his Flat River claims to a certain Crombie, publisher of the *Vancouver Sun,* for two hundred dollars each.

Turner got the name wrong. His customer was probably Robert Cromie, who had created the *Sun* in 1917 and turned it into a major paper by the time he died suddenly in 1936, leaving the paper to his sons, Don, Sam, and Peter. If not Robert, any one of these sons (Don in particular, who ran the *Sun* until the family sold its shares in 1963) could have been touring the north in 1934, assuming the title of "publisher."

Later, when Turner ran riverboats and then piloted his own plane, he earned a living primarily by chartering his services out to people who wanted to be floated or flown into the country around the Nahanni. Many of these people were looking for the lost mine, and it was in Turner's interest, and made his job more exciting, to promote the legend.

But at heart he was a believer. Later in his life, whenever he had some money left over from flying people around, he closed shop and he and Faille flew into some likely area to prospect and look for the lost mine.

After Patterson, Faille, and Turner, many others sought the lost mine. Some were clearly trying to gain publicity by attaching their names in some easy way to the Nahanni legend. One of the most prominent of the latter was "Wop" May, World War I flying ace, famous for his roles in downing the Red Baron and then in bringing Albert Johnson, the Mad Trapper, to justice. Johnson himself, under his real name Arthur Nelson, may have wandered down to the Flat from his trapline at Sheldon Lake to find gold and victims, or so writer Dick North speculates. When he was finally brought down, the Mad Trapper had dental gold in his possession. Is this why heads had gone missing? But heads were still going missing after the Mad Trapper died in 1932.

May's Nahanni adventure found its way into *Pilots of the Purple Twilight,* the purple-prose saga of Canada's first bush fliers in the far north: "Blazing still another air trail over the snow-capped peaks of evil omen [May] descended at last on the frozen surface of an unnamed lake considerably west of Dead Man's Valley." May claimed to be following a map that he had obtained from a Father LeGuen, who had been a missionary at Fort Liard when the McLeod brothers went up the Nahanni to re-find their mine. Willie McLeod had indicated the location of the mine on LeGuen's map, and May told newspaper reporters on his return that it led him directly to an abandoned placer mine, the old sluiceboxes, gold pans, picks, and axes still covered by a skiff of snow. A quick test of the creek nearby showed healthy signs of gold. But May produced no gold as evidence, and he either misplaced or hid LeGuen's map. It turned out that other maps were extant, provided by Father LeGuen as well as other contemporaries of the McLeods, and that each of these maps indicated a different location for the lost mine.

It was probably Wop May who flew Stanier and Clark into McLeod Creek in the winter of 1933–34, but the story is confused. In his own account, given to *Edmonton Journal* reporters, May erased Stanier and Clark as important participants. According to May, Stanier, flying with Stan McMillan of Mackenzie Air Services, had made it only as far as Deadmen Valley.

In February 1947, Pierre Berton, working then as a reporter for the

Vancouver Sun, flew into Deadmen Valley. He was ordered to do so by his publisher, Don Cromie. After the war, interest in the Nahanni legend revived, and there was a media rush on the river. Berton found the name "Headless Valley" more colourful than "Deadmen Valley," and he popularized that name. It was a confusing designation as far as Patterson was concerned, since valleys are often said to have heads and cannot easily lose them. Berton nailed a *Sun* sign on an abandoned cabin – probably Patterson's – and flew out again. FIRST INTO THE HEADLESS VALLEY, the sign said. Presumably this amounted to proof that the *Sun* had scooped the story.

Newspaper coverage of the Nahanni was really the preserve of the *Edmonton Journal,* however. Back in the mid-twenties the *Journal* had started running stories about the McLeods and the search for their mine. Patterson describes these stories – with titles like "Dark River of Fear," "River of Mystery," and "Valley of the Vanishing Men." In particular, the *Journal* single-handedly made the "episode of buffoonery" of 1933–36 into an international event.

As early as 1929, Patterson says, the *Journal* articles had gotten to the point where Flynn Harris, the Indian Agent at Fort Simpson, felt the need to publish a statement in the *Journal* to the effect that the McLeods had obviously died of starvation, that their bodies had been scattered by wolves, and that no gold had ever been found up the Nahanni. He was worried about the number of inexperienced whites dying in the Nahanni watershed. Since many of the newspaper stories featured headhunting Nahanni Indians, he was also worried about possible repercussions for the people in his care. Inexperienced white prospectors were likely to lose their heads in another way on first sight of a wandering band of Indians.

Harris's statement, published on 23 December 1929, did no good. The offending articles flared up again in 1933–34, when the "buffoonery" of the Flat River gold rush started. By 1936, near the end of the rush, Harris was desperate. He appealed to Patterson, who had left the Nahanni area eight years earlier but whose pamphlet on "The Flat River Country," with its accurate maps and compass readings, was making him a reputation as a writer and an expert on the area, to help stop "all these damn fool articles."

Patterson didn't react. Only in 1953, when he wrote *Dangerous River,* did he satirize these stories, written, as he put it, by "the eager young reporter, the type ever prominent on the sucker list." Oddly, for Patterson, this is not an incisive analysis. The articles attracted readers, sold copy, and made money. The reporters were indeed "eager" to milk the locals for every detail, no matter how obviously fabricated it was; undoubtedly, the reporters added details of their own. The real suckers were not the journalists but people who came to the Nahanni looking for gold, for a tribe of headhunting Indians led by a giantess, for a tropical valley, and for a lost mine and a river whose banks were littered with the headless bodies of the men who tried to find that mine.

Berton scooped the story for the *Sun* and his publisher – Don Cromie. In that way Berton was "first" into the valley. His articles were reprinted in newspapers across North America and stirred up even more public interest in the area. Berton then collected these articles into the first chapter of his first book, *The Mysterious North,* a 1956 bestseller and the beginning of Berton's career as a popular historian.

And why not now add to these legendary figures not only Vivien and myself, but also a bunch of Vivien's lumpy-legged, granola-sucking, environmentally friendly fans – hikers and cyclists from suburbs and high-rise apartments all over North America and Europe, people more than willing (as we had discovered) to put out a few dollars or Deutschmarks for a Swiss army knife, a colourful Gore-Tex jacket, a Tilley hat, a VauDe backpack, and an accurate description of routes into and through fascinating areas like Nahanni? Who's to say what some of us latter-day adventurers might find by way of enlightenment, adventure, and even gold? Who's to say what stories of privation, intrigue, stupidity, and even murder we could act out (or invent) in such a famous wilderness?

As if we needed any more encouragement than this, the maps told us that there was now a road into the Nahanni watershed. The road, Yukon Highway 10, turned off the Robert Campbell Highway just north of Watson Lake and followed the McLeod route up the Hyland and Little Hyland rivers to the town of Tungsten at the headwaters of the Flat. Just north of Tungsten, a road turned off Highway 10 and followed the Little Nahanni north, halfway to its confluence with the Nahanni. The road was abandoned and evidently impassable due to giant washouts.

Tungsten was abandoned.

An abandoned road? An abandoned *town?* That, of course, clinched the matter. That road was our obvious way into the legend.

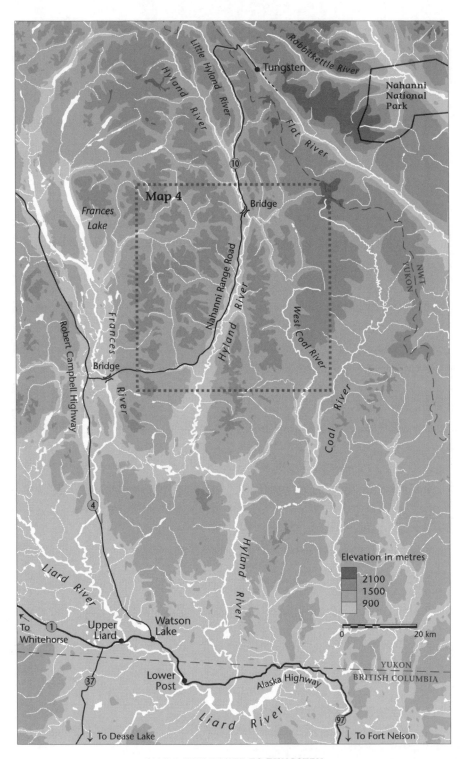

MAP 2: THE ROUTE TO TUNGSTEN

2

Tungsten

As it turned out, the El Dorado dreamed of by the Nahanni
prospectors was not a gold mine after all, but a massive deposit of that
even rarer and more politically strategic mineral, tungsten. The McLeod
brothers probably walked across or very close to that El Dorado, located
as it is on a mountain that stands between the headwaters of the Little
Hyland and Flat rivers. But it was too early in history for the McLeod
brothers to be looking for tungsten.

That didn't happen until the 1950s. Once the deposit was found, a
company was formed and a town was built to extract the tungsten-bearing ore from the mountain. The mine operated until 1986, and then it
and the town, named Tungsten, were mothballed.

The town of Tungsten is, at first acquaintance, spooky.

"This reminds me of *The Omega Man,*" I said to Vivien as we pushed
our bikes up the hill from the locked gates of the town.

"I don't remember it."

"Charlton Heston, I think. New York has been hit by a plague gener-
ated in some medical experiment. The few survivors have turned into
white-haired, red-eyed Luddites who live in the sewers, subways, or base-

ments and come out only at night when they can see. Their eyes are light sensitive. Heston has an antidote that keeps the plague off but can't cure it once you've got it. A scientist with a blind trust in technology despite what it has just done to the world, he hunts down and exterminates the Luddites during the day. Using politically correct, low-tech weapons like crossbows and catapults, they hunt him at night, storming his well-lit stronghold. He fights back with howitzers, machine guns, and (his main weapon) searchlights. During the day, New York is just like it usually is, except no people. Heston plugs along with his submachine gun past miles of parked cars – like those trucks down there – and rows of buildings some with their doors open – like that door marked OFFICE."

"And those other doors across the street."

"But you know that there are people hiding somewhere."

We were glad to have other people with us. One of these people was my son, Wes, twenty-five years old, muscular, five foot eleven, and given to sarcasm – an impulse for which I take no responsibility. He wears his long black hair in a ponytail and is a musician (bass guitar), chemist, and cyclist. Having completed his formal education, Wes was spending his summer deciding what to do with his life, and I was selfishly encouraging him to do what I never would have done at that age – extend the decision-making for awhile. While he was doing this he could, I suggested, join Vivien and me on some adventures. Wes took up our offer, riding his bicycle up Vancouver Island to Port Hardy, taking the coastal ferry north past Prince Rupert, Ketchikan, and Juneau, disembarking at Haines, then cranking his bike from sea-level rain forest up into the alpines of the Yukon. We connected with him at a campsite on the shores of Kluane Lake and hiked for two weeks in Kluane Park before heading east by truck through Whitehorse to Watson Lake and Highway 10.

I was eager to hear what decisions he had come to during his arduous ride.

"I was too tired to think," was all he told me.

The other person with us was my nephew William, only thirteen years old but taller and heavier than Wes. We picked him up at his home in Whitehorse as we were passing through. I had long been promising him an adventure, and I figured that our short and strictly experimental foray into Tungsten would be just right.

Will, too young yet to have a personality, was affectionate and obedient though he had a tendency to pontificate on various topics on which he had been made by his father, my brother-in-law Bob, who really does have a personality, into an expert. These topics were few but inexhaustible: trucks, motorcycles, guns, snowmobiles, jazz, and the merits of eating lots of red meat, preferably in the form of steaks.

A typical conversation between Wes and Will went as follows:

"We should have our motorcycles here." (That was Will.)

"How would we get them over the washout?"

"A four-by-four crew-cab could cross."

"Maybe not."

"Especially if it had a winch on front."

"What would you hook the winch to?"

It was a relief to Vivien and me that Wes was willing to take his cousin in hand, answering his questions and participating in his speculations. Wes was young enough to sympathize with Will and old enough to sympathize with Vivien, whom he knew well as a kind of second mother who, from the time he was fourteen until he graduated from high school and went south, dropped in regularly to make sure I was bringing him up properly, with placemats on the dinner table and cases on the pillows. Wes knew from experience how Vivien was likely to respond to Will's tentative and therefore pushy masculinity. He tried to keep between them. For example, after Will lectured Vivien for the third time on the evils of washing cast-iron frying pans (we carried one in the truck for roadside camping), Wes, fearing an explosion, took Vivien aside.

"You have to remember that Bob didn't have a mother," he told her. "He was raised entirely by his father, and Bob's created the identical relationship with his own son."

Vivien, a child-care worker and so normally a sucker for psychological explanations, nodded wisely. But she also knew Wes. "That could actually be true, smartypants, but if you hear him ragging me about the frying pan again, especially while *I'm* washing the dishes for the third time in a row, get him away from me before I whack him with it."

Wes drove the first lap from Whitehorse to Watson Lake, with Vivien and me up front and Will stuffed into the back of the truck with all our equipment and supplies. Then I drove, with Vivien and Will up front and Wes in the back. I pulled over after an hour, though, pleading drowsiness. Actually, I was afraid Vivien was going to blow up. Will was explaining how all the evidence that red meat causes a build-up of cholesterol was fabricated and publicized by the American chicken lobby.

"Doesn't your dad have heart trouble?" Vivien inquired.

"Aneurism. Nothing to do with cholesterol."

I volunteered to ride in the back, but Vivien intercepted me as I figured she would, abandoning the cab with the eagerness of a cat let out of a cardboard box. Wes resumed driving.

Will had noticed, however, that Vivien was upset about something.

"She never had sons," said Wes. "She doesn't understand men at all, right, Dad?"

"Dead on."

Will seemed relieved. He launched into a monologue on airbrakes. I really did get drowsy then and succeeded in sleeping all the way to Watson Lake.

There, a fellow pumping gas at the Esso station told us that Highway 10 to Tungsten was still washed out. "Only big trucks and heavy equipment can cross."

Rumour was that the townsite, after sitting silent for eight years, was finally being dismantled and removed.

"Last summer I saw one of the town's generators going down the road," the fellow continued. "Later, I saw the town's fire truck heading out."

"They're selling off stuff?" I asked.

"It's too bad," he said, shaking his head. "I was never there but they had a great hockey team. The Flat River Rats. I saw them beat the crap out of our team once." Then he brightened. "But I heard we went up there later and beat the crap out of them."

At a hotel coffee shop we studied the local telephone directory and considered visiting the trucking companies listed therein to ask about trucks going to Tungsten. Maybe we could hitch a ride through the washout. Will favoured this move, thinking that maybe the ride could extend all the way to Tungsten. And maybe all the way back too.

"No way," said Wes. "I want to cycle that road."

Vivien and I agreed. We would have to experience the road firsthand before we could recommend it to cyclists. We decided to simply drive up and look for ourselves. The runoff was still high, so we doubted there would be trucks. We figured we could find a wide, level place somewhere on the creek above or below the washout where we could carry our bikes and supplies over.

The Robert Campbell Highway, Highway 4, runs west and north through mostly uninterrupted bush and muskeg clear across the Yukon from Watson Lake to Carmacks, which is on the Alaska Highway north of Whitehorse. The Robert Campbell is a favourite with the less competitive of the Winnebago crowd, people less interested in miles per day than days per mile, people who want to get out of their machines and do things, like fish. Such people love the empty but well-maintained campsites on big fishing lakes like Simpson, Frances, Finlayson, and Little Salmon. Some of them even make their way up Highway 10 as far as the abandoned government campsite at kilometre 87, perched on a beautiful knoll where the road meets the Hyland River.

An hour out of Watson Lake we made our first contact with the ghost world of Tungsten. The Yukon government has placed a big wooden sign at the junction of Highways 4 and 10:

In 1959 the Canada Tungsten Mining Corporation was formed to develop the rich deposit of scheelite which had been discovered 125 miles north of here, past the Northwest Territory border. This immense deposit of tungsten-bearing ore is the largest in the free world. Located at the headwaters of the Flat River, the area was remote and difficult to reach, with a primitive landing strip providing the only means of access. In 1961 an aerial reconnaissance was carried out, and later that year, without any further survey work, construction started on the Cantung Road, as it is commonly called. Funding for the project was provided by the company and the government, and construction was completed in 1963.

"Some chemist must have written that," I said to Wes. "What's 'scheelite'?"

"Calcium tungstate, after Karl Wilhelm Scheele, one of my heroes."

"He discovered the stuff?" asked Will.

"That and much else. He was probably first to isolate and identify oxygen, too, but he was a Swede and away from the centre of things, so he didn't get credit."

"What's tungsten used for?"

"Don't you read? Every drill bit that you buy comes in a package that says the bit is made out of tungsten. It's for hardening steel."

"I knew that," said Will.

"It's also used to make lightbulb filaments," said Wes. "Its chemical name is 'wolfram.'"

"Why?" I asked, perking up.

"I have no idea."

"The only wolfram I know is Wolfram von Eschenbach, author of *Parzival*, one of the early versions of the Grail legend. Maybe Scheele figured that the Holy Grail must've been made of the same enduring stuff."

"Sounds like a weak connection. Wouldn't he have called it 'graillite'?"

"*Some* chemists read poetry."

We turned northeast onto Highway 10, the Nahanni Range Road. The Yukon government does all it can to warn motorists off Highway 10. A kilometre-long string of signs indicates that Tungsten is closed, that the bridge decks are dangerous, that there is no food or gas, and that the road is washed out. As if to reinforce the message, immediately, before anyone gets too far up the road, the bridge over the Frances River sports a plank deck spotted with gaping holes. Next are the road signs, shot full of high-calibre bullet holes or lying face down on the roadside like fainted sentries or gone altogether. Finally, the bush in places has occupied the shoulders of the road, so that even at slow speeds it seems as though you are hurtling through a tunnel.

"I can't believe that the McLeod brothers came this way," said Vivien, observing the heavy bush on either side of the road.

"Were they tracking canoes up the river?" I asked.

"The books don't say."

"I wonder where they actually veered off and went over the mountains into the Northwest Territories."

"We'll probably never know."

"Unless we find some of their stuff," said Will.

"Keep your eyes peeled."

· · • · ·

WE CAMPED AT the government campsite perched on the knoll above a sweeping curve of the Hyland. The site is marked on the Yukon road maps, but we weren't sure it would actually still be there. The campsite featured a dozen neat sites with preserved-wood picnic tables and iron firepits with grills. The woodsheds were full of cut wood that was serviceable though pulpy. A slightly tilted WATER sign pointed to a path, strewn with windfall and partially erased by a gravel slide, that led down to the river. The campsite also featured a picnic shed with a large wood heater, and two sets of outhouses, sheathed with aluminum to ward off porcupines.

One set of outhouses had toilet paper, and, in the MEN'S, right above the toilet paper, was some graffiti, a pencilled message: *Johann Felix Allgaier/Watson Lake-Tungsten-Nahanni/By Foot/1990.*

I brooded as I sat there. Who was this guy? Did he really *walk* all the way from Watson Lake? That sounded quixotic; he would be using up time he might need to make it into the Nahanni and out again before winter. I decided to keep an eye out for any further traces.

We cooked some thick steaks and sweet onions that we had picked up in Watson Lake, a mandatory hit of fat before leaping off into the bush and a week of fat-free, dehydrated food. It was also a gesture of good faith towards Will, and it comforted him considerably. He even accepted my washing the frying pan, on the grounds that it would be sitting in our truck at the washout for a week and could, if it smelled, tempt a bear to dismantle our canopy.

Of course his preferred solution was to mount a shotgun in the back of the truck with the trigger wired to the tailgate so that any invader would have its (or his/her) head blown off.

After eating and washing up we slid the tables aside and pitched our tent in the picnic shed, throwing some big logs in the heater to fend off the night chill while we slept.

The next morning, just before the bridge over the Hyland, we noticed a cabin to the right and stopped to check it out. In the stove I found a note, dated 10 October 1990, penned on a water-stained paper napkin.

Vivien was amused. "What were you rooting in the stove for?"

"Messages like this," I said, waving it at her, "are always left in stoves. They're the only place in wilderness cabins that are sealed off from rodents, and they're the first places visitors are going to check into."

"I never know when you're kidding me."

"I grew up with that," said Wes.

"Me too," said Will. "I still remember when he told me that the word 'Timbits' came from Tim Horton's fatal car crash. They carried Horton's body off the 401 into the nearest donut shop and the customers looked up and said, 'Timbits.' Boy did I feel like an idiot when I told *that* to my friends."

I sat down at the kitchen table, hauled pen and paper out of my shirt pocket, and started copying the note. Curious, Vivien looked over my shoulder.

"I know who that is!" she suddenly exclaimed. "He stayed with Joanne."

"You must be kidding."

"I'm sure it's him. He was from Germany. I never met him myself, but a few years ago he arrived in Prince George and found Joanne's name on a list of people willing to host foreign travellers. She put him up for three days – way over the limit. Joanne mentioned that he talked a lot – raved actually – about the Nahanni. He was so vehement that Joanne was afraid to tell him that she'd canoed the river lest he fall down and kiss her feet."

Evidently Felix was, in Joanne's opinion, the sort who would have trouble setting a mousetrap let alone route-finding in the bush. In the course of his stay at her place he had shorted out her coffeemaker, flooded her bathroom, and lost the key she had given him so he could come and go while she was at work. The lost key had resulted in a broken window when Felix forced his way back into the house. Joanne paid to have the window fixed, and Felix assured her that he would send her the money when he got back to his job.

"Did she get it?"

"Yes, but somehow he got the decimal one digit closer to the dollar sign than it should have been."

It seemed from the note that Felix had, in 1990, made a serious attempt to walk to the Nahanni. It also seemed that he hadn't actually completed his journey and had written the note on his way out. He wrote that he had run out of food a few days before and so had eaten some oatmeal and dried soup out of the cabin. He planned, true to the northern code, to return the food should he ever come back again to, as he put it, "reach the Nahanni." He pointed out that he had fixed the stovepipe, which had been (and now was again) lying on the floor, and that he had put the door back on its hinges (but it too was lying on the floor). He mentioned that at the time of writing there was already six inches of snow and that the temperature was dropping to minus 10 Celsius at night. He said he was dragging his supplies and equipment on a toboggan that he had taken out of an abandoned cabin near Tungsten.

In short, at the time he pencilled his note, Felix was in trouble. However, we had seen no human remains on the way in and heard no rumours of any deaths on Highway 10.

If we misunderstood him and Felix *had* succeeded in his attempt to get to Nahanni, and if he happened to be a writer and went on (on his return home) to write up a book, it would probably not affect the sales of any book by Vivien. The story of Felix's attempt at Nahanni would not be the sort of guide anyone who had some intention of surviving the adventure would want to read.

"He didn't have to worry about the oatmeal, anyway," said Wes as we left, propping the door up behind us. "There's a big, unopened bag of it in the top cupboard."

By noon we were standing on a pile of gravel and looking down at the washout. During some previous runoff the unnamed creek had taken out a hundred yards of road and three culverts, each one big enough to drive a truck through. The culverts were scattered in the bush below, looking like convulsed tapeworms. The snout of one of them protruded from the edge of the bush, so we climbed into it and discovered that someone had camped on a patch of level sand just inside. A sheltered spot. Felix? It *felt* like Felix. But there was no message, only a fire ring, a burnt-out sardine tin, some leftover wood, and a clothesline suspended on some bolts.

On the other side of the creek, some distance down the road, a yellow bulldozer slept, radiating the heat of the sun. The dozer was obviously used to maintain a smooth grade into, across, and out of the stream. Such attention would constantly be called for, judging by the heavy footfalls of boulders making their way downstream.

"A four-by-four crew-cab could cross," said Will.

Wes looked skeptical. "That water's fast and at least four feet deep."

"Just open the doors and let the water through."

Vivien wandered off downstream, disappearing behind the twisted culverts. I followed, worried as usual that she was not hollering to indicate her presence to bears – a very important safety precaution near creeks – or that she might try to wade across the washout without telling us. It looked like someone had used the dozer to create an alternate crossing downstream, where the creek was wide and flat. However, the side opposite us was a muddy hill, too steep and unstable for truck traffic.

"We can walk across here," said Vivien. "I'll go over first and make a fire. You guys bring all the stuff down. You three will have to do the packing; it'll be all I can manage to get across."

"Why not wade over and start up the dozer?" asked Will. "They always leave the keys on them somewhere."

"That would be theft," said Wes.

"Who's to know?"

"The owner would trace us once he found his engine seized or his hydraulics wrecked."

"Bet I could drive it easy."

Vivien was already halfway back to the truck.

"We'll each need a staff to lean on," I said as we followed her. "I'll get the saw."

Two hours later we were across, dried out, warmed with instant soup, and cranking our mountain bikes slowly northward, brushing through great circular colonies of wild poppies. We enjoyed the warmth of the sun and the quiet after the freezing cold and the roar of the washout. We each had a moderate load – full panniers front and back holding tents, clothes, sleeping bags, and enough food to last a week. Vivien and I set a slow pace, as we always do, having learned to savour our summer days in the bush, that sudden (albeit carefully engineered) disappearance of most of civilization behind a veil of mountains and history. We watched the Hyland Valley open out, the trees thinning, the hills on both sides streaked with snow and dotted with browsing caribou.

"Jesus," said Vivien. "This *is* pretty."

"A good road, too," said Wes as he drifted ahead of us. Will tried to follow close but soon gave up.

"If I had my Honda here I'd be in Tungsten by now," he said when we caught up to him.

"That's a good idea for next year," I replied. "Figure out some way to get it over the washout."

"Bring a chainsaw and find some big trees further up. Drop them across the creek."

"We'll check for trees when we get back. You could also line it across on a skidder tire tube."

"Right on!"

It was peaceful, though for awhile we found it to be an eerie kind of peace. On this side of the washout the road looked like it was still plugged in to civilization. The road signs here were more intact. We were warned to slow for curves and for equipment that might be working just ahead. At one point a ghost road crew had set out their portable signs, telling us to slow down and proceed with caution.

Not far from the washout we found a cabin, situated about 200 metres east of the road in a stand of spruce. The only indication of its existence was a cleared path off the road, which Wes, by that time out of sight ahead of us, had taken the time to explore. The cabin was open and the calendar on the wall was from 1985. A bronze trophy on a shelf told us that the cabin's former occupant had won a tug-of-war competition in that year.

I noted the cabin as a good place to stay if we got wet or cold on the way back. The roof was rotting through in one corner, but otherwise the building was solid.

Much farther along we saw our one sign of real, contemporary residency in the form of a hunting guide's log cabin, again just off the road in the hills to the east. This cabin was securely boarded up with a NO TRESPASSING sign nailed to the front door. Just past the cabin, farther along the road, was a gravel pit, no doubt created when the road was built. It held, in one corner, a corral for the guide's horses. In another corner was a flat-topped stove made out of an oil barrel, and some empty plastic-pipe spools flipped onto their sides to make picnic tables. In a third corner was an outhouse. A busy creek rushed along one edge of the gravel pit and passed under the road through a culvert.

Will parked his bike and inspected the outhouse. "Rotten," he said, then stepped into the bush along the edge of the clearing.

After setting up camp, we sat under an endless, red-streaked, northern sunset, sipping our instant cappuccinos while supper bubbled in the pot.

The next morning drizzled rain, so we got onto the road without loitering over coffee. The road swung east now, with the Little Hyland far out in the open valley to the northwest. The rain picked up as we started our climb to the Yukon-Northwest Territories border. I immediately got off my bike and began to plod upwards. Vivien and Will looked over their shoulders to see where I was and then followed suit. Wes was visible on a switchback far ahead, cranking steadily upward.

The road ascended the north side of the pass. The pass itself was bushy and strung with ponds and small lakes, some of them maintained by beaver, though clearly their supply of scrub willow and dwarf birch was almost depleted. By midafternoon we were at the top of the pass on the territorial border, and the weather was clearing.

Wes was sitting on a large boulder, rain gear spread and drying on the road. He had the binoculars and was taking in the details of the panorama spread below. "There's a cabin on that lake due east of here," he said.

Vivien hauled out the contour map. "That's Mirror Lake," she informed us. "Down below us is the Flat River. Looks bushy down there, but isn't the lake beautiful!"

Emerald green from glacial silt, Mirror Lake drains boisterously into the Flat River. Above the lake hangs a glacier, and directly behind the lake a valley leads up to what looked to us like a circular ridge.

"That could be an access to the Nahanni right there," said Vivien, pushing her finger across the contour map while looking at the ridge.

Wes looked at me sympathetically, handing me the binoculars. "At least you'd have a cabin at the start and end of the trail."

But how good a cabin? Just the edge of the cabin roof was visible above the stand of spruce that clustered at the west end of the lake. It was impossible to tell how much of the rest of the cabin had survived the porcupines. Also, there was no sign of a road or trail going from the Flat up along the creek or anywhere else on the adjacent hillside. Getting from Highway 10 to the cabin would involve two or three hours of bushwhacking hell.

"Those are the Ragged Mountains," said Vivien, "separating the upper Flat from the Nahanni."

"They're aptly named," I said, tracking the binoculars up the ice-rimmed, sandy red pinnacles beyond Mirror Lake.

Will picked up his bike and started down the hill at full speed.

We followed, coasting through scrub forest into the Flat River Valley, keeping our eyes firmly on the road ahead so as to avoid washouts, sinkholes, and the many boulders that had rolled down onto the road from the hills above. We swung south and then had to brake suddenly and hard at a junction. There, the unnamed road or trail we had noticed on the map turned north and carried on past

WES HARRIS CYCLING ON HIGHWAY 10

the Flat Lakes, along the Little Nahanni River, and beyond – far beyond, halfway to Mount Wilson near the headwaters of the Nahanni. Someday we would have to follow that road, but that was something to consider over future campfires.

Much more important now, because we were cold, damp, and hungry (having contented ourselves, as we do when it rains, with trail mix and cold water), was a shack that peeped the peak of its roof above the willows near the junction. It turned out to have everything but a door and windows. It was actually near new, with a stack of dry, clean, two-by-four cuttings out back under a sheet of roofing tin. There was a grill sitting beside some rocks in the centre of the driveway. We put the grill across the rocks for our fire and then, since the rain had begun to spot down again and there was the ominous sound of thunder from the other side of the pass, we covered the fire with roofing tin and spread our foam mattresses and sleeping bags on the shack floor.

I gravitate to shacks, though often, as Vivien points out, they are less comfortable than tents. Tents keep mosquitoes out and are cleaner. In rain, however, there's nothing cozier than a shack, particularly one with a solid

WILL ON THE PASS THAT MARKS THE
BORDER BETWEEN THE YUKON AND
NORTHWEST TERRITORIES. MIRROR LAKE IS
IN THE BACKGROUND.

roof that resonates to the tune of cold water that cannot drip on me. Usually Vivien humours me in such situations because drying out a tent in order to pack it can be difficult. In the rain, it involves spreading a tarp up over a fire and being a human clothesline for an hour. And drying a tent over a fire can destroy the tent's water-proofing.

"Maybe the guy who built this place discovered the lost McLeod mine somewhere up this creek," Wes speculated later that evening as we lay in our sleeping bags.

"Maybe he was going to sell hamburgers to people going in and out of Tungsten," said Will.

"Or cappuccinos," I added.

"Or red wine," said Vivien.

The steady rhythm of rain on the roof washed us to sleep. When we awakened, the morning was clear. We cooked porridge, which Will refused to eat.

"I'm sick of this stuff," said Will. "We're putting out lots of energy. We should be eating bacon and eggs."

"Too heavy and hard to carry," said Wes.

"How about cornflakes?"

"Too bulky. Anyway, you probably don't like powdered milk."

"You got that right."

So Will glumly ate his daily limit of two granola bars with his coffee. Then we broke up camp and set out for Tungsten in high anticipation. According to the contour map, the eight kilometres was almost entirely downhill.

The Flat River here, in its narrow valley, meanders south like an

English brook. We poked our noses into an abandoned house, a much more elaborate shelter than our small one at the junction. It featured a wood heater, a couple of unmade beds complete with pillows, a pile of dusty dishes in the sink, a number of *Playboy* centrefolds stapled to the walls, and an open but full bag of coffee in the cupboard.

"We could've stayed here," said Will, eyeing the centrefolds. "This is a better cabin."

"This coffee isn't that old," said Vivien, sniffing it before she stuck it back in the cupboard.

On the way out I noticed a mud-plastered plastic wagon with a long stick tied to the handle, stuffed upside down under the cabin's porch.

As the road levelled out with the river we caught glimpses of Tungsten through the trees. We were surprised at how big it was. We checked out a windowless building made of heavy timbers and featuring a padlocked steel door. A sign on the door said EXPLOSIVES: NO SMOKING.

The Tungsten town gates were only a kilometre farther along the road.

IMAGINE TUNGSTEN, population 800. Imagine it nestled on the side of a big mountain, from the mist-shrouded upper reaches of which come messages in the form of snowslides; bouncing, car-sized boulders; and the various but always foreboding sounds of intestinal upheaval. That mountain has a grudge against Tungsten, and no wonder.

High on the mountain is the original open-pit mine, an alpine valley turned into a black scar. A switchback road leads to it. Below the open-pit mine is the rust-red ventilation unit for the newer underground mine. Below the ventilation unit, a little above the upper edge of the town, is the underground mine's concrete portal, a structure reminiscent of entrances to the pharaohs' tombs.

A two-lane paved road inside the mountain leads one kilometre due west to where it intersects with the ore zone. Off that road, to the right, there is a large storage area not far from the mine portal, and then, a couple of hundred metres on, an underground shop. The road ends at the face, a vast cavern, but two tunnels swing left out of the face area into an exploratory tunnel that follows the ore zone in a northwesterly direction for a few more kilometres.

The mountain has been gutted.

APARTMENT BUILDINGS AT THE TUNGSTEN TOWNSITE

Up close, the town is not pretty. Too many galvanized steel buildings, a grey-gravel settling pond the size of four Olympic pools, and two or three acres of rusting equipment stored on the flats along the river blot out one of the world's great views: straight down the valley of the Flat River.

To hold the town, four terraces were gouged into the side of the mountain, above and parallel to the Flat River. The terraces were pinched together so the roads on them join at the town's north and south ends. It looks as if the buildings went up first and then most of the space in between them was paved. Roads, parking lots, and front and back yards are generally one expanse of pavement.

On the top or fourth terrace, near its south end, are three identical, brand-new, three-storey apartment buildings. The apartments boast a view of the solid wall of glacier-hung peaks across the Flat. Just south of the apartments and facing south, overlooking the settling pond and that magnificent view of the Flat River Valley, are the two large houses of the mine management, positioned on a circular cul-de-sac.

On the third terrace, below the apartments, are three large townhouse units on the west side of the road, facing fourteen steep-roofed bungalows set close together in two staggered rows. North along that road are two two-room school buildings, one on each side. There are playgrounds around the school building on the west side of the road. Farther north, also on the west side, is a medical clinic. On the other side of the road, facing the clinic, is the rear entrance to the recreation centre, the largest structure in town except for the mill. The recreation centre squats over the third and second terrace. The rear entrance of the recreation centre leads to the bowling alley and the bar. At the north end of the third terrace is the mill, a giant steel building that also squats over the third and second terrace.

On the second terrace, starting at the north end, is the mill, with a half dozen steel buildings clustered in front of it and beside it. These buildings include the mechanical shop, some warehouses, and the building housing the two locomotive-size generators that feed electricity and steam to the mill and town. Across the road from the mill is the main office. Moving south, the eighty-bed dorm on the west side of the road faces the cafeteria on the east side. Then the front of the recreation centre, on the west side of the street, faces an older dorm and the fire station. On this level the recreation centre has two entrances – one at the north end that leads into the library, travel agency, gymnasium, and Olympic-size pool; the other at the south end leading into the grocery store. South of the recreation centre, all on the west side of the street, are some duplexes and the front yards of the bungalows.

The first terrace holds a road from which the back ends of the main office, cafeteria, and old dorm can be reached. Opposite these are some warehouses and lots for parking machinery, trailers, and building supplies. The road on the first terrace continues south around the settling pond to the airstrip, baseball diamonds, picnic site, and hot springs.

Now imagine that town deserted, silent. Imagine the streets buckled by frost heaves that are pushing the six-foot-in-diameter, galvanized-steel service tunnels, with their steam pipes and electrical cables, to the surface. Imagine the covered stairways collapsed due to the snow load of many winters. Imagine the shaking tables and mixers in the mill coated with rust. Imagine the luxurious furniture of the rec centre spotted with grey mould, and the ceiling tiles and gyprock in the eighty-bed dorm buckled and collapsing due to water leaking from the roof.

Imagine entering that silent, disintegrating town. You've just ridden your bicycle along Yukon's abandoned Highway 10, the last eighty kilometres of which are impassable except by foot, bicycle, or heavy track vehicle. You arrive at two white metal gates that are chained across the road and padlocked. A sign near the gates is obviously intended to be intimidating: THIS COMMUNITY AND MINESITE IS SHUT DOWN AND PATROLLED BY SECURITY STAFF. POSITIVELY NO ADMITTANCE THOROUGHFARE NOR SERVICES OF ANY KIND AVAILABLE.

Intimidating or not, you ignore the sign. Didn't you read, back at the start of Highway 10, that the road was built partly by the Yukon government, and aren't you therefore fairly sure that the mining company can have no right, legal or moral, to keep you, a taxpaying Canadian, from the South Cantung hot spring you have heard about or read about in the *Northwest Territories Data Book* or *Hot Springs of Western Canada?* Anyway, you are tired from cranking over the high pass that joins the Yukon and the Northwest Territories. You have stripped down countless times and strapped on thongs to shoulder your bike and bags across washouts. You are damp because of the thunderstorms that seem endemic in the area. You badly need to soak in that hot spring, so you are willing to take a chance on Tungsten's security staff, if there is such a thing.

You lift your bike over the gate. The road leads you up a hill, past a pumping station on the Flat River below, and beneath a row of trucks, vans, and rusted mining machines parked along the edge of the repair shop's yard, their back ends hanging over you.

At the top of the hill you can go down to the first terrace, on gravel, or proceed over pavement on the second terrace. Naturally you pick the pavement; after eighty kilometres of gravel, it feels like a dream, even with the frost heaves. But first you obey a sign on the building beside you. The sign says, in faded lettering, MAIN OFFICE: ALL VISITORS MUST REPORT.

And don't you feel foolish when you *do* report, after noticing that the door is propped invitingly open, to nothing more than an empty counter and a half-dozen empty desks?

So you return, a bit spooked, to the main street, and start south into the silence. But wait! What was that flitting past that open space between the apartments up on the fourth level? A kid, it looked like, almost, on a bicycle. Couldn't be. Probably the shadow of a raven or eagle circling the upper part of town. But now that you think of it, didn't that look (from some distance) like a fishing rod propped over the river by the pumping station, and wasn't that a child's toy bulldozer in the dirt where the office must once have sported a flower garden? Were those pickup trucks, angle-parked here and there along the street, actually left like that when the town was abandoned? And aren't you constantly aware now, as you coast farther into the town, of a steady hum, more a vibration than a sound, as of a well-muffled or subterranean electrical generator?

"Wow," said Wes, pulling to a stop and pointing to a row of glass doors to our right. "This is some building. And it looks near-new."

As we were looking at the building, we heard the sound of an engine starting. The sound turned into an unmuffled roar, and a red crew-cab pickup truck swung out from around the edge of the building and charged towards us. The truck squealed to a stop as we scrambled to move out of the way. We saw the surprised faces of the three men inside the truck. They rolled down the windows. There was an awkward moment on both sides. We were fishing for some excuse for being there. They seemed embarrassed at having almost run us down.

The driver, a tall, thin man in his mid-thirties, grinned. "We're not used to traffic," he said. Stepping out, he introduced himself, shaking hands all around. "I'm Gerald," he said. "Throw your bikes in the back and get in. Company policy is that any visitors have to be chaperoned through the townsite. It's not safe to wander around here."

We drove to the machine shop. The two other men in the truck, Dwayne, a heavy, clean-cut, younger man, and Dexter, who looked to be in his sixties, lean and stooped with a scarred face, clambered out and set to work crating hundreds of bathroom cabinets. Then Gerald drove back to the end of the main street, turned down and proceeded around the settling pond, out and across the airfield, past a baseball diamond, and up to a large, fully enclosed picnic shed in a grassy field beside a creek. The shed had a porch along two sides and was painted bright yellow with green trim. Some of its wooden shutters were swung upward and hooked to the porch ceiling.

"You can stay here," said Gerald. "The creek water's good. It's also warm. Over there's the hot spring. No doubt you've heard of it. Most of our visitors have." He indicated a silver A-frame nestled at the base of the mountain on the other side of the creek. "Just go back out of here and around the baseball diamond. You'll see a road; it crosses the creek on a culvert. Another thing – we'll be busy over here the next couple of days. You'll hear a plane coming in sometime this afternoon. When you hear it, get over to the terminal and I'll take you into town to meet the family. I figure you'll have questions too, so I'll answer them then. Remember: no wandering around town. I know the temptation's great, but it's dangerous." Gerald shook his finger at us for emphasis before he got back in the truck and drove away.

"Poor John," said Vivien. "The biggest junk pile ever and he can't root through it."

"I don't really have the urge. It's *too* big. Maybe I'm intimidated. I envy Gerald, though. Look at all the fun things he gets to do, and all the equipment he has to do it with."

"I wonder if a guy could get a summer job here," said Will.

"The young guy, Dwayne, looks like he could be a student," said Wes.

We opened more of the shutters on the picnic shed, rearranged the inside tables, and put up our tents not far from the space heater. Wes found a stack of pulpy but dry wood amongst some raspberry bushes along the road and brought some pieces inside. Then we headed for the hot springs, stopping for photos of the baseball diamond and bleachers.

"Field of Dreams," said Vivien, planning her captions.

The narrow road from the baseball diamond crossed the lightly steaming creek, then passed some change rooms, a hot-dog stand, and a large outdoor swimming pool with a sundeck, diving-board, and moss-covered intake/outflow pipe. The pipe must have been closed off sometime after Tungsten was abandoned; the pool had only about two feet of water in it, and that water was covered thick with algae. Vivien posed on the diving board for slides.

The road then ran along the base of the mountain to the silver A-frame. Inside was another change room and then the pool. The water was clear, without the faintest sulphur smell. The pool could hold six people, soaking comfortably in about two feet of water. Boulders had been placed in the pool to serve as seats. Light entered from a plexiglass window in the back wall. The water ran steadily in from under the change room and out the back wall into the creek. The pool had been created at the very source of the spring.

We stripped down to our underwear and climbed in.

"A perfect objective for a perfect bike ride," said Vivien contentedly.

"This place is a book," I said.

"Maybe," said Vivien. "We'll have to come back and do the road north to the Flat Lakes and Little Nahanni River. I'll ask Gerald about it."

We were in the pool for two hours, periodically dodging outside to cool off. Then Will said, "I hear a plane."

We dried off and dressed, moving outside as we did so we could watch the plane. An antique DC 3, it buzzed the airstrip once, circled above the town, buzzed the strip again, turned around, and then came in to land. As we were cycling out onto the airstrip, a strange assortment of people appeared on the ground, walking in circles, gawking at the mountains and the hanging glaciers.

"You're not Gerald?" a uniformed man, evidently the pilot, asked, or asserted, as we pulled up on our bikes. He was addressing himself to me.

"No. We're visitors like you."

"Where did you come from?"

"The hot springs over there," I said, pointing.

"That's right!" squealed an anorexic, Mexican-looking girl in halter-top and jeans who was standing at the pilot's side. "They told us there were hot springs." She looked at Wes. "Hey guy, if I get my bikini, maybe you could show me the way."

"On my bike?"

She smiled. "However you know how." Glancing over her shoulder at Wes, she moved towards the plane.

"Me too!" squealed an equally anorexic black girl, also in halter-top and jeans.

"Everybody stays here!" boomed the pilot. "We were instructed to wait at the plane until the caretaker shows up."

"Why?" asked the black girl. "Do you think he's going to drive past the Starship Enterprise? Like he's not going to see this thing here on his runway?"

The pilot gave it a moment's thought. "Bears," he said.

Both girls stopped in their tracks. "No way!"

A blonde young man with a golden tan and neatly trimmed beard, wearing a safari shirt and pants with knee-high socks and hiking boots, nodded at the girls. "Of course there are bears. Didn't you look down? Didn't you see the bush?"

A squat, ancient, Indian man approached. He wore a battered leather cowboy hat, a beaded leather vest, ragged jeans, and moccasins. "Lots of bears in this country," he said to the girls. "Big ones."

"So how about Captain Kirk taxis us over *there?*" whined the Mexican girl, pointing across the airstrip in the direction from which we had just come. "What's the use of standing around *here* by these old shacks? I'm cold."

"Me too," said the black girl. "Or maybe Moses could mumbo-jumbo the bears and they'd, like, go away."

"Yeah. A bear dance, Moses. A *disappearing* bear dance."

"Bears were people once," said Moses. "They decided that talk was foolish, and lived alone. They grew fur and learned to sleep through the coldest months. They're very smart, smarter even than us, so you should always say good things about them, and you never, never step over their shit."

"These people are really weird," said Will in my ear.

"Have you seen any bears?" the Mexican girl asked Wes.

"Nope."

"See!" she shouted at the pilot.

"But they are around," said Wes. "See that pile of black stuff on the runway over there. Bear poop. Will here rode his bike right through it, so he's in trouble. We all carry pepper spray for protection." Wes pointed at the spray holster attached to his belt.

"Ohh. I'm sticking with you."

"You just spray yourself and the bears stay away?" asked the black girl.

"You spray the bear."

A convoy of three red, crew-cab trucks suddenly appeared from around the base of the settling pond and proceeded towards us along the runway. Gerald, driving the lead truck, pulled up, jumped out, nodded at us, and shook hands with the pilot. While they talked, Vivien and I rolled our bikes over to the second truck. Dwayne rolled down his window.

"What's going on, Dwayne?" Vivien asked through the open window.

Dwayne grinned. "These folks are from New York," he explained. "They arranged with head office to come up here to model fur coats for a catalogue. A chopper will be coming tomorrow morning from Watson

Lake to take them up to the glaciers. We're supposed to house them in one of the management residences and see that they don't get into any trouble in the townsite."

"Does this sort of thing happen regularly?"

"No – o," said Dwayne. "But we have seen some strange things over the years."

"Like us?"

"Oh no. You look normal," said Dwayne, smiling. "You're the first to come in on bicycles, though, which has got Gerald worried. The strangest visitors are the Europeans."

"With canoes, right?"

"Yeah. The Flat and the Little Nahanni are like magnets. A few years back Gerald heard two planes fly in unannounced. The planes were gone by the time he got here, but a half-dozen people, all of them wearing buckskin, a couple in coonskin hats if you can believe it, were over there along the bank of the river sorting stuff and loading three kayaks."

Dwayne paused to glance at the models, who emerged on the gangplank lugging their suitcases. "I wonder if girls like that would be just maybe a little bit interested in what it's like to snuggle with a guy who weighs 250 pounds," he said.

"That's the spirit," said Vivien.

"Anyway, Gerald figured that maybe these people in buckskins didn't know much, and the Flat is a tough river, class four in places. He told them about two Swiss guys in buckskins who drowned in the Nahanni just below the Flat. It didn't sink in. Finally he convinced them to get into the hot spring pool over there, which we still maintained back then, and try their technique in case of a roll. That did it. We had to drag them out of the pool. They gave us their buckskins and pushed off. Apparently they made it. Then there was this German guy walking to the Nahanni River."

"Felix!" I said.

"He's a friend of yours?" asked Dwayne, surprised.

We were interrupted by Gerald. "Bring the trucks over and load up the baggage they're bringing out."

Dwayne backed his truck towards the DC 3. Dexter followed suit. We parked our bikes on the porch of the terminal, helped with the loading, and then piled in with Dwayne. The Mexican model, hugging her make-up kit, stuck right by Wes. A photographer and one of the male models squeezed in beside us.

Dwayne continued talking where he had left off. "Then there was an interesting bunch who dropped in to canoe the Little Nahanni, not knowing that the Little Nahanni starts twenty K north of here out of the Flat Lakes. Gerald refused to drive them and their stuff up to the lakes, even though they got desperate and offered him hundreds of dollars. It's not part of his job description. In fact, it's probably a violation of his job description, though he's too paranoid about it if you ask me. I would've taken the money. So they had to radio Watson Lake for a plane, fly out to Watson Lake, then come back in to the Flat in a floatplane."

"That must've cost thousands," I remarked.

"What's that thing hanging around your neck?" the Mexican model asked Wes.

"An Ethiopian ear pick."

"A what?"

"For cleaning out your ears."

"It looks like a tiny spoon. Is it real silver?"

"It is. Viv sent it to me from Africa."

"I thought you were doing cocaine, in very small amounts," said Dwayne.

"Sorry," said Wes.

Our truck roared around the base of the settling pond and raced to the top level of town, into the cul-de-sac with two large houses set across from one another. In the centre of the paved turnaround area was a picnic table. A young woman and two children, a girl who looked to be about ten years old and a small boy, were sitting at the table.

"Gerald's wife Terri," said Dwayne as he wheeled around the picnic table. "Those are his kids, Natasha and Alex. Their favourite hobby is running me ragged."

"You live with them?"

"Me and Dexter have rooms in the basement of their house over there. Terri cooks for the whole crew."

"How did you end up here?"

"I was born here."

Dwayne pulled up beside Gerald's truck in front of one of the houses

– the one "activated," as Dwayne put it, for the visitors from New York. Dexter followed closely. The unloading began, but slowly, the models dickering over who was going to get what room. Vivien, Wes, Will, and I walked over and introduced ourselves to Terri.

"Gerald told me you came in on bicycles," she said. "That's a first."

"We're checking the place out for a cycling and hiking guide," said Will importantly. "Auntie Vivien writes guidebooks."

Vivien frowned. She generally doesn't like to tell people what she's up to when she's researching a book. The appearance of a guidebook about an area can be like a rezoning, and sometimes the locals take offense. But Terri seemed interested.

"We got bikes!" said Alex. He jumped off the picnic table and ran around behind his house.

"It's still broken," said Natasha, watching her brother with only the vaguest interest. "Dad started to fix it, but the models came. I'd really like to watch the models. Do you think we can go to the glacier with them?"

"Maybe," said Terri. "Gerald will be interested in your books, Vivien. We've been trying to convince the mining company that this place has recreational potential."

Alex reappeared, dragging a new bike. The derailleur was hanging loose from its control wire. "It's broken," he said.

"Let's have a look," said Wes. "Maybe we can fix it. Do you have some tools?"

"We got a whole garage. We got tons and tons of tools! We got lifters and welders and everything!"

"Let's go!" said Will.

"Dad got new parts too," said Alex.

"The repair shop is out of bounds," Terri said to Alex. "So is the parts warehouse. Show Wes the tools and stuff in the shed over there."

Wes, Will, and Alex took the bicycle and went around behind the house.

"Why doesn't the company want tourists here?" asked Vivien.

"This place isn't safe. They're afraid someone will be hurt and they'll get sued. They want us to keep people out. We keep telling them it's impossible. *It's a public road,* we tell them. Then they make deals to let people *in,* like this bunch."

"Dwayne was telling us about some of the people who have turned up."

"You wouldn't believe it," said Terri, shaking her head. "The worst was this German guy named Felix, who almost got Dexter killed."

Gerald emerged from the model's house, came over to the picnic table, and sat down. He took his hat off and ran his fingers through his hair.

"How're you doing?" he asked Terri.

"Beat," she said. "You?"

"Yes."

"I put on coffee for everyone," said Terri.

Vivien stood up. "I'll get it. Where is it?"

"Just inside the front door. You'll see it."

"These people are working on a cycling and hiking guide for this place," said Terri.

Gerald nodded. "I thought I recognized Vivien," he said. "She was on television, right?"

"The show was *On the Road Again*," I said. "CBC. Twenty minutes about her travelling in Guatemala and hiking in Canada."

"Remember?" Gerald asked Terri.

"Yes I do," said Terri. "We watched it last winter, back home in Red Deer. She takes the host, Wayne Rostad, on a hike, but he's a smoker and almost dies."

"Hoo boy," said Gerald. He ran his fingers through his hair again. "I don't think we're ready for a guidebook."

Vivien came out with a tray of styrofoam cups full of coffee, with packages of cream and sugar.

"The jig is up," I said to her. "They know who you are."

"And you're going to write a book about this area?" Gerald asked.

"Don't know yet," said Vivien, "but this place certainly has potential."

"The Cirque of the Unclimbables is just over there," said Gerald, arcing his arm back in the direction of the Nahanni. "Every year people come in by chopper or floatplane to climb there. It's supposed to be perfect rock. You could backpack into it from here and save a thousand bucks. There are hundreds of kilometres of mining road and trails for bikers and hikers."

"We go fishing too," Natasha burst in. "It's not like Red Deer at all. Here, you *always* catch a fish, sometimes even without anything on your hook. The Flat Lakes are the best. We got a canoe there and there are mattresses in the bunks."

Gerald continued. "There are a half dozen lakes, all within a few miles, teeming with trout and grayling. You can canoe or kayak the Little Nahanni or the Flat from here, and come out in the South Nahanni. There are cabins everywhere – four on the Flat alone. The hunting is great."

"Don't get him started on that," interrupted Terri.

Gerald ignored her. "Sheep hunters fly into the Flat Lakes regularly, from August to October. They use the big cabin at this end of the lake and go straight up into the alpines above Zenchuk Creek. Then in town here you've got the hot springs and plenty of accommodation."

"Not to mention a gym, a curling rink, a bowling alley, and an Olympic-sized swimming pool," said Terri.

"And spelunkers could explore the mine," I said. Gerald frowned.

Alex came shooting out from behind the house, jumping the curb into the turnaround and circling wildly around the picnic table. "It's fixed, it's fixed!" he shouted.

"Look at the model," said Natasha, nudging her mother and pointing.

The black model had emerged from the other house. She had a Walkman tapedeck in her hand and earphones on her head and proceeded to twist her way, responding to some rhythm that we couldn't hear, to the edge of the road overlooking the town and the valley. At the edge she gyrated back and forth, a strange figure against that immense backdrop of mountains.

Wes and Will came out from behind the house. They stopped and stared at the model.

"I've gotta go to bed," said Gerald. "I'll get Dwayne to drive you folks to the picnic site. That'll be a good excuse to get him away from the models before he goes crazy. Come up in the morning for coffee. We can talk more about this guidebook."

"I can see it now," I said, looking at Vivien. "Banff of the North."

"That's a good caption," said Vivien, hauling her notebook out.

"I'd like to ride down the Flat as far as the road goes," I said to Gerald.

"I'm with you," said Wes.

Gerald nodded. "It's a good road. We go there for wild strawberries. It goes past the landfill to the lumber mill, where they cut timbers for the mine.

There's a house and some other buildings there, right on the river. I haven't been down there for years, so if you see anything unusual, let me know."

"If they were logging there, that would mean skidder trails."

"To tell you the truth, I've never noticed."

Gerald rousted Dwayne out of the models' house and we got into his truck. The black model, still gyrating against the backdrop of glaciers, waved.

"So you know Felix," Dwayne said.

We explained how we had found Felix's note in the cabin by the Hyland River bridge and how we figured that Felix, on his way to Tungsten, had stayed with a friend of ours in Prince George.

"If he got to that cabin, he probably made it out," said Dwayne. "I was wondering about that. I was thinking of killing him myself, but I figured he'd do himself in. Probably his type never does. It's the people who might be with him or around him who would die."

"Like Vivien's hero," I said, "Sir Richard Francis Burton, Nile explorer."

"You sound jealous," said Wes.

"And worried," added Will.

"Nobody's died on me yet," Vivien said.

"Terri told us that Felix just about killed Dexter," said Wes to Dwayne.

Dwayne nodded. "Sort of, but that's not hard to bring about, as Gerald and I have discovered. Dexter's none too swift. Too many years in the pits. Too many fumes. One time Dexter ran into a wolverine in the gas station down on the second level. The wolverine must've been trying to nest in there because he wouldn't move. Dexter tried to immolate the fucker with a can of gas. That's why there's no gas station anymore and Dexter's kinda blotchy and short on facial hair.

"But in this case, with Felix, Dexter wasn't at fault. He was on the upper level in the loader, happily moving a small dirt slide, one of his all-time favourite jobs. He saw a face looking at him from inside one of the apartments. He freaked and rammed the loader into the cement footing at the entrance to the covered stairway down to level three. Luckily we were at the house and heard the crash. We found Dexter out cold on the ground; he'd gone clear out the side of the loader, taking the door with him. When he came to he told us about the face. He was sure it was a ghost, though, some partner of his who'd died right beside him when the rock exploded in some mine back east. We went into the apartment, Dexter stepping on the backs of my feet, and there was Felix, all his stuff spread out on the broadloom. The silly bugger had even crapped into the toilet when it was obviously dry. I got to clean that one up."

"What did Gerald do with him?"

"That was the hardest part. The little fucker was really persistent. We started by throwing his stuff into the truck, dumping him at the gate, and telling him to stay out. Next thing we know we're down in the machine yard welding a snowplough and somebody looks up and there's Felix on a raft going past us on the river. The stupid bastard even waves at us. 'Holy shit!' yells Gerald, and we're off in the truck, trying to intercept him at the bridge. But he's under and gone around the bend by the time we get there. We figured he was heading down the Flat, so Gerald radioed the police and told them, but they weren't going to do anything. It's a free country, etc. Good thing they *didn't* do anything, because two weeks later Felix turned up at the picnic site. Terri was jogging around the airstrip and met him as he came lurching out of the bushes. She just about blasted him with her pepper spray. He was on a makeshift crutch, hobbling around, browsing on berries. Turned out he'd jumped off his raft at the creek that flows out of Hole-in-the-Wall Pass; he was hell-bent to get to Rabbitkettle Hot Springs on the Nahanni. But he sprained his ankle up at Hole-in-the-Wall Lake, near the hot springs there."

There was a pause as Dwayne pulled up by the picnic shed.

"Dexter and I were for whacking him on the head and dumping him in the river," Dwayne continued, popping the truck into park and sitting back heavily in his seat. "We figured he'd disappear under a log jam, or they'd find him at Nahanni Butte and assume he'd flipped off his raft, hit his head, and drowned. Gerald wouldn't go for it. Not in his job description. So Felix got some food from Terri and stayed at the campground. I was supposed to run him out when I left for school, except he hobbled off. Gone. A few days later the game warden at the Flat Lakes, Stefan, radioed in and told us about this guy staying at one of the cabins up there and fishing without a licence. Gerald asked Stefan to put Felix on his quad and bring him down on the Friday before Labour Day so I could take him out to Watson Lake. No way Felix would come. So Stefan started feeding him. Stefan's a lonely guy, a trifle bushed if you ask me. Goes around armed to the teeth with a switchblade in his pocket, a Bowie knife strapped to his leg below the knee, and a sawed-off shotgun slung from his shoulder. Says he's always being attacked by bears and stalked by Indians. But he's some kind of European, so maybe he and Felix could talk."

"Indians?"

"There's an old story around here about the Nahanni Indians, that they like to take the heads off isolated white guys. The thing is, there aren't any Nahanni Indians in the area except for a few big, strapping bucks with brand-new four-by-fours and rifles. We're forever dragging them out of the washout. You'd be more likely to lose your head by surprising Stefan in the bush. He's very fast with the sawed-off shotgun. If you end up at the Flat Lakes, don't walk up to Stefan's shack without making a lot of noise is my advice. Anyway, it seems that Stefan spent September trying to talk Felix out of heading up Zenchuk Creek and over onto the Rabbitkettle River. Too late in the season, and Felix's ankle was still tender. Finally it started to snow, and Felix appeared at Stefan's door, thanked him for all his help, had a coffee, took the gift of a case of sardines, and disappeared into the snow dragging all his shit on a sled."

"Do you think he'll turn up again?" asked Vivien as we exited the truck. "He seems like the determined type."

"I hope not. Gerald's got enough trouble around here. At least, he *thinks* he does."

THE NEXT MORNING, we awoke to the sound of the chopper coming in.

"This place *is* New York," said Wes over his porridge.

Wes and I headed south on the road to the lumber mill, and Vivien and Will rode into town, Vivien to talk to Gerald and Will to watch the chopper and maybe get a ride on it.

The mill road was a good one, and as Gerald said, it was carpeted with wild strawberry plants. We ate our fill and then explored the rifle range – the building was a long lean-to with a wood heater and wooden shutters, hinged so they dropped out and down so the shooters could practise and stay dry and warm. The mill site was between two creeks, the first dammed just above the road by beaver. Along with branches and mud, they used scrap lumber and ends left over from the mill. The mill itself was gone, but between the creeks and right on the Flat River was a two-bed-room house in fair shape, with a fully furnished kitchen-living room. Farther along a road that circled off the main road and up the first creek we found what looked like a barn that had been converted into a bunkhouse. The main road crossed through the second creek, down which ran a num-ber of plastic water hoses. These would have taken water into the house.

Various Flat River travellers had obviously sheltered in the house. The garbage can was full of pieces of nylon rope and dried-out fibreglass patching kits. There was a stack of dishes in the drying rack in the sink.

"We'll have to cross that creek if we want to check for skidder trails," said Wes.

The creek was cold, fast, and about knee-deep.

"Some other time," I said. "By the time we get back, it'll be close to dinner."

"Sir Richard Francis wouldn't have worried about that."

"I know. I've got a tough row to hoe."

"But I have to be frank with you, Dad. You're a hell of a lot more inter-esting now that you're with Viv."

"Thanks, son."

Crossing the airstrip on our way back, we noticed Gerald's truck turn in to the road to the hot spring. We arrived back at Gerald and Terri's place to find everyone in a panic.

"The black model's gone," said Vivien, giving us cups of Terri's end-less supply of coffee. "She was due for a shoot an hour ago and they can't find her. They can't hold up shooting so they're using the guy models now. Moses said she wanted to go to the hot springs but no one would go with her. She got angry and took off, still wearing the hundred-thou-sand-dollar fur coat."

"So you talked to Moses."

"A story in himself. He told me he lives in the Bronx and makes a liv-ing as a stage Indian on Broadway. Says if it wasn't for Dan George he would've been in *Little Big Man.* Said he's registered a claim to Manhattan Island."

"Maybe you should interview him."

"I already thought of that, but he charges, and pictures are extra."

Gerald's truck pulled in. He, Dwayne, and the Mexican model slid

out. Terri came out onto the porch of the house and looked questioning-
ly at Gerald.

"Her bikini's on the line outside the pool, but she's nowhere around."

"She was interested in that gym you guys got," said the Mexican
model. "She's crazy about aerobics."

"She thinks she can use the gym?"

"Can't she?"

Gerald groaned. "We'd better start looking in town," he said.
"Dwayne, go into the house and round up all the flashlights with battery
packs."

"If we have to do this, we'd better split up into teams or it'll take
another day," said Dwayne as he walked towards the house.

"Jesus," said Gerald to Terri.

"It's not your fault," said Terri. "You told them it wouldn't be a good
idea to let such a big party come in."

"You guys mind helping?" Gerald asked Vivien.

"Of course not. You were talking about giving me a tour of the town
anyway."

"I'll take Wes and Will and do the apartments on the upper level," said
Gerald as he distributed the flashlights. "Dwayne, you take John and
Vivien and search the recreational centre. We'll assume for now that she
wouldn't go into the mill. Too scary. Dexter, you get the pilot out of the
house, if he's sober enough, and cruise the streets and the road up the
mountain. Keep in touch by radio."

We searched until eight that evening. We didn't find the model but we
did see the town. Wes and Will reported that the apartments were nice;
all the furniture was gone, but the appliances – stacked washer-dryer
units, electric stoves, and refrigerators, all matching colours – were still
hooked up. Nice carpeting. Will noticed that the names of occupants
were still on the button boards in the lobbies.

"Freaky," he said.

The rec centre was huge, cold, and gloomy. Our lights penetrated the
dark cavern of the windowless gym. The bar was dimly lit, light coming
through plastic sheets tacked high on the back walls of the adjacent curling rink.

"That whole back wall is phony," said Dwayne as we trooped past, pointing our flashlights into any dark corners. "We built it a couple of years ago, after a snowslide took out the real back wall. We have to keep the animals out of these places or we have a mess on our hands."

Dwayne didn't think the company would fix the wall permanently. In public, the word was that the town was mothballed and would be opened again when the price of tungsten went up. Word in private was that the company would keep the lease up indefinitely in order to avoid the cost of removing the town and cleaning up.

"There's an even bigger tungsten claim on Macmillan Pass on the Canol road up by Mount Wilson," said Dwayne. "It's close to the surface, so that's where they'd really want to dig."

In the bar, the chairs were pulled back from the tables, and some of the tables still held ashtrays, glasses, and jugs. On the edge of the counters sat trays of beer glasses. Colour photos of the hockey and curling teams hung on the walls, the teams' trophies prominently displayed.

"The Flat River Rats," I read, remembering the gas jockey at Watson Lake. They looked scary alright.

The grocery store was the same, some lonely cans and packages here and there on the shelves, paper bags scattered near the tills.

"It's like people left in a hurry," said Vivien.

"They sort of did. The union pulled a strike and was immediately locked out. The workers were given a day to pack and leave. Then the gates were closed for the summer. The pickets came and went from Watson Lake and patrolled up by the Flat Lakes turnoff, with a tent city down by Divide Lake. Everybody was having a great time. But in the autumn, after management closed and mothballed the town and flew south, some of the miners came back in and ransacked the place. There's furniture and other shit in every lonely cabin between Watson Lake and Mount Wilson."

"Were you here during the strike?"

"Oh yeah. It was great. School was suspended for May and June and didn't start up again in September. We couldn't go in and out of town by the road; it was controlled by the strikers. So we got to do a lot of flying. Then one day it started to snow. Dad and the others turned off the generators and removed the control panels and some other stuff, and we all got on the planes and left. Next spring, Gerald was sent in with a team of workers. My dad had been transferred to Vancouver, but he came up every year to check on Gerald. I made a few of those trips. Then about three years ago I started coming up here in the summers to earn my tuition."

"An interesting job."

"Only at times like this."

At eight o'clock, with everyone gathered around the picnic table, an obviously nervous Gerald ordered Dwayne to drive the road north to the Flat Lakes road turnoff. Then Gerald went inside to radio the police in Watson Lake.

Wes and Will went with Dwayne. They were back in fifteen minutes, with the model. They had found her in the cabin just outside the gates, the one with the *Playboy* pin-ups on the wall. Dwayne marched her into the house to turn her over to Gerald.

"We saw smoke coming out of the chimney," said Wes. "It seems she met this guy in the hot spring. He invited her to his cabin for coffee. They were there when we pulled into the driveway, but the guy heard us and bolted out the back door with a big pack."

"You saw him?"

"No. She told us."

"There were two cups on the coffee table, and a fire in the heater," said Will.

"What does she mean, a guy? What was this guy supposed to be doing there?"

"He told her he lived here."

The model came out of the house, Gerald and Dwayne following.

"You were supposed to be on the glacier," said one of the cameramen angrily.

"I thought I was done!"

"We didn't get you with Moses, remember?"

"I thought I was done."

Gerald and Dwayne were heading for the truck.

"You'd better come too," said Dwayne as he passed. "I think you'll find it interesting."

"What?"

Dwayne just smiled.

We were in the cabin within five minutes. The place was warm, as Wes and Will had said. There was nothing there that hadn't been there before, except the fire in the heater, two mugs on the coffee table, and, on the bed, a small, neat stack of things: a T-shirt, a B.C.-Yukon road map, and a Penguin edition of Jane Austen's *Emma*.

"Felix?" asked Vivien and I simultaneously.

Dwayne smiled again. "She said the guy was small, wiry, dark, with long black hair and a long, curly beard. That's the Felix we remember so fondly."

"It's him," said Gerald. "That's why he took off when Dwayne drove up. He's afraid we're going to force him to leave."

"So where's he off to?"

"The Nahanni River," said Vivien. "He's single-minded. He tried Hole-in-the Wall and never made it. He had plans to go up Zenchuk."

Gerald shook his head. "He would've gone north at the junction. He knows the cabin there and Stefan was good to him."

"Obviously he likes the hot spring," I suggested.

"Maybe he's going up through Mirror Lake," said Vivien. "I've been thinking of it myself. I believe that route gets you to the top of Zenchuk or even right down into the top of Rabbitkettle."

"I don't know about that," said Gerald. "But either way puts him out of our range."

On the way out, I looked under the porch. The plastic wagon was gone.

WE LEFT THE NEXT DAY, shortly after the models departed, leaving Gerald, Terri, and the kids in peace. Two days later we were back in Watson Lake, having a steak dinner at the hotel.

"So," I said to Vivien as we settled into a bottle of red wine, "have you figured where we're going next summer? I notice you were brooding over the maps while I was showering."

"I want to try to get from Tungsten over to the Nahanni River," said Vivien. "I think Mirror Lake is a good route, but we'd have to cross the Flat River just below the lake. Might not be possible. Zenchuk Creek leads straight into the upper Rabbitkettle River, and there's a road winding east from the Flat Lakes over to the creek. I asked Gerald about that road, and he says it starts behind the warden's, Stefan's, cabin. It's passable, though steep. If we can stay on the ridges, we can be at the top of

Zenchuk Creek in two days. We'll need partners for that trip, though, because it'll be at least a week all the way to Rabbitkettle Hot Springs, and a week back."

"I'm afraid I'll have to be working," said Wes.

"Me too," said Will.

"Maybe Joanne still has Felix's address," said Wes, grinning.

"No thanks," said Vivien. "Dwayne's got him pegged, I'm afraid. But he's got the spirit, God help him. I hope he makes it."

"A toast to Felix," said Wes, topping up our wine.

"Me too," said Will.

Wes looked over his shoulder, checking to see if the waitress was watching. "To keep your cholesterol down, then. I don't want my cousin to pass away young, before he has a chance to make it as a jazz drummer." Wes sloshed a half inch of wine into Will's glass.

"To Felix," said Vivien.

We tapped glasses.

"Another toast," I said. "To our partners, whoever they turn out to be."

"I need more wine," said Will.

"You're supposed to sip it!"

"I thought it was good for me."

Wes sloshed another half inch into Will's glass.

"Any more and you'll be up all night."

"To our partners," said Vivien, touching her glass to ours.

TRAIL INFORMATION

Highway 10 to The Washout

THERE ARE SIGNS at the junction of Highway 10 (Nahanni Range Road) and the Robert Campbell Highway warning drivers that the road is unmaintained and that you travel it at your own risk. Most two-wheel-drive vehicles with moderate clearance can go as far as the Kilometre 146 washout. However, during wet years there are many low spots along the way where a vehicle with high clearance or a four-wheel drive is recommended. Take extra gasoline, and if you are leaving your vehicle for any length of time, wrap it in chicken wire to protect it from porcupines – they often chew brake linings. I have never had problems with theft when leaving my vehicle unattended at the washout for as long as ten weeks at a time, but with more activity in the area, that could change. Ignore all speed signs. They are massively optimistic.

Cycling from the Robert Campbell Highway is also an option. As long as the upper Frances River and Hyland River bridges remain intact, there will be no problem going all the way to Tungsten and points beyond. There are only two or three kilometres of steep upward grinding. The rest of the road is a series of gentle ups and downs (mostly ups) all the way to the pass on the Yukon-Northwest Territories border. You could walk (like Felix) from Watson Lake or the Robert Campbell Highway, but you would use up valuable time that should be used for wilderness excursions around Tungsten.

Driving to the washout takes three to four hours. Cycling to the washout would take two easy days. Crossing the river at the washout can take hours or minutes, depending on the water levels. Cycling from the washout to Tungsten takes one or two days, depending on your strength and the load on your bike. The weight of your panniers will depend on how long you are staying in. You need to carry all necessary supplies. The closest stores and cafes are in Watson Lake.

Conglomerate Creek at Kilometre 78 and No-Name Creek at Kilometre 97 are highly recommended as hike-and-bike trips. The creeks are easy to reach and are also close to the government campsite on the Hyland River.

TOPOGRAPHICAL MAPS: Frances Lake #105H (1:250,000), Little Nahanni River #105I (1:250,000).

EQUIPMENT NEEDED A dependable vehicle is essential – four-wheel drive is recommended for driving to the washout. Carry extra gasoline, a spare tire, and a well-equipped tool kit for minor repairs. Getting a tow truck out here would cost more than a new pick-up. Bicycles should be in good repair, equipped with a repair kit and manual. Mountain bikes are better but not essential unless you are continuing north of Tungsten. The road to Tungsten is almost as hard and smooth as pavement. A leak-free tent and winter sleeping bag are recommended. It gets quite cold in this area and snow is possible at any time of year. Warm clothing and the highest quality rain gear are essential. Take enough food for the entire trip and a few extra days in case you get stuck somewhere. The hot-dog stand at the top of the pass has been closed indefinitely. Take a stove and fuel if you are going into the alpines. Keep wooden matches in a well-sealed waterproof container. Carry a well-equipped first-aid kit with strong analgesics in the event of a painful accident. Pepper spray for bear protection should always be kept handy, even if you are on a bike. Because cycling is quiet, it is possible to surprise an animal.

THE ROUTE

0.0K MINER'S JUNCTION, on the Robert Campbell Highway at the Highway 10 turnoff, was the hub of activity when Cantung mine was in operation. A large log cabin is still in good repair, but the buildings that once served as a restaurant and garage are showing their age. John is hoping to see a cappuccino sign rear itself triumphantly over the entrance to the settlement. Across from the buildings at the junction, a carved wooden sign describes the building of the Nahanni Range Road for the Cantung Mines.

8.3K BRIDGE OVER UPPER FRANCES RIVER. Cross the upper Frances River on an iron-beamed bridge with wooden decking. It is in good repair and can be crossed safely. If this bridge ever washes away, crossing the Frances will require a boat.

12.2K SEQUENCE CREEK

19.2K QUEEN CREEK

35.2K LONG LAKE CREEK

37.1K HOMESTEAD (occupied). To this point, the road is crossed by several creeks where cyclists can get water. Situated on a cliff overlooking a bend in the river is a lived-in homestead with log cabin, outhouse, sauna, and barbecue pits. If you have a life-and-death situation and need shelter, this could be a place to find help.

37.9K LONG LAKE WITH CAMPSITE AT CREEK. Unnamed creek with clear water flowing into Long Lake. There are flat spots for tenting, hunter's firepits, and driftwood left from the spring runoff. The most inviting amenity at this spot is the porcupine-chewed outhouse.

39.5K CREEK WITH HUNTER'S CABIN JUST BEYOND; possible campsite. Dolly Varden Creek crosses the road. There is fresh water.

42.5K It is possible to hike up Dolly Varden, although the road is quite overgrown. There are some wet spots in the first few kilometres that need to be skirted around, and it is not possible to cycle this route. We have not gone to the end of this road so if you go, it is *your* adventure. You can write Tungsten John a letter, c/o his publisher, to tell him what's at the end.

46.6K FRENCH CREEK contains clear drinking water. There were no exploratory roads along French that we could find, so bushwhacking is the only way in.

54.4K NORTH BRANCH CREEK provides fresh water.

58.8K SWAMP and possible washout site in the future. The road washed away in 1997, but the highway department repaired it so that three quarters of the road is passable. The highway department may not continue to do minor repairs in the future, depending on what happens with the mine site itself. If it is abandoned and cleaned up, then the road will also be abandoned.

62.6K SPRUCE CREEK There are a few flat spots on the south side of the road at Spruce Creek, which offers clear running water. Along the sides of the creek you may find firewood.

66.5K SOUTH BRANCH CREEK culvert looks like it could wash out during a wet year. Continue carefully for the next 5.5 K as the road is soft, especially after a heavy rain or during winter runoff.

73.1K THE ROAD TO THE HYLAND RIVER branches off to the right. There are campsites along the road.

78.0K CONGLOMERATE CREEK crosses the road at this point. It is a clear creek with three or four flat spots for tents on the south side. North of the creek is a road going to the west (left) that follows the creek to some incredible alpines. Although the road cannot be driven (even with a four-wheel drive) it can be cycled or walked. See the Conglomerate Creek trail description and "Zenchuk Creek" for details.

78.5K ROAD TO LEFT

85.8K NORTH MOOSE CREEK crosses the road and flows into the Hyland River. Along a road going down to the Hyland from here there are flat camping sites that are close to drinking water and dried driftwood.

86.0K THE GOVERNMENT CAMPSITE, with a covered shelter and outhouses, is a comfortable spot to camp. You can collect drinking water from the Hyland River, a short climb down a steep bank. The trail is behind the covered shelter. The eighteen drive-in sites are on flat gravel pads and are seldom occupied except during hunting season. Traces of hunters can be seen in the logs nailed across trees for hanging dead moose and in the shrinkwrap used to enclose the shelter. Once we found a motorhome parked at the site. A happy fisherman was exercising his skills while his wife watched satellite TV. There is wood available in the bush – the Territorial government no longer supplies the campsite with wood or toilet paper.

97.0K THE ROAD UP NO-NAME CREEK is an excellent hike or bicycle trip. There is lots of water, wood, scenery, ruins, and campsites. See the No-Name Creek trail description.

103.0K HUNTER'S CABIN. The Kaska Mountain hunting cabin is on the west side of the road. It could be used for shelter in the event of a problem.

112.2K HYLAND RIVER BRIDGE. Just before the Hyland River Bridge there is a riverside cabin that could also be used for an emergency. It appears to be unoccupied. Be careful not to damage anything in this or other cabins along the route. These cabins could be critical in the event of an accident. Damage to them endangers your life as well as the lives of others relying on them.

117.0K AIRSTRIP. The airstrip is about a kilometre long. It's possible to drive or cycle along its edge (for variety from the road). There are access roads at both ends of the airstrip.

130.0K LITTLE HYLAND RIVER branches off to left.

133.0K PIGGET CREEK is not a good place to stay due to the fuel drums and other bits of garbage in the area.

145.5K SMALL WASHOUT.

146.0K THE WASHOUT. This is as far as you should take a vehicle unless the water levels are very low. Hunters do take four-by-fours across the washout during the fall, but not usually in the summer. There has been more than one vehicle damaged trying to cross here; the rocks on the bottom are huge and vehicles become wedged between them or hung up on them.

The main crossing by the washed-out bridge has been dug down by vehicles, so unless the water levels are low, it is not possible to ford the river at this spot. To cross the washout, turn left (west) at the culverts about 20 feet before the creek. The trail leads past the bend in the river to where the creekbed has not been gouged by vehicles. The flat creek bottom allows crossing even in moderately high water. Winter runoff usually crests by the end of June.

It generally takes a few hours to transport everything across the river. If you arrive late in the day, it is advisable to stay on the south side of the washout overnight. Crossing takes strength and energy, which are more available after a good night's sleep. On the other hand, since you don't have to worry about early nightfall, you may prefer to push on. There are many camping spots on the other side.

We have crossed the washout by various means including walking and strapping our bikes to our backpacks, ferrying ourselves across with a canoe or a rubber tube, and crossing in the scoop of a frontend loader. The loader was a fluke – Gerald happened to be working on the bridge that washed out the following spring. You should plan how you will cross before you arrive at the water.

Washout to Tungsten on Highway 10

THE LENGTH OF TIME it takes to reach Tungsten from the washout depends on your bicycle load. Two days is average for a heavy (three weeks of food) load and six hours is average for a light load. Carry good rain gear because it rains (or snows) almost every day of the summer in this area. It's very easy to get cold and wet if you are not careful, which will increase the risk of hypothermia.

THE ROUTE

155.0K CAMPSITE. The road undulates up and down the valley, with a bit more up than down, all the way to the pass. Approximately two hours (with a heavy load) after the washout there is a campsite beside the Little Hyland River complete with picnic table and fire rings. Watch for a road going left, through willow, towards the river. There are no markers for this turnoff.

158.0K CABIN. About fifteen minutes beyond the campsite there are two ponds occupied by a large population of birds. Just past the ponds is a hidden cabin. Again, the road going to the right is hard to see, but once on it you will find tons of blueberry plants. The cabin itself is an interesting design and is not locked. You could stay inside if shelter is needed, but please leave it in better shape than you found it.

169.0K TRAPPER'S CABIN. Fourteen kilometres beyond the campsite, on a path to the right, is the outfitter's cabin. A small wooden bridge crosses the ditch and leads to a path that goes through the trees to the cabin. This is not a camping spot. The door is always locked, but it is obvious that the owner frequently uses the cabin.

When Tungsten was in operation, a man tried to reach this cabin after his car died during a blizzard. Wearing city shoes and a light jacket, he left his car and walked through the snow towards the cabin, but froze to death before he found it.

171.5K HORSE CAMP. Fifteen minutes beyond the cabin, on the right side of the road, is a horse camp with an outhouse, leftover cable spools to use as tables, a creek, flat spots, and a frame for a tarp. Aside from the fact that there is little wood for a fire, this is an excellent place to camp. A few steps into the bush there are the remains of a cabin and the wing of a plane.

182.0K MAC CREEK/STEEL CREEK WINTER ROAD. Beyond the horse camp, a road heads west, crosses a culvert, and then goes up a hill to a gravel pit. At the far end of the gravel pit is the winter road leading to Mac Creek and over a pass to Steel Creek. I have never taken this road because my experience with winter roads tells me that I should not go that way unless I have no other choice besides death. However, it is good to know that, if you should decide to come out of Steel Creek by the winter road, this is where you will end up. The culvert (now washed out) is recommended as a campsite if you need a spot to stay before your ascent to the pass.

187.0K YUKON/NORTHWEST TERRITORIES BORDER. Just past the winter road turnoff, Highway 10 turns east and starts the upward climb to the pass and Yukon/NWT border. Near the top of the pass, the road passes two lakes where beaver are often playing in the water. They are fun to watch. There is a sign indicating the border. Shortly after this, the road starts to descend. Past the first curve and just before the second curve is a spectacular view of Mirror Lake with the glacier above it and the valley beyond. The corner mountain, guarding the valley, is one of the most welcoming mountains I have ever seen – when under sunlight. In bad weather, this valley is forbidding.

192.5K JUNCTION OF FLAT LAKES AND TUNGSTEN ROADS. The road zigzags down the hill for 5.5 kilometres to the Flat Lakes Road junction. This is the centre of the Tungsten recreational zone – Banff of the North. There is a small cabin beside a creek at the junction. Supplies can be stored here if you don't want to take them all the way into Tungsten and then back out again. Camping beside the cabin is good, and during heavy rain the cabin offers shelter, even though it is not a good place to sleep due to a pile of dusty insulation batts stacked in the back room.

200.0K TUNGSTEN TOWNSITE. The road to Tungsten is a gentle downhill run, passing beside the headwaters of the Flat River. At this point the Flat is a green stream, offering no threat to anything. Within ten kilometres of its headwaters the Flat becomes a raging class-four river.

As you descend to Tungsten, you will pass a milled-log house, a luxurious accommodation that, due to lack of care, now has a leaking roof. Beyond the milled-log house, on the right, is a dynamite shed made of heavy timber, with a padlocked steel door and no windows.

The next landmark is a gate obstructing passage into the Tungsten townsite. The gate is locked to prevent vehicle access. Ignore the gate, pull your bike through, and cycle along the main road, up the hill, past the air flue and main office to the six-million-dollar recreation centre. From the centre, continue straight ahead until the road divides. Go up the hill, veering to the right, then doubling back until you reach two modest bungalows that are in good repair. This is where the caretakers can be found, and you must check in with them before continuing to the hot springs or the road beyond. You are trespassing.

201.0K TUNGSTEN AIRSTRIP. To get to the hot springs, follow the road down towards the Flat River and past the tailing pond to the airstrip. The road to the hot springs is on the right, just beyond the baseball bleachers. Head for the little A-frame past the outdoor pool. This pool has not been maintained, so moss is growing in abundance, making it slimy.

209.0K LUMBER MILL ON FLAT RIVER. The bridge over the Flat is at the far end of the airport. Cross the bridge and follow that road for about one hour, past a dumpsite. Finally the sawmill and cabin will appear. It is a large, well-built cabin that offers shelter and a comfortable place to stay.

3

Some Episodes of Romantic Buffoonery

OVER THE WINTER, we planned the next summer's trip from Tungsten to Nahanni. We saw on the contour maps two major passes through the Raggeds – that range of the Selwyn Mountains that separates Tungsten and the upper Flat River from the Nahanni.

One pass is called Hole-in-the-Wall. The route starts on the Flat south of Tungsten and leads to Hole-in-the-Wall Lake and down Hole-in-the-Wall Creek to Rabbitkettle Hot Springs, a famous stopping-in or starting-out place for canoeists on the Nahanni, a place remembered fondly by Vivien and Joanne for the sexy young warden, Rick, who took them to climb, in bare feet (mandatory, he claimed), the tufa mounds around the hot springs and then treated them to coffee and cake in his cabin on Rabbitkettle Lake – an act of hospitality that, it seems to me, if it does not contravene the warden code of ethics, should.

The other pass is unnamed. The most plausible route to it starts at the Flat Lakes just north of Tungsten, and follows Zenchuk Creek up. On the pass is a small lake with a small island or rock outcropping near its north shore. That lake is the headwaters of the Rabbitkettle River, which runs down to the hot springs.

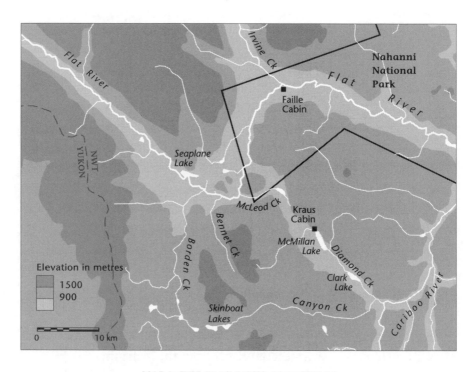

MAP 3: THE FLAT RIVER GOLDFIELDS

The Zenchuk route looked easier and shorter, but it raised many more questions for me. Who was Zenchuk? What did he do to get his name on the creek? Did he simply find it and tell someone? Did he have a claim on it, or a trapline? If we were to find something on it, how might we recognize that thing as Zenchuk's?

My part in the creation of any hiking guide is the historical background. Vivien's fans like to know the history of what they see. I do the research for Vivien because tracking someone or something through a public library or archives is just as exciting to me as route-finding in the bush. It is more comfortable too, though possibly not as healthy. It involves essential visits to great cities like Edmonton, Vancouver, Whitehorse, and Yellowknife. Funky hotel rooms furnished with desks and coffee machines must be located, as well as cappuccino bars, interesting restaurants, and used bookstores.

The first thing I found – or noticed – in my researches was in Dick Turner's *Nahanni:* a group photo of some Liard trappers, including Zenchuk. He is on a boat on the Liard, with many of the others who became a part of the Nahanni legend. Zenchuk is sitting beside a standing Bill Eppler, who is the only person on the boat wearing sunglasses.

Zenchuk has his hands resting on the gunwale, folded formally one over the other in the position used by well-trained kids when they face cameras. He is not looking at the camera. He has dark hair, big ears, a rooster-tail, and a good tan.

"He looks like you before you got gray and wrinkled," Vivien pointed out when I showed her this picture.

"What do you mean? You can't even see his face below the nose because of the guy in the big hat."

"Intuition."

Turner includes Zenchuk's first name, Nazar. The text of his book provides no further information. The photo is dated 1935.

In response to a letter of inquiry, the Territorial Archivist at Yellowknife informed me by fax that Zenchuk Creek and Lake, in the alpines to the north of the creek, were named after Nazar Zenchuk, or more probably Zinchuk. The archivist also included some pertinent pages of the transcript of an interview with one of Zenchuk's colleagues, Gus Kraus. These pages had Zenchuk's name highlighted.

In their books, both R.M. Patterson and Dick Turner mention Kraus. He was, next to Faille and Turner, the most persistent resident of Nahanni, arriving in February 1934 and staying for the rest of his long life. Both Patterson and Turner describe him with affection. The hot springs on the Nahanni, just below the first canyon and Lafferty's Riffle, are named after him; he established himself there in 1941 and stayed for a couple of decades, and the fantastic survivors of his vegetable garden still grow wild in the vicinity.

We learned from the archivist that Kraus *and* Zenchuk, along with some other surviving trappers and explorers associated with Nahanni, including Patterson and Faille, were interviewed in 1976 by historians hired by the Department of Indian and Northern Affairs. They planned on interviewing other important figures like Patterson's trapping partner Gordon Matthews and the bush pilot George Dalziel, dubbed "the flying prospector" by Patterson in his book *Far Pastures* (which describes a 1951 journey up the Nahanni and the Flat in search of Faille) and "the flying trapper" by Turner and Pierre Berton. Matthews was out of the country. Dalziel was busy somewhere in the Yukon.

None of the tapes are available until 2010. About half of the inter-

NAZAR ZENCHUK AT HIS CAMP IN 1934
(COPIED FROM A PHOTO TAKEN BY GEORGE DALZIEL)

views have no transcripts. Zenchuk was the only subject who requested that the transcript of his interview not be opened to public scrutiny until 2010 – an inconvenient date for me as by then my hiking career and possibly even my curiosity will be over. There is no record of why Zenchuk made this request.

What did he have to hide?

"It couldn't have been gold," Vivien pointed out. "When they did these interviews they were all in their sixties and seventies, too old to go prospecting."

"Hope springs eternal." I reminded Vivien that even Patterson notes, in his 1953 foreword to *Dangerous River,* that what he and Gordon Matthews found in their prospecting and exploring in Deadmen Valley in 1927–28 had to remain, "for some time yet," a secret. And by 1953 Patterson knew for sure, and better than most, just how fabulous the talk of Nahanni gold really was.

It couldn't have been fear of libel, either. It was prearranged that the historians would remove from the transcript all potentially libellous references.

We immediately ordered the Kraus transcript. When it arrived, we learned little about Zenchuk and a lot more about Kraus and Turner's crew of Flat River trappers and gold seekers.

Kraus comes across in the transcript of his interview as a sociable man. He was interested in everything and involved in just about every major event that took place on the Flat River and the Nahanni from the time of his arrival to the time of his death. He came from Chicago, through the Peace River country, and into the Northwest Territories, settling for a time at Hay River on Great Slave Lake. There, in 1933, working at the airport gassing and warming up planes and drinking coffee with the pilots, he met Wop May. May told him the Nahanni stories, including the story of gold on the Flat. Kraus made his way to Fort Simpson, and in the fall of 1933 or February of 1934 he flew into MacMillan Lake with Leigh Brintnell, the founder of Mackenzie Air. Turner says that he was trapping, but Kraus says he had no traps; his sole intent was prospecting. He pitched his tent at the far end of the lake, close to the creeks, and started exploring, Bennett Creek first. On Bennett he found old stakes from 1921–22 and 1930–31.

A few days after his arrival, Joe Mulholland, Stan Turner, Bill Eppler, and others turned up at the end of their forty-five-day overland trip from Nahanni Butte. "Oh boy did they eat," Kraus told his interviewer.

Bill Clark, whom he had met in Hay River, joined up with Kraus that spring. Clark had flown into the area a few months earlier, with Stanier, and done some staking, but Stanier, an old man, was unable to continue the partnership due to medical problems. Kraus and Clark worked together on Bennett and McLeod creeks. They stayed in another winter and came out in May 1936 with evidence of gold.

Clark convinced some mining companies, geologists, and well-heeled adventurers like Wop May to put up the money for further exploration. The two partners returned to their base on MacMillan Lake and explored more creeks, all the way up the Flat to the Skinboat Lakes, and also to the southwest over the divide into the headwaters of the Coal River. Their activity stopped in 1939, when all mining was shut down due to the war.

Kraus and Clark's is the most sustained and serious attempt on record to find gold on the upper Flat and to locate the lost McLeod Mine. They found nothing, but Kraus fell in love with the country and started trapping. He was subsequently involved in the investigation of many of the deaths that occurred on the Nahanni or Flat. After his marriage to Mary, a Slavey Indian, he settled for periods of time in places along the Nahanni, including the Butte and the hot springs that bear his name. Pierre Trudeau visited the Krauses in 1970. In effect he was announcing their eviction, though I'm sure the subject never came up. When Nahanni National Park was established the next year, the Krauses moved to Little Doctor Lake, but Kraus became an honorary warden. His primary duty was to warn the inexperienced off the river. He helped locate the bodies of some of those who ignored his warnings.

Kraus's attitude to the McLeod story was skeptical. He got to know Charlie McLeod fairly well and so heard many stories that Charlie came up with to account for his brothers' deaths. About Charlie, Kraus tells his interviewer, "Every time...Charlie'd have a different idea of what happened to his brothers, because he used to go to these seances...Of course, they told him to talk to his dead brothers, and they'd tell him it [the lost mine] is here or there or who polished them off. Well, he blamed Weir for it ... It was always a different story, every time, so I didn't pay too much attention."

Kraus's opinion was shared by the RCMP. An article called "Valley of No Return" in the RCMP *Quarterly* describes how Charlie and "another brother" kept seeing Weir in various places and would notify police of his whereabouts. "Newspapers and magazine writers made quite a play out of McLeod's various Weirs and this, of course, has led to some of the fantastic myths which have evolved."

But what about Zenchuk? Various documents, particularly Kraus's interview and the article "Valley of No Return," tie Zenchuk and the bush pilot George Dalziel to the deaths of three men in the Nahanni area. Kraus implies that Zenchuk was directly responsible for the 1948 death, on the Flat River near the mouth of the Caribou River, of a man named Shebbach. (Kraus says that Shebbach was a Russian, like Zenchuk. This could mean that the conventional spelling of his name is inaccurate; it could be something like Tzebak.) And Kraus's interview, re-examined in light of information contained in the RCMP *Quarterly* article, shows that Zenchuk participated in the search when Bill Eppler and Joe Mulholland failed to turn up in Fort Simpson in May 1936 after a winter's trapping at Glacier Lake, far up the Nahanni River. Eppler and Mulholland had been dropped off at Glacier Lake by Dalziel, who may also have dropped off Shebbach.

Patterson tells the story of Shebbach's death in *Dangerous River,* and he acknowledges Kraus as the source. However, Patterson – wiser perhaps than Kraus in the ways of the world – leaves Zenchuk's name out of the story. Or perhaps Kraus himself left the name out when he told the story to Patterson.

In Edmonton in 1948, the story goes, some time after Zenchuk appears to have left Nahanni (in 1938, white people were banned from hunting and trapping in the area between the Yukon border and the Mackenzie River and north of the Liard, so there was no reason for him to stay) and, significantly I think, a year after Berton made the area famous in his newspaper articles, Zenchuk met a man named Shebbach and told him stories about prospecting on the Caribou River. Probably he told him about the McLeod Mine, too. The two men evidently agreed to meet in the fall at Zenchuk's cabin at the confluence of the Flat and Caribou rivers. They must have intended to put in the winter prospecting – getting their camp set up and their holes started before freeze-up.

Anyway, Shebbach set out from the Alaska Highway, probably from the vicinity of Watson Lake, on foot with a pack and a twenty-two rifle. He ate what he shot and made his way through the Selwyn Mountains and down the Caribou to the Flat. When he got there, he found no one waiting for him and no food in the cache. Also, he was out of shells for his rifle. Winter set in. He waited. He kept a diary, a record of forty-two days of starvation. Finally someone inquired about him, and in the summer of 1949 Kraus and the police went up to see what had happened. They found Shebbach dead, his body torn apart and scattered by animals. Kraus and the police gathered Shebbach together, put him in a sack, and took him to Fort Simpson.

Patterson tells this story only by way of debunking those parts of the Nahanni legend concerning the headless bodies found over the years in Deadmen Valley and up the Flat. He concludes that the corpses were headless because they'd had similar encounters with animals. It seems like a logical deduction. Patterson, most of the time, has a kindly way of bringing the Nahanni legend back to reality, while still finding the reality legendary.

Kraus, in his interview, besides naming Zenchuk as the man Shebbach was expecting to meet, adds something else to the story. He seems to suggest that, after all, Shebbach *flew* in, with George Dalziel. Dalziel was, Kraus says, Zenchuk's one-time trapping partner.

This is interesting because Turner connects Dalziel to the deaths of Bill Eppler and Joe Mulholland. Dalziel flew them in to a trapline at Rabbitkettle Lake in January 1936, according to Turner, and they failed to appear as arranged in May. In November, Dalziel and a prospector, Harry Vandaele it seems, though Turner is not entirely certain about this, flew in to investigate. They saw nothing on the river and found the cabin on Rabbitkettle Lake burned to the ground.

And Dalziel, Kraus seems to say, took Shebbach into the Skinboat Lakes, at the top of Canyon Creek, which flows into the Caribou River. Almost a year later Dalziel, not having heard anything about Shebbach, contacted the police. Kraus and the police flew in on a search.

But Kraus is a confusing talker, leaping great tracts of space and time in a sentence and getting his dates wrong. His interviewers are hard pressed to pin him down. If Shebbach had flown in, how could he have run out of supplies and shells so quickly? Also, if he flew in with Dalziel, wouldn't Dalziel have expressed some opinion or have some knowledge as to whether his partner Zenchuk was likely to appear? Or mightn't Dalziel, after he dropped Shebbach off, have had occasion to confirm with Zenchuk that he was planning to hook up with Shebbach?

In his interview, Kraus also recounts an episode involving himself and Zenchuk, Faille, and others. It says a few things about Zenchuk himself, gives something of the flavour of a trapper's or prospector's life on the Flat, and shows how easily legends could find space to germinate in the scrambled accounts of what was actually happening.

At the beginning of May 1936 (1937 according to Kraus, but the interviewers correct him), Zenchuk and his partner, John Lomar, left their cabin at the mouth of the Caribou River and made their way fifty miles up the ice-bound Flat River towards Faille's cabin, which was on the Flat, near the mouth of Irvine Creek.

The exact location of Faille's cabin in 1936 is impossible to determine. Friends of mine who made a canoe trip down the Flat River from Tungsten told me that there is a cabin, identified as Faille's in the Flat River canoeing guide published by the Park Service, hidden in a tight poplar and willow grove. The cabin is in good shape, with a stove, table, and bed/bench made out of squared timber. My friends even produced a rotted moccasin, found in the vicinity of the cabin and subsequently enshrined in a living room somewhere as "Faille's moccasin." I mention this only as an indication of the credulity of canoeists as compared to their far more meditative compatriots, hikers.

The cabin my friends saw is not the cabin in Kraus's story, which burned in a bush fire. Patterson mentions the burning of the old cabin in *Far Pastures,* an account of his visit to Irvine Creek in 1951. That year, Patterson and two friends struggled their canoe up the Lower Nahanni and then seventy-five miles up the Flat, hoping to visit Faille who, they had heard in Fort Simpson, had spent the previous winter there and had casually mentioned to some acquaintances in Fort Simpson that he would probably stay in for another winter so he could put in a full summer of prospecting and exploring. Folk in Fort Simpson, Patterson found, were worried about Faille, finding it hard to imagine that anyone could cut himself off for so long and assuming that Faille would actually come out sometime that spring. Patterson knew that Faille would do what he proposed. "Situation normal," he thought, so far as Faille was concerned.

Patterson was eager to see his old friend. He was cheered finally, at a point about forty miles up the Flat, when he noticed a dead timber wolf bobbing in an eddy. The wolf had a bullet hole in him. Patterson knew that wolves were always trying to eat Faille – something Faille took as a compliment, while admitting that the cause was probably not so much the sweetness of his person as the fact that he was almost always by himself, a "lone wolf" as it were. Faille and Patterson met, finally, at the swimming hole just a short walk up Irvine Creek, a camping spot frequented by most subsequent voyageurs on the Flat including my canoeing friends.

Patterson and Faille were happy to meet again after some twenty-three years – Patterson, the sophisticated Oxford grad and former banker, and Faille, the friendly mountain man with a passion for a river. But the area was littered with dead timber wolves in various stages of decay, the closest not fifty yards from Faille's mosquito net, and it was also hugely changed, having been swept by a fire at some time in the recent past. Patterson had first to inquire about these immediate matters before they could get down to other talk.

Regarding the wolves, it turned out that Faille had contracted scurvy over the winter and had become pretty weak by spring, when he recognized the disease by the fact that his teeth were loosening. His evident weakness made him even more than usually attractive to the wolves, and for awhile he couldn't go far out of his tent without a confrontation, which the wolves always lost. As to the fire, it had occurred a few years back, during World War II, while Faille was out on a six-year job as an engineer on the riverboat *Thomas Murphy* plying the Mackenzie River. The Irvine Creek cabin had burned, and Faille, when he finally saw the results, was not inclined at that point to build a new one. The beauty had gone out of the place as far as he was concerned. Patterson agreed, but later noted that the area around the burnt cabin now yielded the fattest and sweetest raspberries he had ever eaten. For the next few years, Faille used his tent or occupied one of his other cabins. There were at least two others, one on the Caribou River and one on the Nahanni above the falls.

Starting with these stories, Faille and Patterson talked on into the night, for dinner catching, cooking, and eating a huge Dolly Varden. The next morning they teamed up to toss the wolf carcasses into the river. Faille then waved goodbye and started up Irvine Creek for the upper Nahanni. Patterson struck out through the raspberries into the Selwyns, an area that had always fascinated him.

So much for the fate of Faille's cabin. Back in 1936, at the same time as Zenchuk and Lomar set out for the still-standing cabin, two other sets of partners – Kraus and Bill Clark, and Harry Vandaele and Milt Campbell – were coming down to Faille's from farther up the Flat. This was Kraus's first trip out since flying in in 1934.

Vandaele and Campbell, like Kraus and Clark, were prospectors only, part of the Flat River Gold Rush. Turner describes them in *Nahanni*, and Vandaele can be seen in one of the group photos in the book. He is a good-looking man, about thirty, with a million-dollar smile. Vandaele and Campbell came down to join the trappers because they were hungry – an expected food drop had failed to materialize. The other five were hungry too, as much for society as food. Even Faille, who always trapped alone, welcomed company whenever he could get it, talking nonstop for days to any guest or chance companion. Turner tells of Faille talking through the night to his guests who, one by one, fell asleep to Faille's voice and then periodically woke up to it again, said "Ummm," "Oh," or "Sure," and then fell asleep again, waking up finally in the morning to Faille stirring the fire and still talking.

Turner's theory was that Faille's conversations with himself were a technique to stave off cabin fever, a common cause of death among trappers. Faille often addressed these conversations to what seemed like an especially sympathetic listener: his abandoned wife Marion.

The men met, too, because following the ice out was a dangerous procedure, particularly if anyone got too eager and tried to stick too close to, or get around, the retreating ice. And usually they were fairly eager. You wanted to get out just behind the ice and just before the thaw hit farther up on the hills and tons of water, soil, and timber crashed down hundreds of creeks into the Nahanni.

The trappers and prospectors were also, this particular spring, short on civilized comforts, which made them even more eager. Kraus and

Clark, bearing the additional strain of Vandaele and Campbell, had run out of tobacco, tea, and milk weeks before and had been eating nothing but meat, which, when it is the only item on the menu, has to be eaten half raw to provide the vitamin C needed to stave off scurvy. By the time they got to Faille's cabin, Faille was out of everything too, except for a pail of beans that went well with the two moose that Kraus shot just a few minutes before arriving at the cabin. Split between seven men, however, the beans didn't go far. Zenchuk and Lomar had bare cupboards also, except for twenty-four pounds of flour that they had left in their cache on the Caribou. Everyone was eager to eat some of that, but the ice was holding from Irvine Creek on down, making travel impossible.

So they waited and talked. Gold was the main thing on the minds of all these men. It was behind almost every story they told, though their energetic pursuit of gold is – as Patterson's, Kraus's, and Faille's examples prove – no indication of how seriously they took the legend of its existence.

Kraus and Clark, for example, during that winter of 1935–36, had been sluicing on Bennett Creek. Kraus mentions how they laboriously dredged the gravel out from under the ice and washed it down in early spring in two boxes placed on top of the ice in runoff water. They had a half ounce of gold to show for their labours; not much, but evidently enough to keep their interest in the creek alive.

Vandaele and Campbell were concentrating on McLeod Creek. Kraus makes no mention of their finding any gold.

Zenchuk and Lomar were trappers. There is no indication that they had much interest in prospecting. Faille too was a trapper, but he was interested in the McLeod Mine and he did do some prospecting. He believed that gold *and* the lost mine were to be found near the Nahanni above the falls. He trapped Irvine Creek because it provided access to the upper Nahanni.

At Irvine Creek, the men were expecting two other trappers to turn up. Kraus doesn't mention this in his interview; the details are to be found in the RCMP *Quarterly*. About six weeks earlier, in mid-March, Kraus and Clark had received supplies by airplane. George Dalziel, the pilot, told them that he had just recently flown Bill Eppler and Joe Mulholland in to Glacier Lake, about a hundred miles north on the upper Nahanni. The men were trapping marten and were planning to walk out down the Nahanni, then over to the headwaters of Irvine Creek and down to Faille's cabin. Presumably they would get Dalziel to haul their pelts out later, though why they'd make such a complicated arrangement is a mystery. Surely a better idea would be to raft their furs out, coming straight down the Nahanni in June or at low water in August. Turner says they planned to build a skinboat for this purpose, but it may be they wanted to hook up with Faille and the others to do the difficult lower Nahanni in a real boat and with an experienced boatman.

Kraus and the others arrived at Irvine Creek about 28 April and left on 8 May. During this time they saw no signs of Mulholland and Eppler.

While waiting for the ice to move, Faille, Kraus, and Clark prepared Faille's canoe, stuffing it full of hides and equipment, including Faille's outboard motor, which was his usual means of getting up the river. It was also long out of gas. They left just enough space for the three of them to sit. Zenchuk, Lomar, Campbell, and Vandaele built a large raft and loaded it with hides and what was left of the moose meat.

The ice moved, and, shortly after, they followed, hoping that it had gotten down past the Caribou River and Zenchuk's flour. But somewhere close to the Caribou River they caught up to the ice, and there followed a few frustrating days during each of which they made a mile or two, the ice jamming, then breaking and moving, then jamming again. About five miles above the Caribou River they found a sheet of ice arched solidly across the Flat, leaving a four-foot-high space between the arch and the water. The ice arch was a long one, but they could see through to the other end and figured if they kept their heads down they could be out from under in seconds. But nobody had the nerve to try. So they ditched the raft and slid the canoe, hides, etc., across on top of the ice and then built another raft and got back on the water for the last few miles to the cabin and the flour.

Kraus made the whole bag of flour into sourdough biscuits. If there were any left when the ice moved on, they could take them along and eat them on their way down.

At their cabin, Zenchuk and Lomar had the 24-foot scow that they had come in on. They launched and loaded it, and when the ice moved a few days later, the trappers made their next lap easily, down to the mouth of the Flat. From there they could see that the Nahanni was blocked. The river looked like a frozen lake, except that the gigantic chunks of ice covering it were rearing and bucking like penned mustangs.

The men camped on a gravel bar too close to the ice. That night the ice blocked the river's flow, and water started to rise. There was nowhere to go but up the cutbank behind them. They found a small flat spot about fifty feet up the cutbank and managed to hoist their stuff up. They slept until about three o'clock in the morning, when they heard a rumble. The ice went out and within minutes they were letting the canoe down until it was sitting on an expanse of broken ice and slimy silt at the base of the cutbank.

Kraus was fed up and wanted to laze around and wait for the ice to get down through the canyons on the Nahanni. A trip out should take only two days; why prolong the agony by trying to anticipate the ice? Also, it was dangerous. You could get sucked under the ice. But everyone else was eager to move on. For all they knew the ice was already into the Mackenzie and on its way to the Arctic Ocean, and all the other trappers, including Eppler and Mulholland, were drinking, examining gold nuggets, and trading stories at Whittington's hotel bar in Fort Simpson.

It was at the mouth of the Flat, according to the RCMP *Quarterly,* that Kraus, Clark, and Zenchuk noticed freshly cut trees and signs of a recent campfire. Zenchuk, the last person to pass that spot the previous autumn, testified that the cuttings and the campfire remains had not been there in the fall. The trappers assumed that Mulholland and Eppler were just ahead of them, going over the ice or along the adjacent hills.

But if Eppler and Mulholland had reached the mouth of the Flat a few weeks earlier, finding the Nahanni still iced over, why would they not have waited for their friends?

Kraus, Clark, Faille, and the others launched and loaded their canoe and scow and started off again, the three in the canoe in the lead with the scow following. In Deadmen Valley just above Meilleur Creek, the ominous spot where, almost thirty years earlier, the headless bodies of Willie and Frank McLeod had been found, they ran into an ice dam that extended across the entire river. Both boats got sucked into the whirlpool immediately in front of the dam and were quickly in so deep that the men were looking up at the edge of the swirling water. Then, by pure chance, the pool coughed them back up and they made it to shore instead of slipping under the ice.

After that, Kraus got his way. They gave the ice lots of time to get out before they proceeded on down the river, noting more signs of Mulholland and Eppler, and they made it out safely.

Shortly after, the RCMP *Quarterly* says, they were interrogated as to the whereabouts of Mulholland and Eppler, who had not arrived in Fort Simpson. This happened just after 1 June, when Dalziel reported to the RCMP that he had taken the two men in to Glacier Lake in February. Dalziel said that when they failed to appear in early May, he was asked by Joe Mulholland's brother Jack (Jack and his wife Daisy, with Eppler, owned the trading post at Nahanni Butte) to fly in and check on them. Dalziel had done this and found the cabin burnt to the ground, with no sign of human remains in the rubble.

An RCMP officer immediately flew in with Dalziel. They found nothing except the burnt cabin. "Not having suitable tools along, the pair did not disturb the rubble." It seems that nothing essential to survival, like the men's rifles, was conspicuous in the rubble or the vicinity, and the RCMP assumed that the men had tried to make their way out. From June 6 to 9, Dalziel and a partner, William Cormack, flew the river and other adjoining areas, finding nothing. Meanwhile, Faille, Kraus, Clark, and Zenchuk were questioned.

In August, Corporal Regis Newton made another patrol up the river in search of the missing trappers. "He confirmed Dalziel's remarks that neither [Eppler or Mulholland] had perished in the cabin fire at Glacier Lake, and [he] interviewed Faille and, from the latter, learned that the strange camp fire at the Nahanni and Flat River junctions was undoubtedly made by the missing pair as everyone else in the area that year had been accounted for."

The RCMP concluded "that Eppler and Mulholland either perished in the waters of the South Nahanni, or were trapped in a snowslide while attempting to cross the mountains near the junction of the Flat and South Nahanni Rivers. No trace was ever found of their bodies."

I could flesh out Kraus's story with informed speculation, making the story more engaging. The materials certainly provide for that option, given that just about everything said by Kraus and the RCMP about the disappearance of Mulholland and Eppler contradicts what Turner says. Turner says that the men were at Rabbitkettle, not Glacier, Lake. He says that Vandaele, not Cormack, flew in with Dalziel on the search. He says "they took enough canvas and paint to build a canoe…Their plan was to come down the river as soon as the ice went out." The RCMP took Dalziel's word that their plan was to walk down the upper Nahanni, over to Irvine Creek, and down Irvine to Faille's cabin. Turner also hints that Eppler actually made it out and fled to Vancouver and then to Australia, afraid that he would somehow be implicated in the death of Mulholland. The RCMP say nothing about this.

However, when I speculate I have to second-guess, and this almost certainly gives a personal slant to history. It is tempting, but Vivien wants nothing in her guidebooks that is not close to fact.

So my research came to a stop, but I had gotten enough facts on Zenchuk to pique the curiosity of any of Vivien's readers who might want to head up his creek, and I had established the fact that no one had walked into the Nahanni and written about it. Shebbach, of course, according to Kraus in the version he gave to Patterson, walked in, and his diary might contain some account of that adventure. When asked by interviewers about Shebbach's diary, Kraus, who had brought it back with the rest of Shebbach's remains and possessions, speculated that the RCMP had probably turned everything over to Shebbach's next-of-kin.

Someone else is no doubt on that trail. Vivien and I had another trail to follow – the dotted line on the contour map that went above the south end of the Flat Lakes towards the alpines above Zenchuk Creek.

4

Zenchuk Creek

THE ONLY DISTINCTIVE thing about Birch was that he wore, at all times, a safari hat and hiking boots. Otherwise he looked like your typical hulking, inscrutable, acne-infected teenager.

The school Birch attended, occasionally, badly wanted him, at six foot six and 200 pounds, on its sports teams, but Birch was as interested in sports as he was in arithmetic, French, or any other academic study. Some time ago the school deduced that Birch was "intellectually challenged," probably as a result of smoking too much dope. He was often reprimanded or punished by teachers for smoking the stuff in public, and by police and judges for the same offence as well as for possession with intent to traffic. He consequently spent a lot of time at a special facility called Camp Tracking.

Camp Tracking is for young men whom the courts wish to detain, but not in a regular jail. It is located in the rolling pine country south of Prince George, on sky-blue Lake Tracking. Politicians, school authorities, probation officers, and members of the general public who happen to go to the camp recognize the irony of condemning boys to a place that looks like an expensive resort.

Camp Tracking has a log bunkhouse attached to a log kitchen, dining room, and lounge. It has a swimming raft about a hundred feet off a pier that extends out into Lake Tracking. In summer, a row of red and green canoes graces the sandy beach in the vicinity of the pier. In winter, a row of snowshoes and cross-country skis decorates the pile of shovelled snow in front of the bunkhouse. At night, the soft glow of low-pressure propane lights illuminates the windows and casts on the grass or snow the shadows of boys playing pool or working at desks.

No matter what the authorities or public think about the attractions of Camp Tracking, it is, judging by the large number of escape attempts, adequate punishment in the minds of most of the boys incarcerated there. But Birch had no record of escape. In fact, Birch's record at the camp was impeccable. Birch cut mountains of firewood and stacked it in the shed. He shovelled snow – tons of it. He helped with projects like building picnic tables and outhouses. He went out with the camp leaders canoeing, hiking, fishing, and star-spotting. He attended special lectures on all these topics and more. Other inmates pined for phone contact with girlfriends, friends, and even parents, and still others pined for the streets of town or the arcades, pool halls, and malls. Birch did not pine for anything.

Vivien quickly caught on to the obvious fact that Birch liked Camp Tracking.

Dragooned last year by one of the camp leaders to present a talk with slides (the camp has a small portable generator for such purposes), Viv devised and delivered a dramatic show about Kluane Park. Birch sat in the front row, mesmerized. He growled at anyone in the room who was inclined to disturb Vivien's show or ask goofy questions. He asked questions about distances and times. He produced twenty dollars for Vivien's guidebook and demanded a signature.

"Go the distance," she wrote to Birch.

Birch lugged Vivien's stuff out to our truck. "Take me with you," he said.

In 1996, when it came time to plan our ascent of Zenchuk Creek, Vivien remembered Birch.

"So basically this kid's a pothead," I commented.

"I believe that he deliberately gets into trouble so he can stay out at camp. That's exactly the sort of thing I did as a kid. Anyway, I like him, and without him we can't go unless we find someone else."

"I'll buy him a Swiss army knife."

Taking Birch on a hike was like adopting him. A social worker and a probation officer had to be consulted. The social worker took us through what she saw as the relevant highlights of Birch's dossier and arranged for Birch's parents, long divorced, to visit us.

Obviously uncomfortable in one another's presence, they sat stiffly at either end of our sofa, Birch in between, so they had to look around him to see one another. This made things difficult for them; they wanted to show a united front when it came to Birch. Probably they had learned to do this over many years of dealing with social workers. I was immediately attracted to Birch because of his efforts to facilitate their front, nodding and smiling at their comments on his food preferences, eating and sleeping habits, and love of the bush. It seemed that there was no question of either parent objecting to Birch's going with us, though they dutifully scanned the maps, sat through ten minutes of slides from our initial trip into Tungsten, and examined the equipment we would provide for Birch. They treated their visit more as a job interview, their role being to provide good references for a son who had lucked onto a rare chance.

Their attitude made me nervous. "Your son could die up there!" I wanted to shout. "We could all die!" But I knew that Vivien would not approve of any such outburst.

Both parents knew of Vivien from her travel column, and both seemed to regard journalists as a higher order, within earshot of the gods. The fact that I taught at the college didn't seem to hurt.

We learned that Birch lived with each of the parents alternately, but with the mother for longer periods of time because she had steadier work and a permanent address. His movements from one parent to the other seemed to be based on their fluctuating ability to cope with him on top of life in general.

The father, finding occasion to assist me when I returned some equipment to the basement, told me that Birch wouldn't talk to save his life, but generally understood what he was told. "You just gotta say everything loud and minimum three times," he advised.

Birch's mother, finding herself at one point alone with Vivien, told her that Birch was a good boy at home, his only problem being bad dreams, from which he awoke drenched in sweat and screaming.

"What does he dream of?" Vivien asked.

"Bears, mostly."

The visit ended with handshakes all around. The father agreed to loan Birch his own extra-large sleeping bag, and the mother to provide new rain jacket and pants. The family left separately – the father in a beat-up pickup truck, the mother in a small but fairly new car, and Birch on his bicycle.

"Bears?" I said to Vivien when she told me of Birch's nightmares.

"We'll give him the big can of pepper spray."

Birch rode in the back of our truck all the way up the Alaska Highway, embedded in an arrangement of sleeping and clothing bags and evidently asleep most of the time. At a cafe at Pink Mountain he noticed buffalo meat on the menu and had to try it. Buffalo meat is popular along the Alaska Highway, more among tourists than locals. Birch loved it.

"It's grass-fed," he said happily as we returned to the truck.

At Liard Hot Springs, where we soaked for a couple of hours before moving on to Watson Lake, Birch stretched out on one of the submerged benches and, staring through the circle of tall trees at the sky, said he could almost imagine the place as it was when only the Indians gathered there for prayer and healing.

I entertained Birch with my impression of a rheumatic come to the springs for a cure. "I can walk!"

Vivien attached herself to a distant group of visitors.

At Watson Lake we stocked up on extra goodies to store in the truck and at the Flat Lakes. The healing effect, at the end of a long hike, of a can of smoked oysters or bacon, equals that of any hot spring. Also, on our stops up the Alaska Highway we had rediscovered what a teenage boy's appetite can be. Satisfying Birch was not going to be easy. Birch never actually asked for anything, but any offer was bound to be accepted.

"How about some ice cream on the apple pie?"

"Yes, please."

"One scoop or two?"

"Two, please."

Birch found a cafe advertising buffalo burgers and led us in. He had, it seemed, acquired a simplistic but nonetheless admirable concept of what he called "organic food." This was anything green or indigenous. We had found out in our two nights in campsites along the way that he could identify Labrador tea and knew how to mix it with rosehips to make tea that didn't taste entirely medicinal. I added scotch to mine, but both Vivien and Birch put their hands over their cups.

"It'll kill the vitamin C," said Birch.

Vivien nodded, looking at Birch with approval.

Birch also knew high- and low-bush cranberries and shaggy-mane mushrooms. Vivien got him chewing on the tender young shoots of fireweed.

"That could result," I told her, "in serious overgrazing of the Yukon's floral emblem."

"But it'll also take the pressure off the north's dwindling supply of wood buffalo meat."

We had planned a preliminary hike on the civilized side of the washout, just to test Birch. If he hated hiking, we could easily get him back to Watson Lake, load him up with a bag of take-out buffalo burgers, phone his mother, and stuff him on the Greyhound bus.

When we first studied maps of the area around Tungsten, we noticed two mining roads running west off Highway 10, one up Conglomerate Creek and one up an unnamed creek. On the map, we could see that the two roads rose rapidly out of the bush that shrouds Highway 10 and the Hyland River, arriving in the alpines and ending at the crossed pickaxe symbols that indicate mine sites.

We decided to go up the Conglomerate Creek road. The only reason for our choice was that Conglomerate makes a picturesque debut on Highway 10, featuring a small, stone-step waterfall visible from the highway on the right side of the creek. Conglomerate was marked when we were there the year before – most of the creeks in the area originally were marked, though many of the markers are now face down in the bush along the highway's shoulder.

It took Birch a long time and considerable assistance to get rigged for the hike. We had outfitted him with an ancient but solid external-frame pack that Vivien had given to her husband one Christmas. She always

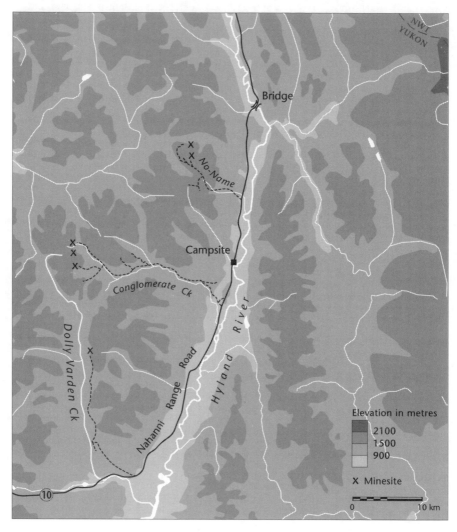

MAP 4: CONGLOMERATE CREEK

said, with withering sarcasm, that it had never been used. Not even once! So when they separated, she had naturally hidden it away and then made off with it.

Experienced packers are intimate with their packs, having learned where to put each item for maximum convenience and how to manage each zipper and strap. Watching a cluttered campsite disappear in seconds, each item to its appointed place, is like watching ballet. For the most part, however, Birch stood there dumbfounded, his hand on some item and his pack flat on the ground in front of him.

We understood and took over. "Roll all your clothing tightly, like this," Vivien said. "Place it in your plastic clothes bag and put the bag into the bottom partition of your pack."

"Snap your cup onto your shoulder harness using the plastic shower-curtain hook that I stuck on its handle."

Birch tried his pack on. Vivien adjusted the straps. "You've got about thirty-five pounds. On Zenchuk, that'll turn into forty pounds, half of it food. I've got about the same. John carries a bit more because his pack is much better than yours and he always brings 900-page books."

"Give me Dickens," I said, "or Dostoevski. I want the real stuff when I'm in the bush risking my life."

"You carry books?"

"Always," I said. "So does Viv. There's a box of them in the truck. I'll show you."

I dragged the box onto the tailgate and opened it. Birch glanced at our collection: Atwood's *Robber Bride,* Richler's *Solomon Gursky* (which I recommended for its northern content), Mistry's *A Fine Balance,* Shields' *Stone Diaries* ...

"If I don't carry a book I can carry something else," said Birch, turning away.

We continued stuffing Birch's pack, working around him like a couple of Arabs loading a camel.

"Your bear spray velcros onto your pack harness."

"Your bug spray is in your bottom sidepocket. You can reach around with your right hand and get it without taking off your pack."

"Soon you'll do all this without even thinking about it."

Once loaded, we lurched up the road, packs and boots creaking. We made the usual dozen or so initial stops for adjustments and to shed clothing.

"If you're uncomfortable – too hot or too cold or a boot hurts – stop right away and fix it," Vivien advised. "Don't let a sore or blister develop into something worse. And don't worry about slowing us down. We'll be doing the same thing."

The mining road up Conglomerate began just north of the intersection of the creek and the highway. Not far up the road, on a switchback that ran through a stately grove of spruce, we found the remains of a mining exploration camp. The shack was in bad shape, the roof completely rotted through, but the core-sample racks, built to hold their incredible weight of stone, stood solid.

We downed packs to make a close investigation. Birch slid out one of the heavy drawers for a look. I explained the process of drilling test holes and then I wandered off to inspect a bear cache, a heavy plywood box built on a trestle-like tower.

"Shit!" yelped Birch when I was halfway up the tower.

I looked over and saw him hopping around, holding onto one foot. He had dropped one of the core samples on his foot. Vivien was running over to check him out. "Sit down and take your boot and sock off."

"It's okay."

"Just let me have a look."

It was okay, though Birch was limping slightly as we moved off.

"What are you carrying that core sample for?"

"Can I take it with me?"

It was a foot-long hunk of sparkling quartz with ribbons of orange rock swirling through it. It had to weigh at least ten pounds.

"You could leave it here and pick it up on the way back."

"Good idea." Birch lovingly returned the stone to its drawer.

A little farther on we noticed, on our right, a teardrop lake. A road seemed to provide access, first curving around a garbage pit, into which I immediately descended.

"John likes to see garbage," Vivien told Birch. "It makes him feel at home."

"A beer can on the side of an abandoned road is an ambassador of civilization," I said. "In tough circumstances, it could be useful. A cutting edge, a container. Flatten it out and nail it onto your shack – it's a perfect shingle, impervious to rain and time. Nature doesn't make objects like that."

"Birchbark," said Birch.

"That's right," said Vivien. "Combine it with pine pitch and you can sheet roofs and canoes."

I shook my head sadly at them, poor fools, standing there in Gore-Tex, attempting to pretend that the evolutionary path of humankind leads anywhere other than to a technological Eden or Armageddon. I climbed down into the pit for a closer look while Vivien and Birch continued on to the lake. I noticed some five-gallon oil buckets half-buried in the gravel, a few of them obviously intact. Most of the plastic items were broken. Plastic really *is* junk, I thought sadly. Usually you can't even burn it for heat; it just melts.

While I was still poking around, Vivien and Birch returned. "The road ends on a hill overlooking the lake," Vivien announced, hauling out her notebook. "There might be a trail down to it, but it's not obvious."

"You didn't go down anyway?" I asked, my attention riveted on a piece of angle iron protruding through the gravel. What was on the other end of *that?* I wondered.

"The lake's in the middle of a bog, smartass. If this turns out to be a good hike, we'll come back some other year and see if there's a way to get to the shore. Leave that junk alone and let's go."

We walked on. As we walked we could hear an increasing commotion from Conglomerate Creek. We soon encountered a side road leading left. The road passed through a space that looked like it had been pared by a bulldozer. Scraps of plywood and lengths of drilling pipe indicated that this had been an exploration site. At the edge of the cleared space we looked down through a rocky canyon at a mushbowl, a seething circular patch of white water, on the creek below.

Our day ended on the banks of a wide gravel washout, in a cleared space featuring a forty-five-gallon oil drum, dozens of large nails scattered on the ground, some rusted stovepipes, and the remains of plastic tarps. A fire ring indicated recent occupation by hunters. We dropped packs to explore.

It turned out that a large tributary of Conglomerate Creek, flowing in from the north, had swept away a wooden bridge and then carved itself a few extra channels between our spot and the slope opposite. We could see a road or trail curving up into the bush on that slope, but couldn't tell if it was our road or a side road. At first we thought it possible that we were actually on Conglomerate and that the creek had decided to move over and occupy the road. We beat our way north up our side of the creek, past some faded, brittle, flagging tape hanging from willow branches, but the bush continued to get thicker and there was no sign of a road veering off. We returned to the washout and set up camp.

"Here we see the advantages of garbage," I said, flattening out a piece of stovepipe and using a rock and ten-inch nail to pound holes in the pipe to make a grill so our cooking pots sat more securely over the fire. The forty-five-gallon drum, set level, made a good surface for our cooking utensils.

Birch proved adept at gathering firewood, snapping pieces in two and sniffing the ends to check for sap or moisture. He knew to go for the lower branches of spruce if there was nothing dry on the ground. Finally we had to stop him. The woodpile was getting too high. A cup of instant cappuccino did the trick.

"So. End of your first day," Vivien said to Birch after we had settled around our fire. "What do you think so far?"

"This is great," murmured Birch, sweeping his eyes in a circle across the wild scene, the raging creek, the gravel banks up its far side, spruce lying head-down in the water, crossed by other spruce leaning at crazy angles, the snowy peaks of distant mountains visible above the treetops.

Vivien smiled, then turned to me. "We could've taken our bikes this far."

I nodded.

"Pretty steep," said Birch doubtfully.

"We'd have to push them most of the way," Vivien admitted. "But on the way back we'd be all the way out from here to the truck in an hour."

"That would be fun," said Birch.

"We know of one guy that comes into Tungsten pulling a wagon, but that's not efficient. You can't carry much more on a wagon than you can on a bike, and a wagon's much slower."

"A kid's wagon?"

"Yeah. And all the way from Watson Lake and back."

"One year he stayed in so long he had to drag his stuff out on a sleigh," added Vivien.

"I'd like to meet that guy," said Birch.

"You probably will if you keep coming back here."

"I'm coming back."

Viv told Birch what we knew about Felix while I concentrated on stirring our dehydrated food into the large pot of boiling water. When Viv finished talking, I settled back and started talking about Patterson and Faille. "In the old days they dragged loaded canoes into places like this. It's called lining. Here, for example, they would've lined up the Hyland and then up this creek as far as that canyon we passed. Usually they were prospecting, so they had lots of equipment. Lining was tremendous work, and dangerous, clambering up gravel washes, portaging over cliffs, and inching around the faces of rock bluffs with a bucking, fully loaded canoe attached by a drag line to your waist. But they got in with a lot of stuff, and they were able to get out fast with their furs, gold, whatever they went in to get. We do something like that with the bicycles, thanks to these mining roads."

"How'd they rig the lines on the canoes?" asked Birch.

I explained, using a stick to scratch a diagram in the sand.

"Wouldn't it be dangerous having a canoe tied to you?"

"It is dangerous. You could get dragged into the river by the load. On the other hand, if you were just holding onto the rope and happened to let it go by accident, you'd lose your canoe and supplies. You'd probably starve before you could walk out. If there was more than one guy, one pulled and the other rode in the canoe to steer it and jump out and push if it got grounded."

I then talked more about Faille and Patterson, a mistake on my part, as it turned out. I was planting the seed of an idea in Birch's young and therefore inadequate mind.

In the morning, after fording the creek at the road and walking up the opposite bank, we found ourselves almost immediately in sub-alpines, the trees giving way to willows and dwarf birch, with the odd black spruce projecting through. We passed a flattened frame cabin and a road forking off to the north. We could see it on the hills above, switchbacking into the alpines. Vivien consulted the contour maps, estimating the alpines at about 1750 metres. The maps showed the road ending up there, probably at the remains of a drilling platform. We decided to push along the main road to the mine site and then maybe, if we were still interested, explore any side roads on our way out.

Farther along, a twin waterfall poured down the slope opposite into Conglomerate Creek. Then the road levelled out, passing through a thinly vegetated area with the snow-streaked alpines now in clear view ahead of us.

At the end of this plateau we faced the apparition of a white, aluminum ATCO trailer.

"Does that ever look weird in this setting," said Vivien.

"Like a lawyer on public transit."

"Like you in shorts and hiking boots."

"Like Patterson in a Stetson."

We crossed a spongy field to the trailer. Its door was hanging open. Inside we saw a musty-smelling ruin. The roof must have been leaking in places, and animals had been going in and out to shred things.

A kitchen, a shower, a toilet – it was hard to imagine how things would have been hooked up. A propane furnace. In the office-bedroom at the back end was a desk decorated with core samples.

"Look at this," said Birch, still in the kitchen area.

It was a scrawled message, dated 1985, parts of it faded to oblivion, and it said something about turning back, "only one skidoo working."

A hint of danger.

Vivien located an old box of pasta and a jug of cheap pancake syrup hardened to sugar. "We'll take some of this pasta out with us," she said.

She was thinking of Birch's amazing appetite, of conserving our homemade, dehydrated meals for the ascent of Zenchuk.

"Maybe we can hit Gerald and Terri up for some food when we finish the hike," I said to her.

"I'd hate to do that, but they have stuff flown in regularly, so maybe we can put in an order."

Farther on the road forked in three directions, and we stayed to the right, making for some buildings indicated on the map. Late in the afternoon we saw the camp below, scattered along the headwaters of Conglomerate

Creek. At this elevation the creek was reduced to a thin black ditch in the green alpine. There were a couple of shacks, a yellow bulldozer, a large flat-deck truck, and a lot of junk.

"Home," I said, rubbing my hands in anticipation.

While still above camp and in the open, we hauled out the maps and reconnoitred.

"The mine's above the camp, below that ridge," said Vivien. "It's probably in those rock piles up there. There's a lake too, maybe the source of the creek. One of the roads that forked off back there must go to the other side of that ridge and another mine."

The road ran down to the camp through a thick stand of dwarf spruce. Birch stopped on the way, rooted in the bush to his right, and dragged out a plywood sign. We barely made out the faded lettering:

> SLEEPY HOLLOW
>
> YUKON
>
> POP 11

Vivien and I camped on open ground between the shack and the creek. Birch decided to occupy the shack. He wondered why we were camping outside, and I said that the weather looked good and the shack looked dusty. "Vivien's sensitive to dust."

"I'm going to sweep it out. There's a broom."

"Go ahead. It looks solid and you've got a choice of four comfortable army beds. If you're going to light a fire in the stove, though, check the chimney first to see if it's solid. You'll need those mosquito coils on the shelf there, so don't lose sight of them."

While Birch worked on the shack, Vivien and I jumped the creek and walked up to the open-pit mine. The miners, with their usual thorough-ness, had created an erratic wasteland of boulder piles.

"Disgusting," said Vivien.

"Small price to pay for the road in, though," I said. "All they did here was sort tons of gravel."

"I guess you're right. There'd be no way into here without the road, and these alpines are beautiful. We could've done the entire trip on our bikes, actually."

"Just shoulder them across the washout?"

"Right."

Returning, we could see smoke coming out of the cabin chimney. The whole scene suddenly looked domestic, safe. Birch had hot water boiling in a big aluminum kettle, enough water for tea, cooking, and washing. He proudly showed us his work, after allowing Vivien to treat and bandage a deep gash (from a stovepipe) on the palm of his hand.

"I found an axe, a broken saw, and plenty of nails, all in the toolshed over there. There's enough stuff around here to really fix this place up. The table and chairs were outside under a tree. There's an old oil drum up in the tree. I don't know what it's for."

We went out for a look. The five-gallon oil drum, lashed onto a tree branch about seven feet off the ground, was part of a shower unit. An intake pipe with a tin can carefully placed over it, and a ladder leaning against the tree, allowed the miners to fill the drum, probably with water heated on the cabin stove. A tap was welded to the bottom of the drum, and a juice can, open at the top and perforated at the bottom, was wired onto the tap to serve as a showerhead. Flat on the ground beneath the whole unit was a pallet board. A clothing rack and soap dish were attached to the tree.

"That would've felt good to those dusty miners," said Vivien.

That evening Birch set to work reactivating the shower. The next morning we spent an hour filling the apparatus with warm water from the kettle and cold from the creek and washing ourselves.

"Heaven," said Vivien.

Then we packed and left. At the top of the road, Birch looked sadly over his shoulder for a last view of Sleepy Hollow. "A guy could live there," he said.

"In the winter?"

"There's lots of firewood. I'd have to learn how to hunt and trap."

In a long day of steady grunting, looking neither to the left nor the right all the way except to remind Birch to retrieve his core sample, we were back at our truck and bicycles on Highway 10. Our minds were now on Zenchuk. We drove the truck to the government campsite just before the washout and pitched our tents in the picnic shed; the floorspace we had cleared the previous summer was still cleared.

"Birch is alright," I said quietly to Vivien as we settled to sleep. "He's

strong and eager and generally knows what to do."

Vivien nodded. "The
only thing that worries me
is he keeps hurting him-
self," she whispered. "That
gash is going to be okay,
thanks to our powdered
antiseptic, but it's a nasty
one. Also, he leaves his stuff
lying around. I don't know
how many times I've picked
up his knife and handed it
to him. He's got some
important stuff, so keep
your eye on him when he's
packing up and check the
spots he leaves from."

VIVIEN LOUGHEED AT SLEEPY HOLLOW

By midmorning the next
day we were pulling Vivien's old canoe off the top of the truck canopy
and dragging it to where Highway 10 disappeared into the creek. We
had already piled our bicycles and supplies there. We stripped down to
shorts and thongs and attached one end of a long rope to the front of the
canoe, one end to the back.

"Now you'll see how lining works," I said to Birch, moving upstream
to where a gravel shoal extended out into the water.

"How it *might* work," Vivien corrected. "By the way, I'm getting in."

"Why?" I asked. "This is just a test."

"You're not drawing enough water to make the boat do what you want
it to do. Besides, it's my canoe and if it goes I'm going with it."

The technique worked fairly well, though Vivien was correct about
the canoe needing a load. Also, the farther across I was able to manipu-
late the canoe, the more it leaned towards me, threatening to swamp.
Vivien compensated by leaning and finally by paddling the last few feet
over to the other side.

She jumped ashore, dragging the canoe after her, untied my rope from the back of the canoe, and tied another rope there. Then we were easily able to pull the canoe back and forth across the washout. Birch loaded and unloaded, riding back and forth to hold onto things which didn't fit snugly into the canoe. Finally I jumped in and was pulled to the other side.

We lit a fire, dressed warmly, and consumed some instant soup. Then we stashed the canoe in the bush nearby, loaded our packs and panniers, and began our ride to the Flat Lakes.

With loaded panniers front and back, and backpacks loaded to about thirty pounds, the trip took us two full days. Again we camped in the gravel pit near the trapper's corral, and again we got hit by a squall on the pass. We checked out our little shack at the junction north of Tungsten and found it exactly as we had left it, including the piece of tin roofing over the firepit in the driveway.

"*Nobody* comes in here," said Vivien.

"Isn't it great?"

The part of the road that was new to us, from the junction to the Flat Lakes, delighted us. It ran along the west side of Divide Lake. Along with the glacier above Mirror Lake, Divide Lake is the ultimate source of the Flat River. The lake featured a picnic site and two floating docks. From a rise about halfway between Divide Lake and the Flat Lakes, we saw the Flat Lakes in the distance. Soon we came to a creek flowing into the Flat Lakes from the east. On the other side of that creek was a framed cabin with a fearsome human-bear visage painted in white on the door.

"What's that supposed to mean?" asked Birch.

"KEEP OUT, I imagine," said Vivien.

"Or it's a warning to the bears to stay away," I said. "This is probably the warden's – Stefan's – cabin that we heard about last year. It's one of four cabins around the lake."

"Looks deserted."

"I guess he hasn't come in yet."

"Let's look."

We took off our packs, removed our boots, put on our thongs, and waded across. The cabin was locked, its windows nailed over with plywood and its door nailed shut. What looked like a garage beside the shack was also padlocked. We could see, through the crack between the doors, a four-wheel-drive all-terrain cycle and a propane-powered freezer. Between the two buildings and the creek was a firepit with an elaborate adjustable grill big enough to hold half a moose.

"Look at this," said Birch.

The cabin's doormat was a large piece of 3/4-inch plywood with nails sticking up through it.

"Some welcome."

"Dwayne told us last year that Stefan had bear trouble."

"What kind of bear trouble?" asked Birch, scanning the bush along the edge of the cabin's yard.

"Imaginary, in Dwayne's view," I answered. "Stefan reported blasting one grizzly right through the door of the shack. The griz was bent on breaking in. Stefan also reported shooting one that intercepted him between the shack door and the outhouse. It does all sound a bit exaggerated."

"I dunno," said Birch, worried. "I've heard other stories like that."

"Don't worry," said Vivien. "If he had bear trouble, it was probably due to barbecuing moose steaks on the grill here."

"Or grayling."

"Our dehydrated food doesn't smell at all, until we cook it. Even then it hardly smells."

Vivien hauled out a contour map. "The road divides here. One branch goes along this creek to the lake and the other around the lake and farther north along the Little Nahanni River, which runs out of the far end of the lake. The cabin that the Pitts were talking about is probably accessible from the road that goes around the lake, but let's go down to the lake first and take a look."

We crossed back over to our bicycles and packs. Noticing that the creek had, at some time in the past, overflowed its banks and occupied the road, we left our thongs on. In a few minutes, pushing our bikes through a foot of icy water, we arrived at a point on the east shore, near the lake's south end.

"Wow!" said Birch.

"Beautiful!" said Vivien.

"A picnic table!" I said, sitting down gratefully.

The Flat Lakes are really one lake, severely pinched in the middle. The north shore is a steep, heavily wooded hill that drops straight down into the lake. The south shore is eminently hospitable, with many bays and coves, some of which feature gravel beaches and inflowing creeks. Beavers building at the south end have thinned the willow and dwarf birch. The distant north end of the lake mirrors much more distant, whitecapped mountains.

Directly across from us, not more than a hundred metres away on the lake's west shore, was a cabin with a full front porch. A set of moose antlers added a rustic touch – they were mounted on the gable above the porch roof. The willow and dwarf birch had been cleared between the cabin and the shoreline. A half-dozen large spruce trees surrounded the cabin. A small pier extended out into the lake.

"It's lovely!" exclaimed Viv.

On our side was the picnic table, a pole frame for a house-tent, a dozen bright-orange forty-five-gallon drums of aviation fuel (mostly full, as Birch quickly ascertained), a long floating dock, and a red fibreglass canoe.

"That's the Pitts' canoe," Vivien explained. "They're the family that looks after Tungsten, and they come here to fish. The gas belongs to the outfitter who flies in sheep hunters; that's why there's a warden stationed here."

"Can we use the canoe?" asked Birch.

"Don't see why not," said Vivien. "As long as we're careful. We can cross over to the cabin. But we don't need to take our stuff; the cabin should be accessible from the road."

"The road running north," I added.

"We hope."

We crossed, Birch at the front, Vivien at the back, and me in the middle.

"You could wade over to the cabin," I observed, looking down at the lake bottom.

"Look at those fish!" exclaimed Birch.

"Grayling," said Vivien. "Fat ones, too. They're feeding here where the creek runs in."

"You don't see the fish in Lake Tracking," said Birch.

"There's another creek coming in just to the left," I said. "The lake's entire outflow must be at the north end."

"Dwayne set us straight on that."

"Yeah."

JOHN HARRIS IS IN THE CANOE AS IT IS LINED ACROSS THE WASHOUT

Birch jumped out at the small pier and held the canoe in. Vivien and I disembarked and Birch pulled the canoe up onto the beach beside the pier.

"You're okay in a canoe," said Vivien admiringly.

"I've never done any rivers like you, though," said Birch.

The cabin was a ramshackle affair, but tight, with no evidence of animal activity inside. It had a bedroom with two built-in bunks with mattresses, and a kitchen with a table and chairs, a wood heater, a sink, a counter, cupboards, and a propane range. The range was disconnected, as were the propane lights, one in each room. Each room had a chrome-and-orange-vinyl easy chair. The porch featured a bench.

"The big chairs and the bench are courtesy of Tungsten," I said.

Vivien nodded. "The bench is identical to the benches at the baseball diamond in Tungsten," she explained to Birch. "These chairs are from the recreation centre."

"I think I saw a path out back," I said. "It probably goes to the road. I'll follow it and see."

"No more than twenty minutes," said Vivien, checking her watch. "And stay on the path. And take your pepper spray. And keep blowing your whistle."

I circled the shack before taking the path. There were two large piles of lumber, one of them mainly cedar siding. There was an outhouse in the bush behind the cabin. There was a small shed for an electrical generator under one of the giant spruce, and another shed that held an old washing machine and some firewood. The path to the road was wide but crossed by windfall, most of which I was able to toss out of the way, but some of which I had to climb over or walk around. I realized that it would be impossible to get the bicycles down the path.

After a steady climb of about ten minutes I broke through some thick willow onto the road. I scraped a mark across the road with the heel of my boot and returned to the cabin.

Vivien was in the kitchen. "Did you find the road?"

"Ten minutes up the hill."

"There's some useable tea, coffee, porridge, and spices. The cocoa and instant soups are cement. It looks like the place is used once in a while, probably by the floatplane guy."

Birch came in with firewood. "There's an axe in the shed," he said, "but no saw."

We put a fire into the heater, dampened it down, filled a large pot and a kettle with lake water, and put them on to warm, then canoed back over to our bicycles. After we put the canoe back in its place on the shore, we waded up the creek to the warden's cabin and main road, and cycled around to my bootmark. From the end of the lake to the trail, the road climbed steeply.

"We can't take the bikes down until we find a saw and do some clearing," I said. "But it's easy walking."

We couldn't see the lake from the road because the slope was so heavily wooded. On the other side of the road was a stone bluff. Tired but relaxed, having found a secure home for the night, we walked to where the road crowned. A creek roared down off the bluff and through a culvert beneath the road. We caught a glimpse of the north end of the lake.

"The road's still quite good," said Vivien, looking north. "Except for a few washed-out culverts, you could drive a truck from Tungsten to here. Do you know what that means?"

"Banff of the North."

Birch looked quizzically at us.

"Vivien's got plans for this country," I explained. "A guidebook. Adventure cycling and trekking. With cabins. People in shorts crawling up the cliffs and trails and hurling their trail bikes up and down the road. I'm going to start a cappuccino shop, maybe right here at the lake."

"I thought it was going to be back at the corner."

"This is prettier."

I pulled Vivien gently off the road and pointed her towards the path. We unloaded the bikes, stashed them in the bush, and lugged our packs and panniers to the cabin.

Next morning I sat on the porch bench, bundled against the cold, cradling a hot coffee in both hands, watching Vivien. Half obscured by the mist hanging over the water, she was fishing off the dock, her coffee steaming beside her. Birch, who had planned to fish too, was still asleep.

In ten minutes she had three fish. I returned to the kitchen to lay some

THE CABIN AT THE FLAT LAKES

canned bacon in the frying pan. The bacon was part of the stash from our panniers that would stay in the cabin awaiting our return from the Rabbitkettle. Birch woke up as soon as the delicious smell spread through the cabin.

We made a late start, assuring Birch, who still wanted to fish, that on our return we would spend a day or two convalescing in the cabin. We hiked up the path to the road, made sure our bicycles were stashed securely in the bush by the trail, and then headed off down the road to Stefan's cabin.

"This is going to be a grunt," said Vivien as we put on sandals to cross the creek to Stefan's cabin.

"How far on this road before we hit bush?"

"I figure we'll camp at the end of this road. It zig-zags almost to the alpine, but there'll be an hour or more of bushwhacking from where it ends up to the alpine. It'll be steep too. We can save that for tomorrow morning."

The road, more of a trail, looked like it had been made by a small bulldozer in a hurry. It climbed steeply, crazily in places, high along a gorge down which the creek, that flowed so peacefully past Stefan's cabin and into the lake, roared. In places we could step to our right just off the edge of the road to the edge of the canyon, but only rarely could we see all the way to the creek at the bottom.

"There's a lot of bear shit on this road," Birch kept saying.

"The freshest has a skin on it, so it's at least a couple of days old," I said, poking at a pile with the toe of my boot. "If you find some warm stuff, let us know."

I piped steadily on my whistle.

After a couple of hours we caught some views of the Flat Lakes, our cabin a tiny sparkle at the south end.

"There's another cabin right near ours!" exclaimed Birch.

Sure enough, the far shore of the lake swept in tight beneath the road, making a small bay, and tucked into the bush not more than a hundred or so yards from our cabin was another, smaller, silver speck.

Vivien hauled out the binoculars. "There's a path between the two," she said. "It runs along the shoreline. That creek we saw up on the road, where the trail starts down to our cabin, flows into the lake between the two cabins. Could be some good fishing there, too. Can you see the road?"

"For sure." The road was clearly visible above the second cabin, as the slope there fell straight down into the lake. Otherwise, a straight, dark streak in the green forest indicated the road's presence right to the north end of the lake and beyond.

Our trail forked. We took our packs off and investigated. The right fork led down through thick, high willows to a small creek, probably the top of the one we had followed up. Across the creek, the trail seemed to curve south.

"We want to go above and to the north of that hump over the lake," said Vivien, so we returned to our packs, shouldered them, and continued up the left fork. In a few minutes we arrived at a large open space in an ocean of dwarf birch.

"Another picnic table!"

We ran to the table and sat down.

"It's still a bit early," I said. "What should we do?"

"Stay here," said Vivien reluctantly. "See the bush up there between us and the alpines?"

"I noticed."

"I'm kinda tired," said Birch. "That was some climb."

So we made a leisurely camp, gathering dry branches from the trunks of a few squat spruce that stuck their heads above the willow.

At around midnight, we were shocked awake by a loud bawling.

"An elk?" I asked Vivien.

"An elk that swears," said Vivien, listening closely. Sure enough, there were some four-letter words mixed into the elk's cry.

"Birch! Birch!" yelled Vivien, poking her head out of the tent. "What's wrong?"

The bawling stopped.

"I was dreaming," said Birch, after a long silence, his voice still raw and sobbing.

"Did you take your pepper spray into your tent?"

"I think I forgot it in the outhouse at the cabin."

"We'll bring you one of ours."

I delivered my spray can to Birch's tent.

Back in my sleeping bag, I whispered to Vivien, "Should we go back tomorrow and get the spray? Without packs we could be there and back in a day."

"No," she said, rolling back to sleep.

"Do you mind if I call your safety practices into question?"

"Call them what you want. If we went back and got the spray, he'd just leave it here or somewhere else. We haven't got time to waste. It looks like this will be slow going, and our food won't last past two weeks."

It turned out she was right on all counts.

Birch seemed okay in the morning. When he rolled his tent and bag while I made breakfast, he placed the pepper spray on the picnic table, and I quietly grabbed it and attached it by its string to my pack strap. I always carry it this way, the string tied long enough so the spray can fits neatly into my shirt pocket. My reasoning is that if a bear whacks me and I still have a head and am conscious, my spray will be within reach.

It was, unfortunately, a warm morning, the wrong kind of weather for serious bushwhacking, though better, of course, than rain. The bugs, numbed during the night, came out early and in full force. We kept looking up at the alpines, imagining the bug-clearing breezes sweeping across them.

It was two full hours up into those breezes. In places we climbed straight over rock bluffs that we couldn't make our way around due to the bush. As we ascended, moving as consistently as we could to the northeast, we could see the full length of the Flat Lakes below us. Near the lake's south end, on the far shore, the two silver dots, the cabins, shone in the sun. Behind them, a streak in the forest indicated the road. But now we could see that streak running past the outflow of the Little Nahanni River and following that river north into the mountains. Directly across the lake from us, the hills that divide the Northwest Territories from the Yukon swept north and south, all similarly configured, like the toes of some monstrous foot.

Once on the alpine slope we moved quickly, eastward now, and Zenchuk Valley opened up. First Zenchuk Creek, entering into the Flat Lakes not more than a few yards from where the Little Nahanni flowed out. Then a strip of canyon through which the creek tumbled towards the lakes. Then the valley itself, a jungle of glistening ponds, golden-brown moraines and eskers, and dark-green willow. Then the serried slopes that ran up the far side of the valley. Finally, as we looked due east, our backs to the Flat Lakes, we could see, at the top of the valley, a mountain that looked like an elephant's head. A mountain that also looked to be far away. Then our alpine slope ended in bush, and we faced our first ravine.

At dinner time we found a rocky knoll with a large rock in the centre. The rock was gouged on top, making a natural firepit. There was wood aplenty, and just enough space around the central rock for our tents. A short distance to the east, a creek flowed past and down into a large pond on the valley bottom. We took water from the creek until Birch, scavenging firewood, found a small spring in the side of the knoll.

While we sprawled around the rock savouring our instant cappuccino, Birch pointed out the rippling wake of an animal swimming the pond below. It emerged on the other side as a moose and fed there in full view for an hour.

"If you had a rifle," said Birch, "you could live here. All you'd need is your tea and coffee, maybe some rice."

"That's what Faille and Patterson did," I said. "And rice was exactly what they chose to carry."

We ate, cleaned up, and retired early to our tents to escape the bugs. I made sure Birch got the pepper spray. Vivien caught up on her journal, referring to the contour maps for distances. She estimated that we had done eight kilometres that day.

"Our chances of making the Nahanni are as good as nil at that rate," she said.

"Maybe we'll see it."

"Not unless we climb a mountain."

"It'll get easier at the head of the pass," I said, putting aside my *Life of Dickens* to look at the map.

"But look what's ahead on the Rabbitkettle."

She was right. Farther ahead, the river entered the treeline, and there was a canyon. It looked like we could climb over the bluff on the north side of the river, but it would be steep and bushy. After the canyon, two rock glaciers flowed into the river from the south.

"At that point we won't be able to choose sides," I said. "The river won't be crossable."

"We want the north side anyway. That's where Rick the warden's cabin is."

"What have they got there?" asked Birch from his tent.

"Cake!" I said.

"What have they really got there?"

"A cabin," said Viv. "And a cable and skiff that they use to take people across the Rabbitkettle to the tufa mounds."

"They take them over?"

"It's a protected area," I explained. "Also dangerous. It's suspected that some of those old trappers and prospectors, like maybe the mysterious Bill Eppler and his partner Joe Mulholland, disappeared in those mounds, trying to get a warm bath in the hot springs."

"We've got to make twelve kilometres tomorrow," Vivien said decisively. She pointed at a small lake on the map. The lake sat at the foot of a rock glacier and had a small island in its centre. It was the headwaters of the Rabbitkettle River. "We've got to be there by tomorrow night."

Next morning we decided to try for easier hiking higher up. We followed the creek up and instantly ran into a comfortable old camp at the base of a bluff, some sawed sticks scattered around, and a full tin of safflower cooking oil jammed into a crevice in the bluff.

"A prospector," said Vivien, "and not too many years ago, either."

We found a game trail that skirted the bases of a number of moraines, and we made good time for three or four kilometres. Then we made another four or five difficult kilometres, crossing steep slopes covered with slimy cladina moss. We camped by a small, three-step waterfall, high above Zenchuk Creek, nowhere near Vivien's goal.

We were excited, however, by the appearance of a large waterfall up Zenchuk Creek. We had earlier taken it for a patch of snow or ice, but then realized that there was no other snow or ice in the vicinity and focused the binoculars on it.

"We'll spend some time tomorrow taking pictures of that!" said Vivien.

"Considering the size of the creek, it's one hell of a waterfall," I said.

We were at the falls by noon the next day. We had dropped low to avoid another wide and steep-sided gully and to see if there were some game trails along Zenchuk Creek. After an hour of torture along the creek, we found a trail. It led us back up onto the slopes, and then up the valley into sub-alpine. I was plodding along in the lead, head down, engaged in my usual game of trying to remember the lines of famous poems, when I noticed an old pressure cooker tangled in the dwarf birch to one side of the trail. I looked up; a Swede saw with an extra blade and a frying pan hung from a nail pounded into a dead poplar.

We entered a clearing and slipped our packs to the ground. Without a word to one another, we began to poke around. Birch found a full tin of white gas under a spruce. Vivien found the garbage pit that had been unearthed by bears. Rusted tins were scattered beneath the dwarf birch.

"Glory be," I said, picking up a cappuccino tin. "A fellow traveller. A sensitive person. This calls for a cappuccino in honour of our absent friend."

There was an airtight heater under a nearby tree, but it was rusted beyond use. I flattened a rusted stovepipe to use for a grill, and Birch took the Swede saw and cut firewood. Vivien found a small creek nearby and fetched water.

"Maybe this is Zenchuk's camp," Birch speculated.

"There may be some sign of him buried deeper in the pit, but I'm afraid there was no instant cappuccino in Zenchuk's time, poor bastards."

After a snack and libation to the unknown prospector, we headed for the falls, leaving our packs in the clearing.

"It's a lot easier having a saw," said Birch as we made our way around a bluff towards the centre of the valley.

"They make a light, collapsible model," I said. "When we get back, we'll check one out."

On the other side of the bluff we found ourselves above the falls. Moving down the alpine towards them, we noticed a number of grave-sized holes dug in the gravel.

"Test pits," I explained to Birch.

The falls spilled over two large steps of jutting stone and were at least thirty feet high.

"Zenchuk Lake's over there," said Vivien, pointing north. "It's on the other side of that ridge, so I don't know if it's the source of the creek or not. It doesn't look like it from here."

"Maybe we'll see the lake from the head of the pass."

Our photography session was interrupted by a rain squall. We rushed back to our packs, but by the time we got our raincoats on, the sun was out again, so we repacked our raincoats and headed for the top of the pass. It was boggy in places, but the trail was clear and marked by claim sticks, pieces of lathe with aluminum tags tacked onto them.

We camped on the pass in another rainstorm, cooking under our tarp on our gas stove and getting quickly into our tents. The rain eased but continued steadily until two a.m. – I was waiting for it to stop so I could climb out to pee. Shortly after I climbed back in, a large boulder came rolling past from the direction of Elephant Mountain. We heard it coming for a long way; it sounded like a three-legged moose crashing through the willow and birch, and it passed about fifty feet below the tents.

"What the hell is that?" Birch cried over to us.

"Just a boulder."

"How big?"

"Sounds about the size of a Mazda truck."

"Fuck, man!"

By noon the next day we were circling the little lake at the head of the pass. It was fed by a rock glacier that nuzzled the south shore. A tiny island protruded near the north shore. One by one we stood for photos at the east end of the lake, where the Rabbitkettle started out on its journey to the South Nahanni.

"If I piss into this little stream I'm pissing into the Nahanni," I announced.

"Don't you dare," said Vivien.

Crossing passes makes me nervous, more aware of the difficulties overcome that will have to be re-overcome on the way back, albeit from uphill and with some knowledge of the terrain. Vivien experiences the reverse: total exhilaration at entering new country. But this time that exhilaration was tempered by the knowledge that our food supply would permit us only two or three days on the Rabbitkettle.

We descended for three hours, to where a small creek ran from the north through a stone chute and beneath a grove of thick, stunted poplar into the Rabbitkettle, which at that point was just wide enough to be unjumpable. We found a flat space on a small bluff above the creek. Between the bluff and the creek was an outcropping of shale, which gave us a place for an efficient firepit and cozy seats.

"We'll be at the canyon tomorrow night," said Vivien. "Then we'll drop packs, take snacks and raingear, and climb over, maybe making another five kilometres to the first rock glacier before we have to turn back."

"You don't want to make a four-day dash to the Nahanni, beg food from Ranger Rick, and use our Visa to fly out with the first plane that drops a load of canoeists into Rabbitkettle Lake?"

"Don't tempt me. And don't propose what you'd never do yourself. What if I said yes? Birch would probably vote with me."

"You bet I would," said Birch.

"Okay, okay," I said. "We all know it would be suicide. Maybe Ranger Rick isn't home. Maybe there won't be any planes. Maybe they don't take Visa. The result? Three more headless corpses on the Nahanni."

"Headless?" asked Birch.

"Starving to death would be rough," admitted Vivien. "As for murder, even if it involved getting your head chopped off, not that bad a fate considering the alternatives, like dying hooked up to a hospital bed. And we'd get our names into another Nahanni book."

"Wouldn't you rather *write* the book?"

"I guess so."

That evening, just before we were ready to tuck in, Vivien noticed Birch fumbling with a zipper on his tent. "What's wrong?"

"I think it's okay."

"No it isn't. The zipper's completely off. There's some spares in the blue kit in your pack."

"I think I lost the kit," said Birch.

Vivien ransacked Birch's pack. No kit. "Damn it," she said. "That's got our spare stove parts, our spare buckles for the pack harnesses, and our tool kit. It's not safe to hike without it."

Birch kneeled, glumly silent, in front of his tent. Vivien stood a moment by his pack and then returned to sit by the fire.

"She's mad," said Birch.

I felt sorry for him. He was a good hiker, just inexperienced. "She's mainly upset that we have to go back," I explained. "She'll be okay. But meanwhile you're going to get eaten alive by mosquitoes."

"I've still got lots of lotion."

"Good. Climb in and put it on your face. I'll spread the tarp over the entrance to the tent and weigh it down with stones. That'll keep some of the bugs out."

I set Birch up for the night and then joined Vivien by the fire. Thunder sounded from over the Zenchuk side of the pass.

"Let's get into the tent," I said.

"He won't even be able to keep the rain out of his tent. The fly zipper is half gone too."

"I spread our tarp over it. He'll be okay."

We changed into our sleeping clothes and headed into our tent. Vivien worked on her trail notes while I read. Finally she whispered, "I'm glad you looked after Birch. I was too hard on him."

"Yeah. He's just starting, and he's just a kid. I told him you were mainly upset about having to go back."

"Not entirely true. But now we really do have to go back, and we'll start tomorrow. No day hike. It won't be safe to fool around here for another two days. That stuff is too important."

"Maybe we'll find it somewhere close."

We turned back the next morning, after Vivien talked to Birch, taking his coffee to his tent to wake him up.

"He's okay now," she said to me when she returned to the fire.

"He's going to be a mess of bites, but he said he had enough lotion."

Vivien smiled. "He doesn't really have *any* lotion. I gave him some of minc a couple of days ago. He lost his somewhere back there, and then he lost what I gave him. How much do you have?"

"Plenty."

In four days, harassed by rain but moving quickly, we were back at the Flat Lakes cabin. En route we found no sign of the repair kit, but then we located only two of our old campsites.

We fished and ate for two days, Birch deftly pulling in some large grayling. We cleaned up our cabin and visited the neighbouring one, intending to clean it up also. Unfortunately, the local chipmunk had long ago eaten his way inside and was busy shredding the place from the inside out.

On our third day, restless, we decided on a day bicycle trip to Tungsten. The call of the hot springs was irresistible, and we wanted to tell the Pitts of our adventures up Zenchuk Creek.

It felt good to be on the bikes again, relatively unloaded, speeding on ahead of the bugs. The trip took two exuberant hours.

Birch was surprised when he saw the town. "They just *left* all this?"

We could hear the generator running as we skimmed past the recreation centre. It seemed a good sign that things were as usual this summer.

They were, except Dwayne and Dexter were gone.

"It's just us now," said Terri, serving us coffee and thick slabs of homemade bread. "We don't like it as much. It's not as safe."

"What happened?"

"The mine changed hands. We're not company employees like Dwayne and Dexter. We contract out to babysit the town. The new owners renewed our contract for this summer."

"Good thing too," said Alex.

"He likes getting out of school early," said Natasha. "So do I."

"You *don't* get out of school early," said Terri. "You get a pile of work that you're supposed to do, and you haven't finished half of it yet even though it's July. So get back to your rooms for another hour."

"We want to visit!"

"We're going to the hot springs now and we'll be back to visit later in the afternoon," said Vivien as the kids took their bread and milk and returned to their rooms.

"What's Gerald up to?" I asked Terri.

"They've got him going through the core collection, which is housed in a building near the administrative offices. The trouble is, the building's not heated. He's got the lighting rigged to a generator truck, and a couple of electric heaters in one of the offices, but when he's out in the collection it's cold work."

"So the new company wants to know what it's bought."

"Yeah. The geology guys phoned."

We left for the hot springs. After an hour, Vivien and I returned to town. Birch decided to stay for another hour.

"Don't overdo it," advised Vivien. "If you stay in too long, we'll have to tow you back to the Flat Lakes."

"Okay."

Back at the house, Gerald was on the radiophone to the new head office, and Terri and the kids were off in the water truck. We got more coffee and sat outside at the picnic table. Gerald soon joined us.

"So you have to start your 'Banff of the North' campaign with a whole new set of mining executives," I suggested as we shook hands.

"Yeah. But they already know about the sheep hunting. Some of them are coming in September."

"Terri was saying you miss Dwayne and Dexter."

"Especially Dwayne. I tried to get them to let me take him on, but they suspended all maintenance operations until they have a chance to inspect the site. What about your plans for a book?"

"On," said Vivien. She described our Zenchuk hike.

Gerald was especially interested in the prospector's camp. "Probably he would've been in there when the mine was operating."

"What would he be looking for?"

"Gold, lead, zinc, copper. Prospecting is a complex business now. He must've thought he was onto something if he staked as much as you said, but I guess he was wrong."

Vivien told Gerald that that next day we planned to head north on the road from the Flat Lakes, on bikes. We would travel for a day, stay overnight, return to the Flat Lakes, then head out for home the next day.

"I've flown the road as far north as Steel Creek," said Gerald. "At Steel Creek the road turns west to the Yukon border. There's a mining exploration site, indicated on the contour maps, at the border. There's also an airstrip. The place is called Howard's Pass. I don't know if they cleaned it up or not, but it was once a big operation. The road goes past Howard's Pass to another airstrip, but I've never flown that far. Your main problems will be the wooden bridges, four of them, probably all of them partly washed out, between here and Steel Creek. They're on creeks that you'd have trouble crossing, at least early in the season."

"Any cabins?"

"Not that I know of."

"If those bridges are even mostly there, that would be great," said Vivien.

"They might not be there for long," said Gerald. "Same goes for the cabins on the Flat Lakes. The territorial government asks me about them once in awhile, which means they're probably considering having them removed, which means I'd have to 'copter in with some helpers and lots of kerosene."

"Why would they want them removed?"

"Name of the game," said Gerald. "The mine owners are responsible for a complete clean-up. 'Complete' is the operative word. Is this your helper coming up the hill?"

"Yep," said Vivien. "And it looks like he stayed in the springs too long. I hope he can make it back to the Flat Lakes."

"That's okay," said Gerald. "Terri wants to feed you and then we'll throw your bikes in one of the crew-cabs and take you home. The kids want to go fishing this evening and we've only been there once this summer."

I was wondering how Gerald was going to negotiate the two or three washed-out culverts between the turnoff on Highway 10 and the Flat Lakes. I found out when I helped him throw a pile of four-by-fours from the propane loading dock into the back of the truck. He used these to fill in around the culverts so he could drive across.

After dinner we loaded our bicycles on top of the four-by-fours and were on our way. It took only a half hour to get to the lakes. Gerald, Birch, and the kids went out in the canoe; Terri turned the truck around and drove Vivien and me to the trail above the cabin. She came down to the cabin with us to drink tea and watch the fishing. Finally, Gerald and Birch docked the canoe at the pier and everyone had instant cappuccino. The brighter stars were visible in the endless northern twilight before Gerald and the kids crossed over to dock the canoe and we walked Terri back to the truck.

"It's nice having people around," said Terri as we said goodbye. "It gets pretty lonely up here."

"We'll be back. Next summer we're going to the end of this road."

"Me too," said Birch.

Next morning we loaded our panniers lightly – some clothing, lunches and dinners for a couple of days, bags of trail mix, bicycle tools, and spare tires. We strapped tents and bags to the racks on the back of our bikes.

The road was rideable except for the usual washed-out culverts and fallen trees. Some stretches were not easy due to water running off the hills above and down the road, softening it. The vegetation got thicker as we moved north, but local wildlife had kept a path open along one or the other of the wheel ruts. We were glad of the obstructions, actually. What merely slowed down a bicycle would make the road impassable to any normal person with a four-wheel drive.

Once past the north end of the Flat Lakes, where a gravel-pit or turn-around allows a perspective, the road followed the Little Nahanni as it wound – slowly at first, then picking up speed, and finally in places thundering over big rocks – towards the Nahanni. The hills are steep and thickly wooded; without the road, overgrown and washed-out as it is, the country here too would be inaccessible. The dominant vegetation is stunted spruce, taller and thicker down by the river, and squat and sparse above the road. The spruce stick up through a jungle of tall willow.

Just at dinner time we came to a fork in the road. The main road continued to a small wooden bridge, while the branch to the right led to a clearing, on the very edge of which, beneath tall spruce, stood a small cabin.

"It's locked tight," said Birch. "We'd need a crowbar. I broke the blade on my knife trying to pry the latch off."

Far stronger than us on a bicycle, Birch had been riding ahead for most of the day. We'd had to remind him not to go on too far, even though he had reclaimed his can of pepper spray from the outhouse behind our Flat Lakes cabin. He was getting comfortable in the bush.

Birch helped us push our bikes around some spruce that had fallen across the road into the clearing. "The river's right through the trees over there. There's a path. You can't see much through the window, but the cabin's full of wooden boxes. There's a firepit right there, with a grill.

The outhouse even has toilet paper!"

I peered in the cabin window. "The boxes are for setting traps," I said.

"I'd like to look at those," said Birch.

We pitched our tents and lit the fire, using kindling and wood from some boxes by the side of the cabin.

After dinner we examined the bridge. It was made of twelve-by-twelve timbers set on log pilings with a plank deck, the whole structure held together by bolts and steel cables. The bridge looked out of place, a straight line in that tangle of trees, and bleached silver in a world of green and black. It crossed a creek that we could easily have forded, but at some cost of time.

"I can see what Gerald means about these bridges," I said, examining the substantial pile of driftwood lodged against the supports. "They take a big hit in the spring."

A breeze blew up the creek off the Little Nahanni, keeping the bugs clear of us. We sat for awhile on the sun-warmed timbers.

"Maybe later we can lobby the government to leave these in," said Vivien.

"Or even, after your book attracts hundreds of cyclists and hikers, to improve them."

"I want to do this road with you next summer," said Birch seriously.

"It's a deal," said Vivien.

"What we've found here," I said, "is about two hundred kilometres of traffic-free cycling trail, with cabins."

"I wish I could stay here all winter," said Birch. "Like Faille and Patterson."

"You'd need a rifle for sure," I said. "And a chainsaw. You'd use a mountain of wood through the winter. I wonder how deep the snow gets."

"I could learn to trap, too."

"That's how they all did it. Once we're in Watson Lake you could get Turner's book; he describes the trapping in some detail."

We left Birch sitting on the bridge, and returned to the cabin.

"You've hooked another victim," I said to Vivien.

"He was already hooked. But the talk about staying here through the winter makes me nervous. That would be suicide."

"He knows that."

"I wonder."

The next morning we cycled back to the Flat Lakes, and the morning after we made our way in one long ride to the washout. We camped beside Gerald's bulldozer, lined the canoe across early the next morning, and by midafternoon were taking long showers in a hotel room in Watson Lake. Vivien and I phoned our kids. We also, through the radio operator, contacted Terri to tell her we'd made it out.

"We found another cabin," I reported. "About twenty-five kilometres north of the Flat Lakes, right on the Little Nahanni."

"No way!" said Terri. "Gerald will be very interested in that. Could you drive to it?"

"No."

Birch went to explore Watson Lake. I gave him a list of books by Turner and Patterson. "I've seen them for sale at Hougen's General Store," I said. "You could check into a guy named Dalziel, too. Both Turner and Patterson talk about him. Dalziel was Nahanni's first bush pilot and a partner of Zenchuk's who trapped up the Beaver River just north of here."

"I'll check it out. Write down his name."

"How about six o'clock for dinner," said Vivien. "I think I'm ready for a buffalo steak if they have any."

"I'll eat the rest of the buffalo."

TRAPPER'S CABIN ON THE LITTLE NAHANNI RIVER

Birch arrived late for dinner. Vivien and I had already made our way through a bottle of wine, and he sat down with the air of someone bearing glad tidings. He had the books by Patterson and Turner. He also had a job at one of the local gas stations.

"Don't worry," he said. "I checked with Mom."

"I hope you don't mind if I check with her too," said Vivien. "We're responsible for you until we hear different."

"I'll give you her number," said Birch.

"I've got it," said Vivien, grabbing her notebook and heading for the lobby.

There was an awkward pause.

"I read about the McLeod brothers in Patterson," said Birch.

"Have some of those stuffed mushrooms. What do you want to drink?"

"Milk," said Birch, pushing four stuffed mushrooms into his mouth in quick succession.

I signalled the waitress and told her to bring milk and another plate of stuffed mushrooms.

"A lady at the museum showed me a sketch of Dalziel," Birch said. "They don't know much about him. But they say his house is right across from the old hotel, and his kids still live here, though they sold the house."

"Really?"

"I could get in touch with them once I'm settled in."

"That would be great. Settled in where?"

"There's a residence for kids who come here to work. Most are university students. It's easy to get a job here in the summer. The guy who sold me the books sent me to this office, and they sent me over to the garage."

Vivien returned. Birch looked up expectantly.

"Okay. She says you can stay. Are you sure you want to do this?"

"I've got nothing else to do."

The waitress arrived with the milk and mushrooms. When she left, Vivien leaned over close to Birch. "Just do me one favour. Don't go back into Tungsten and try to stay around there. I know you want to do it. *I* want to do it. But it would be suicide."

"Don't worry," said Birch, reaching for his milk. "I'm not crazy."

TRAIL INFORMATION

Dolly Varden Creek

Kilometre 39.5 on Highway 10

TOPOGRAPHICAL MAPS: Mount Murray #105A15 (1:50,000), Mount Billings #105H2 (1:50,000)

THE ROUTE: You can travel by bike for a few kilometres, but then the trail goes around the base of a hill, the ground becomes boggy, and bikes become more trouble than they are worth. It is no problem to leave your bike at the bog. We have not gone farther than the bog.

Conglomerate Creek

Kilometre 78 on Highway 10

MAJOR MINERAL EXPLORATION was done up Conglomerate Creek, especially above the gorge. The bluff above the gorge was scraped to investigate sedimentary layers, and some drilling occurred. There were also plans for a small hydro facility at the gorge.

The entire route, approximately 34 kilometres, is on hard-packed gravel without potholes or soft spots. The times and distances are approximate and relative to weather conditions and mode of travel.

TOPOGRAPHICAL MAPS: Mount Billings #105H2 (1:50,000), Tyers River #105H7 (1:50,000)

EQUIPMENT NEEDED: A bicycle will get you to the far end of the valley quickly. Cycling takes about five hours in and two hours out. The hike from the hunter's camp across Conglomerate to the mine site is about five hours each way. You will need overnight gear and food for a minimum of three days. Light boots are okay for this hike/bike. There is a little lake above the mine site should you decide to stay an extra day to explore. Carry water, as it is not always available on the trail.

THE ROUTE

0.2K FORK. Shortly after you leave Highway 10, a creek crossing is the first obstacle on the trail. It is followed by a steep upward climb to the fork. Take the left-hand fork and curve around to the creek. Do not continue straight ahead as this trail just ends near the top of the mountain. Views of Conglomerate Creek start after the curve.

4.0K CORE-SAMPLE RACKS. One hour beyond the fork there is a second creek crossing. Then the first landmark, a mining exploration camp, appears. A core-sample shed containing rows of core samples filed in drawers stands close to the cabin, which is not in good enough shape to be used for shelter. There is also a bear cache where food could be stored about ten feet above the ground. Fresh water is available, so this is a potential camping spot.

10.0K REED-RIMMED LAKE. The road continues to the top of the hill, which gives views of the surrounding peaks and occasionally a glimpse of the creek's canyon. After a few kilometres the road descends to a swamp, where a bulldozer trail leads to a reed-rimmed lake. A few metres past the lake turnoff is another creek crossing and then a few trickles before a fourth creek crossing.

10.2K CONGLOMERATE CREEK GORGE. Five minutes past the fourth creek is a road to the left that leads to the Conglomerate Creek Gorge, where roiling pools of water churn into cauldrons of stone at the bottom of the canyon. This is a spectacular spot.

13.0K START OF THREE LAKES. Returning to the main road, you will pass three lakes. There are possible camping sites at the third lake. The road continues past the lakes, under a few deadfalls blocking the way, before ending at a hunter's campsite where there are many tent spots, a burning barrel, and lots of wood for a fire.

14.5K END OF THREE LAKES.

25.0K CREEK CROSSING AT HUNTER'S CAMP. Unless the water levels are low, it is not advisable to ford this creek with a bicycle. Besides, it would be difficult to cycle the road on the far side of Conglomerate, and it is possible to walk to the mine site and back in one day. The other option is to stay at the lake above the mine site for a night.

Ford the creek about 100 metres up from the hunter's campsite and find the road on the opposite side. Follow the right-hand trail at the first fork.

26.0K WATERFALL. The road meanders up and down through the woods, past a set of twin waterfalls on the opposite side of the valley. At the second fork after crossing Conglomerate, veer to the left into the creek valley and walk along the flats. From there mountain peaks dotted with ice beckon the hiker to come for more exploration.

27.5K ABANDONED TRAILER. Another hour of walking will bring you to an abandoned trailer, which could offer shelter in a storm. A note written on the wall in 1985 says, "I left because my skidoo is the only thing working."

32.0K SLEEPY HOLLOW. The trail turns north up Conglomerate Creek Valley and leads to Sleepy Hollow, population 2. Follow the road down the hill to the mine site, where there is a cat, a truck, some sheds, some core-sample racks, and a sluicebox. The most interesting artifact is an ingenious shower made from a five-gallon drum and a couple of tin cans, one with nail holes pounded in the bottom and used as the showerhead.

34.0K ALPINE LAKE. After crossing the stream at Sleepy Hollow, continue directly ahead to reach the little alpine lake.

The return trip is by the same route. If you have extra time, take overnight gear and explore both sides of Conglomerate.

No-Name Creek

Kilometre 97.0 on Highway 10

This fifteen-kilometre trail can be cycled as a long day trip or hiked in two to three days. Since the Valley of the Cirques is so magnificent, I do recommend spending at least one overnight there.

TOPOGRAPHICAL MAP: Flood Creek #105H8 (1:50,000)

THE ROUTE

0.5K CABIN. The first landmark on the trail is the remains of a substantial log cabin. There are firepits and ready-made seats but no water, so camping in summer is not possible.

2.5K UNDERGROUND STREAM. There is a fresh underground stream on the left side of the trail. Just before you get to the underground stream there is a creek on the right, but it is too far away to obtain water. Fill your water bottle at the underground stream for the stretch into the next valley.

7.8K PASS TO VALLEY OF THE CIRQUES. Shortly after the underground stream there is a creek crossing that requires a bit of work. The trail goes up a steep hill, over the pass, and into the Valley of the Cirques. Beyond the pass is a little lake, but it is open to the elements and so is not very hospitable for camping.

8.7K PASS TO MOOSE CREEK. A trail to the left, marked by a rock with some unreadable graffiti, leads towards North Moose Creek. However, once back into the tree line on North Moose Creek, the bushwhacking would be horrific. I did not do it! You can get exceptional views of the surrounding countryside from the drilling platforms above the road on the side of the hill. Below the drilling platforms, in the valley, there is an old camp where a grove of poplar trees offers shelter for tenting. However wood is scarce, so you will need a stove for cooking. Watch out for the huge grizzly living in the area.

15.0K BASE CAMP. Continuing ahead along the side of the hill (rather than towards Moose Creek), the valley opens. Most of the trails going up the hills lead to dead ends. There is a barrel stove at the forks at the far end of the valley. This is on the eastern slope of the hill. You can make a base camp here. As you continue along the trail around the far side of the mountain, a huge slide area comes into view.

If you are going down into the valley, follow the road to the creek beyond the barrel-stove base camp, cross the creek, and immediately turn left. The road continuing straight ahead stops at a dead end, but the left-hand fork leads to the far end of the valley, along the valley floor, and to another pass.

To the Flat Lakes from the Junction

THE FLAT LAKES are the best place I know to relax, enjoy the weather (while under a roof), and eat yourself silly before heading for (and after returning from) a gruelling hike.

TOPOGRAPHICAL MAP: Shelf Lake 105I-1 (1:50,000)

THE ROUTE

1.5K DIVIDE LAKE. From the junction (Kilometre 192.5 on Highway 10), follow the road down the hill to Divide Lake. A trail leads to the shore of the lake, but there is no reason to stay here except to fish or watch the birds, of which there are many.

6.0K CONSERVATION OFFICER'S CABIN. The road continues up and down hills, past a couple of creeks and another set of unnamed lakes (on your left), and eventually passes the conservation officer's cabin. It is on the opposite side of the creek which is not difficult to cross. The cabin is in excellent condition, even though animals are starting to explore the inside whenever the door is left ajar. There are no plans to station another conservation officer here. The Zenchuk Creek trail starts from this cabin.

7.5K FLAT LAKES CABINS. The road continues straight ahead to the lake, and the Flat Lakes cabin can be seen across the water. The road itself has been occupied by the creek. A road branching to the left carries on around the lake, up a steep hill, and on towards Howard's Pass. Near the top of the first hill, a trail to the right leads through an overgrown gravel pit and then down to the Flat Lakes cabin. There is a large gully with a creek crossing the road just after the gravel pit; if you get this far, you have missed the trail to the cabin.

Besides being used by us, the Flat Lakes cabin is used by an outfitter. Please repair anything that needs repairing as payment for your rent. The cabin has a good stove, beds with mattresses, kitchen table and chairs, and an outhouse.

To get to the next cabin on the lake, follow the lakeshore to the north around the corner and over a little creek. The second cabin is small and has been invaded by squirrels. It is also an excellent place to stay, but you will need to clean it up to make it habitable. We have never been able to board up the entry holes well enough to keep the animals out.

The third cabin along the lake is on the south shore of the upper (north) lake. The cabin, yellow in colour, has been wrapped in metal sheeting and is in magnificent shape. It is almost impossible to see the cabin from the road but the trail leading from the main road is marked by an old gumboot stuck on a broken willow branch.

Zenchuk Creek

ALTHOUGH THIS HIKE will test all your skills, it will also leave you with unsurpassable memories. Once at the headwaters, where the Rabbitkettle goes down the other side of the pass, you get the sense of being in touch with the Nahanni, as the Rabbitkettle is a major and legendary tributary. It is possible to go down the Rabbitkettle River as long as you stay on animal trails. I have been down the river past both rock glaciers and about five kilometres past the river's elbow.

I would also highly recommend a circle hike from the pass between Rabbitkettle and Zenchuk Creeks over to Kuskula Creek and down to Mirror Lake.

TOPOGRAPHICAL MAPS: Shelf Lake 105I-1 (1:50,000)

THE ROUTE

3.0K END OF ROAD. Start your trek to Zenchuk Creek and the headwaters of the Rabbitkettle River by following the road up the hill above the conservation officer's cabin (see To the Flat Lakes trail description on page 124). The road follows a ridge above a roaring creek and ends at a gravel pit, where a picnic table helps make camping comfortable. There is water about ten minutes east of the gravel pit.

5.0K TOP OF KNOLL. To get to Zenchuk Creek from the end of the road, look north for the knoll at the base of the treeline. The knoll is on the mountain south of Zenchuk Creek Valley. An animal trail on the far side of the gravel pit leads part way to the knoll. Aim for a draw with some white rocks. Carry water as there is none until you get to an underground spring past the knoll, about two or three hours from the gravel pit.

Once on the ridge above Zenchuk Creek, the Flat Lakes and the Little Nahanni River flowing north are in full view. Follow the ridge, staying above the willows. This makes walking fairly easy. The yellow lichen called cladina is slippery when wet, but the only alternative to walking on it is the inhospitable valley below with thick willow and alder. Look for and use game trails. They make travel up this valley possible.

8.0K SHELF ABOVE LAKE. Continue along the shelf past the lake below. There are flat spots and small creeks where it is possible to camp. You will need a stove as there is almost no firewood in those places where camping is good. Beyond the lake are many spruce groves and small streams. Continue past some cliffs, and follow close to the base of a moraine. About three or four kilometres past the lake is a trail that makes walking easy. Across the valley and over the opposite ridge is Zenchuk Lake.

15.0K WATERFALL. The waterfall on Zenchuk Creek is visible as a white dot for a long time before you reach it. Be certain to explore it as it is spectacular, with shelves from six feet to twenty feet spanning the width of the creek. The creek curves around, digging a trench into the valley as it goes. There are campsites near the falls.

16.5K PROSPECTOR'S CAMP. Stay on the trail that skirts above Zenchuk Creek all the way to a prospector's camp, where there is comfortable camping. The prospector's camp is tucked beside an open field, with a creek coming in from the south. Zenchuk Valley is to the west, a rock bluff is to the east, and a stone wall is to the north. The camp has saws, dishes, tin cans, a fry pan, and a pressure cooker. I call this Zenchuk's camp, even though the midden shows that tins from more recent times have been discarded there. We were unable to discover why the creek was named after Nazar Zenchuk, one of the Nahanni characters from the 1920s and 1930s.

21.5K RABBITKETTLE PASS. Walking from the camp to the pass is a bit difficult, but there is lots of water and plenty of flat spots for camping. A mountain that looks like an elephant head marks the pass. Aim for that mountain. There are two little lakes just before the pass. Stay on the south side of the valley for the entire hike. There are claim stakes all through the area, but none are very recent.

There is a tiny glacier-fed lake on the pass, shadowed by dark, unvegetated mountains. On the north shore of the lake you will pass a rock outcropping. This lake is the source of the Rabbitkettle River.

This is one of the most beautiful passes I have ever stood upon. The floor of the pass is a soft green alpine meadow inhabited by a metropolis of marmots. Numerous valleys lead from the pass towards the south, one of which goes to Mirror Lake.

The pass is long. Once on the Rabbitkettle side the canyon closes in within three or four kilometres, and the vegetation becomes more abundant, making the trip down to the Rabbitkettle Hot Springs a challenge.

If you are not going down the Rabbitkettle, return by the same route or go over to Kuskula Creek and Mirror Lake.

Mirror Lake

THIS IS A BUSHWHACK, and if you do not find the cabin, there are no flat places to camp around Mirror Lake until you get to the top end. You could cross the creek that flows out of the west end of the lake and camp on the north shore. I did not do this. However, the valley at the top end near the glacier is spectacular, and I highly recommend this trip. If you are going all the way to the Rabbitkettle River or the Cirque of the Unclimbables, this is the route to take.

TOPOGRAPHICAL MAPS: Shelf Lake 105I-1 (1:50,000)

THE ROUTE

0.0K JUNCTION OF FLAT LAKES ROAD AND HIGHWAY 10

1.8K Leave road and bushwhack. Go to the sharp curve in the road, past the junction but before the milled-log house near Tungsten. Head towards the Flat River through thick willows, aiming for the two sandy cutbanks that are above the river and near a small stream. After twenty minutes of willows, the bushwhacking becomes easier. When you reach the Flat River, you must bushwhack upstream to a wide spot above the small rapids. The rocks are slippery, so be careful.

3.7K CABIN. Once across the Flat, head straight up the hill in the direction of Mirror Lake. Ascend to above the spot where the lake drains into the creek and start heading up the valley towards the centre of the lake. Your goal is the remains of a cabin on the side of the hill above the lake. If you can't find the cabin, return to the lake and follow its shore until you see a trail going up the hill. This will lead you to the cabin. Pitch your tent inside the cabin or on the small flat spots beside the cabin. There is a firepit outside, and some kitchen dishes and utensils were left in the stove inside the cabin to prevent the animals from breaking them.

6.2K KUSKULA CREEK. The lake is swampy and it is not a good idea to camp beside it unless you cross to the north side or go all the way to the upper end. However, the hike up the valley to the glacier is a great walk with spectacular views. An alternative return trip is to continue up the valley to the end, with another few hours of bushwhacking to the headwaters of Kuskula Creek. There are lots of gravel bars to camp on when you reach Kuskula. Once you are past the bush, the entire valley is spectacular. It crosses over a few kilometres of rock to some tiny glacier-fed lakes and finally to the Zenchuk Creek/Rabbitkettle Pass.

19.2K RABBITKETTLE RIVER.

5

Mercury

G.C.F. (GEORGE) Dalziel is not a member of Canada's Aviation Hall of Fame. Nor is he one of the fliers commemorated on a bush-pilot's monument, a shaft of stone on Dome Rock on the shore of Slave Lake, unveiled in Canada's centennial year. The ceremony was attended by more than a hundred of those fliers who, according to the inscription, "penetrated the age-old isolation of remote ... regions ... and thus during the nineteen twenties and thirties played a vital role in northern development."

Dalziel was not one of the fliers at the unveiling. Maybe he was not considered "vital." Maybe he *was* so considered, but declined the invitation to attend.

As Viv and I mulled over the many pieces of the Nahanni story, it occurred to us that Dalziel – referred to by Turner and the other Nahanni old-timers as Dal – was central to certain critical events that took place in the area during and after the Flat River gold rush. He flew in Eppler and Mulholland, who disappeared, and he was central to the search for these men. According to Kraus, he flew in Shebbach, who also died. Kraus mentions another death – that of William Gilbertson, who died in 1940 after Dalziel flew him to a lake near the Flat River. Gilbertson "was an aero engineer for Dalziel." Yet none of the storytellers ever found time to describe Dalziel or tell his story. What they say about his activities is often contradictory.

When a road trip took us through Edmonton, we stopped over to do some research. Edmonton, Pierre Berton writes in *The Mysterious North*, was, in the first half of this century, the real capital of the Northwest Territories. People heading for the Territories came to Edmonton by rail and then moved north through the Peace River country by boat, plane, freight wagon, or sleigh. People leaving the Territories went out through Edmonton. Dalziel – or Dalziell, as his name appears in some sources – would have flown in and out of Edmonton regularly. In fact, according to Berton, his reputation persisted at the Edmonton airport into the late 1940s. "They still talk of the day that J.F.C. Dalziell, the famous flying trapper, flew in with a record hundred and fifty thousand dollars worth of stone-marten pelts."

We would find a cheap hotel downtown, maybe one frequented by the Fort Simpson trappers and gold seekers – the Strathcona, for example, the King Edward, or the Leland. We'd go to the archives and the public library. We'd hit the coffeehouses and the bookstores.

We chose the Strathcona, on the edge of a funky cafe/bookstore district of the same name.

"This place can't have changed much," Viv remarked, examining the hotel lobby as the man behind the desk registered us.

"This place never changes," said the man.

We occupied the room next to that of a woman who must have been dying of emphysema. Throaty coughs punctuated the classic country-and-western that she listened to all day and most of the night. In the early afternoon of our second day there, we watched the cleaning ladies, who were also dying of emphysema, roust our neighbour out of her room so they could do their job. Our neighbour, anorexic and in her sixties, stood by the door chatting, smoking, and coughing while her room was being cleaned.

"Wish we had some good photos of Dalziel and the others to show to our neighbour and the hotel staff," I said to Viv that night as we were being lulled to sleep by Johnny Cash.

"She does look like the remembering type."

The archives, our first stop after we settled into the Strathcona and found an interesting cafe and cappuccino joint, were barren. At the public library we found that the *Edmonton Journal* was not indexed. We had no time, on this particular trip, to crank our way through miles of microfilm.

"Sometimes research is a pain in the butt," I said.

"Not as much pain as grunting a sixty-pound pack over the hills. If we were heading for trailhead somewhere, you'd be a lot more interested in sitting at that microfilm machine."

"I wonder if they'd let me bring in a cappuccino."

"See that sign?"

"Shit. Do they have your books in the catalogue?"

"*Chickenbus* and *Forbidden Mountains.*"

"Mine?"

"I was hoping you wouldn't ask."

The used bookstores, back out near the Strathcona, yielded four books that contained interesting, though brief, references to Dalziel.

The first was *Airborne from Edmonton* by Eugene Louise Myles, published in 1959. Myles knew what she was doing: her book was indexed, unlike most books of local history written by locals. She also produced the epithet "the mystery trapper" to add to "the flying trapper" and "the flying prospector":

> Most widely known of those who operated a machine for their own work was G.C.F. Dalziel, the "mystery trapper" of the far north.
>
> After one summer's convincingly quick trip out with Wop May, Dalziel enrolled as a pupil with Captain Burbidge, earned his "ticket," and flew north with his own plane. "The whole northland," he chuckled, "will be my trapline from now on."
>
> When he presently flew back with a load of furs to sell, the fuselage of his machine was badly scarred with claw marks inflicted by a curious or hungry grizzly bear.

The above quote is from the end of the chapter "1937–8." Since Dalziel flew Eppler and Mulholland into either Rabbitkettle or Glacier Lake early in 1936, the "convincingly quick trip out with Wop May," as well as the flying lessons, probably took place in the summer of 1935. Burbidge *is* in the Aviation Hall of Fame. Maurice "Moss" Burbidge was an RAF vet who stayed in the forces after the war, training pilots. In 1928 he replaced Wop May as chief flying instructor of the Edmonton and Northern Alberta Flying Club.

Myles's book indicates, too, that Dalziel was a novelty, and that he did work for a time out of Edmonton rather than selling his furs at Nahanni Butte or Fort Simpson.

Another book with a brief mention of Dalziel, *and* with an index, is Tommy Walker's *Spatsizi*. In this book, Walker describes how he and his family settled at Cold Fish Lake in Spatsizi in northern B.C. in 1947. On the lake they found an old dock and a drum of gas. Locals told them the dock was Dalziel's: "He has a tiny plane and flies everywhere, trapping and fishing."

A little later, Dalziel descended from the sky with his son and some fishing tackle. In the conversation that followed he told the Walkers he was worried about wolves reducing the goat and caribou supply. He said he lived in Telegraph Creek all winter and moved to a log cabin on Dease Lake as soon as school was out. He flew passengers for twenty-five dollars per hour, freight for twenty-five cents per pound.

So a dozen years after he started to fly, Dalziel was no longer centred in Alberta. He was not far from the Nahanni, though. If Kraus is correct, the year after Dalziel met Walker, he flew Shebbach to his fatal non-encounter with Zenchuk.

Dick Turner's *Wings of the North* says little about Dalziel – it's an account of Turner's own career, starting in 1958, as a "flying prospector" and "flying trapper." Not *the* "flying prospector" or "flying trapper"; Turner is careful to point out, and somewhat proud of the fact, that Dalziel was his immediate predecessor in the Nahanni area. "He had to be the toughest man I ever knew," says Turner. By way of illustrating this toughness, he briefly describes Dalziel's operations in the Mackenzie Mountains, trapping marten with a packsack and pack dogs. He also tells how one autumn Dalziel left Lower Post on the Liard River in B.C. and turned up in March at Fort Norman on the Mackenzie River.

So Dalziel was another who, like Shebbach, had walked into the Nahanni watershed. Then he crossed the Nahanni and moved on to reach the Mackenzie. God help me if Vivien ever got it into her head to duplicate that journey!

Turner also says that "when Stan McMillan [another Hall-of-Famer and a pilot for Mackenzie Air Services] flew into MacMillan Lake during the pseudo gold rush of 1934, Dalziel was already there, having walked over from the Yukon."

Was Dalziel in on the rush too, another of Patterson's "romantic buffoons," sucked in by the McLeod story? Or was he merely en route to Fort Norman, trapping? Turner's account doesn't give a date for the Fort Norman trip.

Either way, Dalziel's walks were amazing feats. He probably went up the Coal River and over the divide into the Caribou – the route that Shebbach, if he walked as Patterson says, may have followed thirteen years later. But there are other trails on the old Yukon maps. For example, there's a trail across to the Beaver River and over to the Caribou, or up the Hyland and over to the Flat, the probable route of the McLeod Brothers. On the Fort Norman trip Dalziel probably angled north after leaving the Flat, crossing the Nahanni somewhere between Rabbitkettle and Virginia Falls, and hitting the Mackenzie upstream from Fort Norman.

But this, or the MacMillan Lake trip if it was a separate one, was Dalziel's last spectacular feat on the ground. Soon after, Turner says, Dalziel used the proceeds from his marten trapping to take flying lessons and buy a Curtiss Robin.

Aviation Digest describes the Robin as a high-wing cabin monoplane, very popular with pilots. Seven hundred and fifty of them were manufactured between 1928 and 1930, when production halted due to the Depression. The plane had a payload of 450 pounds, cruised at 102 miles per hour, and could go for 500 miles on its two wing-tanks that held 25 gallons each. The purchase price was $7500 at the factory in St. Louis. The Robin was used to set endurance records in 1929 and 1935. It was a dependable and stable plane, ideal for bush flying.

With his Robin, Dalziel trapped and explored by air. Turner also says that, after World War II, Dalziel started BC-Yukon Flying Services at Watson Lake and flew a Beaver with "Eat moose meat. Ten thousand wolves can't be wrong" written on it. In his Watson Lake home, Dalziel collected "full mounts, head mounts, and half mounts of everything from a Himalayan mountain sheep to a polar bear."

So Dalziel was also a world traveller. He must have been fairly wealthy

in his middle years. He seems, too, to have had three homes at the time
– at Telegraph Creek, Dease Lake, and Watson Lake.

Turner's panoramic view of Dalziel's life is filled out a bit by Larry
Whitesitt in *Flight of the Red Beaver.* Whitesitt, raised in the U.S., had as a
youth fuelled his imagination on Jack London's stories of the Klondike.
He also knew all the details about the McLeods, their lost mine, and the
men who sought that mine. In 1964, having completed his flight training,
he became a Canadian. He headed north. In 1968, working for Omineca
Air Service out of Smithers, he flew into Cold Fish Lake, met Tommy
Walker, and heard about Dalziel. A year later Whitesitt landed a job with
BC-Yukon Air Service in Watson Lake. Dalziel had sold the company by
then, but still had the house in Watson Lake. By 1969, however, Dalziel
had switched from trapping and operating flying-service companies to
outfitting. Whitesitt sums it up: "Dal ran a guiding service, flew a Super
Cub, and was still very active."

Finally, in 1969, Whitesitt met Dalziel at the latter's hunting camp at
Bluesheep Lake in B.C.

> Dal had lived many lives, and I judged him to be in his mid-sixties.
> He owned the oldest original building in Watson Lake, a log home.
> He was here in the 1930s and was the first to fly in and explore the
> Mackenzie Mountains extensively. He didn't say much, but I
> sensed he had many stories, experiences and knowledge beneath his
> calm exterior. His wife June was a friendly and gracious host.
>
> Inside his log home was a fantastic trophy room. He had the sec-
> ond and fifth largest stone sheep in the world, fully mounted, ani-
> mals from Africa, a tiger, various sheep, including one Marco Polo
> sheep from Afghanistan, bears, moose, and other animals that he
> had shot.
>
> In the early days Dal shot game and flew it into the mining camps
> so they could have fresh meat. He started B.C. Yukon and had one of
> the first Beavers in the country. He now flew a Super Cub with long
> range tanks so he could keep tabs on his large hunting area and get the
> camps set up … Dal ran a first-class operation and was well organized.

Still later, Whitesitt flew sportsmen into Little Dal Lake, presumably
named, along with Dal Lake farther north, after Dalziel. These lakes are

about fifty miles northeast of the Nahanni River and about two hundred miles from Watson Lake. If their location indicates part of Dalziel's route in his epic journey of 1934, he did cross the Mackenzie Mountains a fair distance north.

Whitesitt's wife Kathy, a Hollywood-style beauty as Whitesitt proudly claims and as the photos show, got a job expediting for Dalziel; she drove clients from the Watson Lake airport to his house, set them up in hotels, etc. The Whitesitts and Dalziels enjoyed some pleasant social evenings; the book includes a photo, taken in the Watson Lake house, of the two couples together. Whitesitt doesn't date the photo, but Dalziel, a small man, does look to be "in his mid-sixties."

Whitesitt then tells how, in his retirement, in 1989, he made a nostalgic solo flight from his home in Washington State to Tuktoyaktuk and Old Crow. On the way back from the Arctic Ocean, he stopped in Dease Lake and visited the Dalziels' summer residence at the south end of the lake. It was a sad experience for Whitesitt; the house was boarded up and deteriorating. "Now it seems tired, like the old buildings in Dawson City, and is slowly sinking into the earth." Dalziel was long dead by 1989.

Whitesitt's comments, "He didn't say much" and "Dal had led many lives," are a good summary of something that all four books make very clear. Dalziel's accomplishments were impressive enough to speak for themselves. First, a flying-outfitting empire, "a first-class operation." Second, a major air-service company, BC-Yukon, that continued to exist after Dalziel moved on. Third, a list of feats of personal strength, endurance, and determination that impressed even the most rugged of northerners.

However, not one of the authors of these books indicates any feeling of either affection or dislike towards Dalziel – only respect and admiration. Nor are there any remarks about his personality: his sense of humour, if any; his loyalty, if any, to friends and family; his generosity or lack of it. It's as if he were a force of nature rather than a human being.

After the Edmonton bookstores, armed with a growing list of questions for anyone we should encounter who might actually have known Dalziel, we moved on to the Aviation Museum at Edmonton's Municipal Airport.

The lady at the museum entrance, when we asked about the archives, said "Archives? You want to talk to one of the old guys. I think Bernie is back there." She buzzed the coffee shop. "Bernie. Someone wants to see you up here."

"The old guys," said Vivien. "I like that."

In a couple of minutes, we saw a portly but spry man emerge from under the wing of a Beaver and make his way towards us past the restored fighters and floatplanes.

He had on a nametag: Bernie Richardson. Alberta Aviation Museum Association.

"What do you want to know?" he asked after we introduced ourselves.

"We're interested in a bush pilot who operated out of Edmonton and Fort Simpson in the thirties. George Dalziel."

A smile lit up Bernie's face. "You'd better come with me."

We were led back down through the restored planes, under the wing of the Beaver, and into an office. "I've got a picture of him in here somewhere," Bernie said. He opened a filing cabinet and shuffled through the files.

"Here it is. That's Dalziel in the centre. The tall guy on the left is Grant McConachie. Frank Burton's on the right. The plane behind them is a Robin. McConachie's just sold it to Dal. That'd be in '35."

It was the Curtiss Robin that Turner mentions, former property, it seems, of Grant McConachie, probably the most famous of the pioneers of commercial aviation in Canada and the first president of Canadian Pacific Airlines.

In the photo, Dalziel looks proud. He's holding his hands in a funny, formal way, like he's unused to being photographed. McConachie's brow is knit and his stance aggressive. He looks like he's chewing on an invisible cigar. It might just be a momentary twitch or shift of position caught by the camera, but McConachie looks impatient.

"Can we photograph the picture?"

"Sure. Can I get a few copies?"

"Sure."

"We're interested in the history of the Nahanni region," I explained to Bernie, then asked, "Did you know Dal well?"

"Not really. I worked with him for a few months, for Peace River Air.

We flew meat from Peace River into Yellowknife and delivered it to Peace River Meat. Ted Amos was the agent, and the shop was right where we landed, next to the MAS [Mackenzie Air Services] dock."

"So you and Dal were colleagues?"

"Yeah, but I didn't see that much of him. We did once go by train together to Fort Erie. Jack McNeil, the company president, took us. He bought a Waco and we flew it back. That'd be July 1938, I think. The company soon got into trouble and Dal disappeared. Frank Burton took over as president. I quit after awhile. The meat wasn't inspected. The other airline companies turned us in."

"All of the other pilots who flew into the Nahanni are mentioned in the histories," I said. "Some are famous. But there's nothing on Dalziel."

"That's because he was a nuisance," said Bernie. "A kind of sorcerer's apprentice. Ultimately, they were sorry they ever licensed him and sold him a plane, but he bugged them until they did."

"He lived here then?"

"Yeah. Had a wife and kid, I think, and earned money selling newspapers around the airport."

"So what was the problem? He didn't pay?"

"Hell, he paid. Never any problem that way. One way or another, Dal succeeded with everything he did. If anybody lost, it was the competition. He undercut them. He took customers off them. Mackenzie Air Services and Canadian Airways were always getting the police after him."

"Was he licensed to haul passengers?"

"Oh yeah. He had a private and a commercial licence. He even had his mechanic's ticket, so he didn't have to carry anyone with him. But he was always ahead of the law, doing things they hadn't even thought of yet, so they tried hard to catch him up on one infraction or another, mostly in connection with trapping."

"We learned from the archives in Yellowknife that all airline trapping was prohibited in 1937, and that this change severely inhibited Dalziel's operations."

"They specifically mention Dalziel?"

"Yes."

"Ultimately they closed the whole Nahanni area to white trappers, and it stayed closed until the fifties. You couldn't say that move was directed at Dal, but the archives are probably correct if they assumed that some of the laws prohibiting the use of planes were passed with Dal in mind. In fact, if I remember correctly, his name came up in Parliament. As the papers reported it, the complaint came from the Indians and Indian Affairs Department. The Indians gave up trying to compete with him, which meant the government had to pay them more pogey."

"It's been suggested he made a practice of stranding customers in the bush."

Bernie showed no surprise. "Dal put men on his lines once he set them up. He didn't actually run most of them himself. It was pretty casual. Dal would meet a guy who had nothing to do and ask him to trap one of his lines. Dal would provide the supplies and equipment, fly the guy in, and train him if he needed it. Dal took half the fur. There were also the prospectors, some of them totally inexperienced in the bush. I know that one of the Peace River mechanics wanted in there. I remember the guy. He was hot to do some prospecting."

"Gilbertson?"

"Bill, yeah. He was another Peace River Air employee."

"Did you ever fly with Dal?"

"Once in the Waco and then a second time when we went up to his trapline at Rabbitkettle to clean it out. That was in the summer, just before Dal disappeared into B.C."

GRANT MCCONACHIE, GEORGE DALZIEL, AND FRANK BURTON IN FRONT OF THE
CURTISS ROBIN DALZIEL BOUGHT FROM MCCONACHIE, 1935

"Weren't you a bit worried, knowing his reputation?"

"I made damn good and sure everyone knew where I was going and with whom."

"Do you remember anything about the camp?"

"Not really. A lot of rusty traps and some pelts. Don't really understand why he bothered with it at all, unless he was *ordered* to clean it up. What I do remember is the trip out. He flew right down the river, down over the falls and through the canyons, just over the water most of the time. He told me he was checking things out. And there were fires burning then, so at times you couldn't even see the wingtips. He was a good pilot, I'll say that for him. And he was prepared for emergencies. Well supplied. I remember his rifle in particular, an under-over .22/.30."

Bernie had things to do, so we took some photos of him with us and told him, "We have to be getting home, but we'll be here again in the spring. Meanwhile, we'll send you copies of the photos."

"If it helps, I heard that Dal worked for the U.S. Army, building the Alaska Highway. I lost track of him after that. My ears went on me in the fifties, so I lost my ticket. Took up long distance trucking, mostly Edmonton to Vancouver. That job was a hell of a lot scarier than bush flying. But I also heard that when Dal died down around Victoria or Vancouver there was a fuss over his will. He tried to cut out one of his kids, and she contested the will. It was in some of the northern papers, including the *Journal*."

"That'd be the B.C. Supreme Court. The Victoria law library should have the transcript. We're heading down there for a visit to my son."

"Could you make a copy for my files?"

"You bet," said Viv. "And if you remember anything else about Dalziel, let us know at this address." Vivien handed Bernie her card. Bernie hauled out his wallet and handed her his card.

"Send the court stuff here."

We found that if Dalziel was a nuisance to the authorities, the work he and Bernie did for Peace River Air was much appreciated in Yellowknife. The local newspaper, the *Blade*, ran an obituary for the company, which we discovered in Jock McMeekan's book *Yellowknife Blade*, another of our finds in the Edmonton bookstores. McMeekan states that the farm products brought in by Peace River Air were less expensive and of better quality than those available from "far away." He describes these latter products as "third-grade commercial beef, poor grade pork, sausages that tasted like stale sawdust and eggs that were sometimes literally explosive." He blamed the demise of Peace River Air on "rival transportation companies, notably Mackenzie Air Service." He implies that MAS told the authorities that uninspected meat was being sold, and the authorities shut Peace River Air down.

Dalziel, in short, was providing a needed service to the community.

The court records we found in Victoria tell a story that doesn't reflect so well on Dalziel, though as the judge in the case noted, Dalziel was sick and depressed during the last couple of years of his life. The story, which says a lot about Dalziel's business activities and his family life after he settled in B.C., concerned his attempt to keep his older daughter Bonnie from the inheritance she would normally have received as one of his four children.

As the transcript explains, Dal's problems with Bonnie (his *legal* ones, at least) started in 1960, when Dal sold BC-Yukon Air. One of the buyers died a year later, and the company came up for sale. Dal informed his daughter and her husband – a flier who had once worked for Dal – that the company was available, and they made a successful bid, Dal providing a $50,000 loan to supplement their $10,000. But the sellers reneged on the binding contract, and Bonnie and her husband sued. After some complex legal battles, they were awarded $40,000 in damages, an award that was appealed by the sellers but then upheld. In his summary, the judge who upheld the award made special note of the couple's seriousness in trying to purchase a commercial aviation business, mentioning that they had looked for one as far away as Australia.

Dal was angry about the failed purchase of BC-Yukon. He did get his $50,000 back, as the judge makes clear in his 1985 decision reinstating Bonnie in Dal's will. But Dal, the judge goes on to say, didn't want Bonnie and her husband to claim damages instead of "specific performance." In short, Dal wanted them to ask the court to force the sale. The judge notes that Bonnie's husband made the decision to claim damages based on good legal advice and on the fact that share values were dropping. The judge also says that Bonnie tried to convince her husband to claim specific performance. She supported her father.

Did Dal want to get his company back, using his daughter and her husband as a front? And if Bonnie backed Dal in this, why was he so angry at her at the end of his life – by which time she had been divorced from her pilot husband for years?

There is a hint, in the judge's summary, that Dalziel might have wanted some of the damage money:

> Bonnie's husband recovered $40,000 damages but his net recovery after legal expenses etc. was $28,000... Most unfairly, in my view, it became accepted in the Dalziel family that Bonnie had cheated her father out of $40,000. This was quite incorrect and unfair, but she has carried this burden ever since and, like many misconceptions which sometimes become self-authenticating, it may have affected the ultimate testamentary disposition made to Bonnie by her father.

The judge also considered Dalziel's treatment of his four children and their children, and his state of mind when he made up his final will. It's a *King Lear* story – Dal kept picking favourites among his children and grandchildren and changing his will accordingly, mainly in connection with the disposition of his shares in the Dease Lake outfitting company and of the certificate that gave him exclusive hunting and guiding rights for big game in the largest designated territory in B.C.

> The value of the certificate was substantial and he owned 95% of the shares of an operating company which owned two airplanes, 10 or so hunting cabins, guiding and hunting equipment, horses, traplines, a building in Dease Lake and about $130,000 in cash.

Dal's oldest child and older son Robin – a lawyer and outfitter – was effectively ruled out as heir when Dal gave him an interest in an outfitter's territory, and Robin subsequently sold his interest; this angered Dal. Younger son Byron, a pilot and guide, "was probably too independent for his father's liking." The judge (another fan of Jack London and Robert Service?) admired Byron's "typically northern indifference to family politics." Cherryl, Dal's younger daughter, "was said to be her father's favorite." As well, Cherryl's husband, Myles Bradford, "was Mr. Dalziel's right-hand man for many years."

The judge then recited a long history of wills and codicils. Even Bonnie, for a short while, was back in grace when one of her sons, Chris, "became the heir apparent," and then when one of her daughters, Cara, earned her grandfather's affections and the nickname "Fox." The judge considered Bonnie's brief periods of parental favour as important in his deliberations on Dal's treatment of his children in his final will: "A grandfather like Mr. Dalziel does not give an attractive teenager a nickname like 'Fox' if he does not have a real fondness for her." In short, Dalziel had strong feelings for Bonnie's children, and to disinherit Bonnie was to disinherit them.

Ultimately, Dal prepared the documentation needed to transfer all his shares to Cherryl as of 1 January 1983. But he died, at seventy-four years of age, on 26 December 1982, the transfer incomplete.

Dal's other properties and possessions, and some of the company cash that Dal claimed as a dividend shortly before his death, were not so much in contention. Dal's first wife, June, had died in 1974, shortly after she and Dal retired to Fulford Harbour on Saltspring Island. She left her 5 percent of the company shares to be divided equally between the four children. Dal's second wife, who had been his long-term assistant in the Dease Lake outfitting company, was written into the early wills as the executor and as the recipient of various bequests. But by 1981, Dal and his wife "were not getting along, and a divorce petition was issued but not proceeded with." Dalziel executed a codicil disinheriting his wife. After his death, she too made a claim under the Wills Variation Act and reached a "substantial settlement" with the estate. The estate agreed to provide her with a house and a living allowance. This settlement, the judge noted, "reduces the value of the estate and makes redistribution, if any, difficult."

Cherryl inherited the company, minus the cash but with the hunting and guiding certificate. The other three children split what was left – not much, the judge thought, especially after legal expenses.

In summing up Dalziel's character and his actions concerning his final will, the judge, an echo of Service's "Law of the Yukon" in his mind, said:

> Like so many from the north, where only the strongest survive, he was a stubborn, strong-willed, and somewhat insensitive man … In 1981, Mr. Dalziel was wintering at Saltspring Island with his wife.

He was not well; he was drinking too much; he was brooding because his pilot's licence had been revoked for health reasons; and he was getting old.

The judge concluded that Dalziel was of sound mind when he made his will, but was acting with typical impulsiveness in disinheriting Bonnie, who was divorced at the time, forty-seven years of age, supporting kids, and without any visible means of support. Dalziel's action was "a thoughtless decision which a judicious father alive to his parental duty would not have made under these circumstances." Dalziel, the judge concluded, "did not always show kindness to those who displeased him."

Vivien and I had little time to brood over Dalziel's story, though on our way home to Prince George we went to Fulford Harbour, only a half hour on the ferry from where Wes was living on Vancouver Island, to check out Dal's neighbours. Byron, we learned, still visited the island to go fishing with friends and was a popular figure. But Dalziel himself was remembered as a very private, even unfriendly man. In fact, his reputation seemed to have preceded him to the island, creating suspicion. Neighbours told a story of him going trapping with a partner and coming out alone with "too many" furs, a lot of them "not cut the way Dal was known to do it."

"He shot his partners and stole their furs," one man said conclusively. That same man had heard that Dalziel had acquired some of his foreign trophy heads by flying into Kamchatka and eastern Siberia at an altitude low enough to escape detection by Soviet radar.

BY JUNE WE WERE on our way to Tungsten. We wanted to check in with the Pitt family, soak in the hot springs, and stay a night or two in the Flat Lakes cabin. Then it was off to Whitehorse and Kluane, a summer of finding and photographing new routes to the Lowell and Donjek glaciers in preparation for a new edition of Viv's guidebook.

At Watson Lake, while Viv visited the food store to stock up on canned bacon, oysters, pancake mix, and other delicacies, I slipped over to the museum and found a phonebook.

There was a number for Byron Dalziel. Curiosity got the better of me and I plugged some coins into the payphone.

He answered. He was interested in talking, but was busy selling hay at that moment. We agreed to meet when Viv and I got out of Tungsten.

"My nephew just went in there," he said.

"Hiking?"

"Hunting."

I volunteered to leave a copy of my rough notes and a copy of the photo of his father and McConachie for Byron to examine.

"Where are you phoning from?"

"The museum."

"Leave the stuff with the people at the front desk. They know me."

After hanging up, I put my notes and the photo into an envelope and took it to the desk. An elderly lady, "Rhea" according to her nametag, agreed to hold it for Byron.

"Sure I know him. His father was one of the people who contributed to the founding of this museum. One of the best things they ever did in this town. The old house just across from the hotel was Dal's, and then Byron's. Byron may have sold it. He lives out of town now, and the house is boarded up."

"Is that where the collection of trophies is?"

"Used to be, anyway. You know, you're the second guy in so many years to come in here looking for information on Dalziel and the trophies."

"Who was the other guy?"

"Young, big. I see him around town once in awhile. Know him?"

I shrugged. Not knowing what Birch had been up to over the winter, I decided I had better keep my mouth shut. "Did you know Dal?" I asked instead.

"Sure. Everyone in town did. I flew with him once, over his trapline. He used to check it by air. Too close to the ground for me. I'd call him a daredevil."

She turned her attention to the crowd of tourists gathering behind me.

That evening we drove out Highway 10 to the government campsite on the Hyland River and pitched our tents, once again, in the picnic shelter. The next day we drove to the washout, carried our bikes and gear across, and cycled into Tungsten.

Gerald and Terry weren't there. They had contracted out their work as caretakers in order to spend more time at their woodworking shop in Red

Deer. The man looking after things wasn't sure when they would be back.

We asked him if there had been any visitors.

"None that I've *seen*," he said. "But I heard a plane come and go. The next morning I found footprints through town and up the road north. It makes me nervous. They're supposed to radio for permission to land."

The footprints mentioned by the caretaker were visible all the way to the Flat Lakes. They passed the path down to the cabin and continued towards the north end of the Lakes.

"It's about ten miles from Tungsten to here," I remarked.

"That would be nothing for a Dalziel."

The cabin at the Flat Lakes was unchanged, except for the depredations of a chipmunk, resident of a nearby spruce tree. I evicted him by sawing up some planks and nailing them under the eaves. We lazed around for two days, eating, sleeping, reading, and writing.

When we arrived back in Watson Lake, Byron Dalziel was not in. We left a couple of messages on his answering machine and headed to Whitehorse, but we couldn't help thinking: maybe he's avoiding us. Maybe we shouldn't have left the notes. Especially the stuff about the trials.

In August, heading home for a winter's work, me at the college and Viv freelancing for the local paper, we turned off before Watson Lake and took the Stuart-Cassiar Highway south, hoping to find Cherryl Bradford in Dease Lake. If she and her husband still had the company, they would have been running it for fifteen years since Dal's death.

Cherryl was in the Dease Lake phonebook as "Sherry." She was at home.

"We got your notes from Byron," she said. "I read them. You're surprisingly accurate, except for a few facts. Do you have time to talk?"

I was relieved. "We thought your brother might be avoiding us," I said.

"Oh no," she laughed. "He came down here to fly for us. Some government contracts. Can you come over?"

Sherry lived in a rustic house at the south end of the lake, on a hill above Dalziel's old house. Though the place was undergoing renovation, it was still recognizable from Whitesitt's photo.

What we found in Sherry's house was the last thing we expected. Dalziel, the man of few words, had told his own story. It was in the form of a neatly typed, 250-page manuscript.

"My stepmother typed it for him," Sherry explained. "It was based on these notebooks and was to include the photos in this album." She showed us a half dozen faded, leather-bound notebooks full of illegible writing, and a fat album of clear black-and-white photos.

I thought of Whitesitt. "Dal ran a first-class operation and was extremely well organized." That statement seemed to apply to everything Dalziel did.

There was also a clipping file, put together by Dalziel's first wife, June. None of the clippings were dated, and most of them were from the *Edmonton Journal*. The file showed that Dalziel was a famous man in Edmonton for the first few years of his career as the "flying trapper."

Sherry easily read our thoughts as we flipped the typed pages and examined the notebooks and photos. "The press portrayed him as a renegade and adventurer," she said. "He was the first to recognize the potential of the airplane to trappers. Reporters waited for him at the Edmonton Airport and took down everything he said and changed it. If he didn't turn up, they wrote articles speculating on where he was. He wasn't just the 'flying trapper,' 'flying prospector,' or 'mystery trapper.' He was also the 'mad trapper.' You'll see it in one of those clippings, a story that made it all the way to the *New York Times*. They picked up somewhere that the Nahanni Indians feared him because of his uncanny ability to survive and the speed at which he moved through the bush. So the reporters made the obvious comparison. Probably that's why they decided that Dad was stranding people up the Nahanni. They also liked to build mysteries and exaggerate the dangers, so that whenever Dad did an emergency landing or went through the ice they made a big story out of it. This made him look like a daredevil."

"Some people would have died for that kind of attention," said Vivien.

"He didn't like it. He didn't think of himself as an adventurer. He used to quote one of his favourite adventure-authors, Stefansson I think: 'An explorer meets adventure only when he makes a mistake.'"

"He read lots?"

"Always. He always carried a book. I remember Dickens, Shakespeare, Byron. That's how my brother got his name."

"I think you know what you have here," said Vivien, still turning the pages.

"I hope to find a publisher for it, soon, so I'd appreciate any advice you'd have. I'd have published it long ago, but my stepmother had it and was possessive of it as well as of a lot of things that belonged to my mother or to the family before my mother died. You'd understand if you knew my stepmother's history. I understood, so I was patient, and finally she turned it over."

"This is his life story?"

"No. It covers his childhood, but he seemed to know that he was important mainly as an explorer of the Mackenzie Mountain area. Most of the book deals with that. The story stops when he leaves the area."

So the story wouldn't include Shebbach, I thought.

"He also wanted to set the record straight," Sherry continued. "As you perceived, there are a lot of half-truths going around."

"He sounds a bit like Patterson," I commented. "Do you know his book?"

Sherry smiled. "One of the books you missed was *Trail to the Interior*. In it you can see some of the relationship between Dad and Patterson. He was one of Dad's best friends. He and his wife visited often, especially after Mom and Dad bought the house on Saltspring. The Pattersons were a nice, funny old couple. I was very fond of them. Patterson's Grumman canoe is still out there in the yard."

"Can I touch it later?" asked Viv, laughing, but really, I knew, serious.

"Dad liked people who knew what they wanted and who worked hard to get it. He included Patterson in this category. To Dad, Patterson was a great writer. Adventure was his subject matter. Dad never really understood leisure. I remember once driving with him and he saw some joggers and commented that it was too bad all that energy wasn't used to generate electricity or something. Dad was not a warm person. He warmed to you – and that included us kids – only to the extent that you were useful. I remember the first time he flew with me after I got my licence. When we landed, I asked him if he'd been afraid, and he said no, the plane was foolproof."

I turned up a photo of Zenchuk. "Nazar Zenchuk was said to be your father's partner. Do you know anything about him? We first tried to get to the Nahanni by going up Zenchuk Creek, so we'd like to find out something about him. There's very little, at least so far."

"He was one of Dad's best friends. He said Nazar was the best stick man he'd ever met. Being a stick man meant you knew the bush and could survive. You could take whatever pain came your way and accomplish what you set out to do. It was the greatest of all compliments, especially coming from Dad."

I knew that the phrase "stick man" had other connotations – sexual ones. But these originate in an entirely different place, the south.

"He was Dad's trapping partner over the years. I remember him as a big, raw-boned man, very gentle. He spent his last years in Watson Lake and died in a seniors home in Whitehorse. We visited him there often."

"Does he have family?"

"Yes. He married a Native lady and had kids. I don't know where they are. One, Phillip, was killed in Stanley Park. It was some kind of drug deal gone wrong. His wife left him and ended up with one of his trapping partners. But Zenchuk wasn't a sad figure. He loved the bush, and that's where he lived, and he seemed out of place anywhere else. Once he got drunk in Watson Lake and slept out and lost a finger or toe to frostbite. Everybody thought it was ironic – nothing like that had ever happened to him in all his years on the trapline. If you look in the clipping files you'll find some articles that mention him in connection with Dad."

And so six hours went by in Sherry's house. It was late August, and already the leaves were turning. The woodstove in the kitchen crackled steadily. Sherry had spent the morning scanning her father's notebooks and manuscript for answers to the many questions highlighted in my notes. She read us the relevant passages, filling in with any extra information she happened to remember.

George Dalziel was born in 1908 in Winnipeg and raised in Vancouver. His parents were well-off and dedicated to their kids, but the marriage was troubled and Dalziel's parents split up when he was in his early teens. Dalziel completed school – a private school – and planned to become a doctor. He was determined to do it on his own, and he knew how to do it: he would trap his way through medical school, selling furs to pay his tuition. In those days the Boy Scout movement was less about building self-esteem and more about making a living. In the Scouts, Dalziel had learned to trap and hunt. He ran a trapline on False Creek that, he says in his manuscript, sometimes netted him more in cash for a week's work than his teachers were making.

When he finished school in 1925, he and a group of friends headed north. Dalziel had the Cassiar area in mind. He knew about it from stories of gold discoveries and gold mines in the area. He ended up at Telegraph Creek, trapped there for a year, and then moved on to Lower Post on the Liard River. From Lower Post he began his incursions into the Mackenzie Mountains.

At some point he made a momentous decision. He decided to give up on medical school and continue his trapping and exploring. One consideration was his family. He was supporting two sisters at nursing school. Another was his love of the life, the feeling that surviving in the wild tested all of his abilities to the limit. "I can walk all day and all night if I have to," he writes. Another consideration must have been financial. Furs were worth lots of money, even during the Depression.

Dal trapped from 1925 to 1935, with Zenchuk as a partner much of the time. In 1934 he set out, very deliberately, to explore the country from the Liard, near the territorial divide, to the Mackenzie River. One of those journeys, from Lower Post to Fort Norman, alluded to by Turner, took place between 20 July and 6 September and was done solely for the sake of exploration. He made careful notes, took excellent pictures with a sophisticated camera, and drew maps based on compass readings. This material was requested by the government and used in the Canol Pipeline and Road projects of 1943.

Dalziel used pack dogs in summer as well as winter. On his summer trip there were eight dogs, and four completed the journey. Dalziel writes that he "had to kill the bitch," and he "lost three of the weaker dogs."

The dogs were important because they carried almost everything; Dalziel carried a rifle. He writes that he and the dogs needed lots of "fat meat," which meant moose and moose only. Caribou, he writes, would not do. The grocery list included ten pounds of flour, two pounds of salt, twenty pounds of sugar, ten pounds of white beans, two pounds of raisins, and three pounds of lard. Dalziel averaged twenty miles a day – over twice the distance that Viv and I can make on an off-trail hike. He went up the Coal River and over to the Flat. There he encountered some prospectors, among them Kraus and Clark. He wrote in his notebook that they had found no gold and were prospecting on unlikely ground.

"He never liked mines," commented Sherry, "and he didn't think much of prospectors. They were gamblers, looking for a quick fix. Worse, they often didn't know how to survive in the bush."

This meeting with the prospectors is almost certainly the source of Turner's comment that Dal was at MacMillan Lake at the start of the gold rush. But it's clear that Dalziel was not part of the "episode of buffoonery," though he undoubtedly would be tempted to stake some claims. Dalziel was exploring the Mackenzie Mountains, and he had been through that way before.

Dalziel seems to have moved up the Flat to Hole-in-the-Wall Pass rather than the usual route up Irvine Creek. He named the pass and the lake, photographed the lake, and found the hot springs at the south end of the lake. He went through the pass to the Nahanni River and rafted across below Rabbitkettle Hot Springs (he describes the springs). East of the Nahanni he encountered signs of earlier Indian habitation (tent rings and cuttings on trees), but nothing recent; he concluded that the recent absence of Indians was due to the influenza epidemic of 1908. He found and named Dal Lake and Little Dal Lake, as well as June Lake, named after his wife. Kraus says he also named Sunblood Mountain, Stonemarten Lake, Flood Creek, and Skull Creek, though some of these names could have come from flights after he got his plane. He rafted down a creek into the Mackenzie, where a series of comic misadventures and a shooting contest with Wop May marked his return to civilization. Dalziel says he won the shooting contest.

The "convincingly quick trip out with Wop May," then, mentioned in *Airborne from Edmonton,* could have been the flight out from Fort Norman. Maybe Dalziel won the flight in the shooting match. But Sherry didn't read the part of the manuscript that covered leaving Fort Norman. In connection with the shooting contest, though, Dalziel says in an aside that it was Wop who encouraged him to fly and continued to encourage him through his training and after he got his licence. May's death in 1952 was, Dalziel says, a sad occasion for him.

Dalziel's book includes a chapter on his training in the summer of 1935. Evidently he was a troublesome student; "Moss" Burbidge kicked him out of the Aeroclub at one point after Dalziel tried six rolls in succession when he was supposed to be practising only one at a time. The irony was that there was a lot of money in such hijinks. Dalziel describes a circus in Lloydminster where a number of Edmonton pilots accumulated small fortunes by taking people up at six dollars a head – more if you wanted to fly over your farm or experience some fancy flying. McConachie was using his large tri-motor Ford – purchased from Sir Harry Oaks, Klondiker and wealthy prospector, murdered in the Bahamas in 1943. The fliers were regarded as heroes and treated to numerous drinks in a subsequent all-night party. The next morning, Dalziel, McConachie, Frank Burton (McConachie's engineer), and another pilot decided to return to Edmonton in Dalziel's Robin. McConachie wanted to pilot the plane on the grounds that the plane was overloaded and he had the most experience. Dalziel stated it was his plane and he would fly it. But the overloaded plane had trouble getting off the ground and Dalziel had to fly under the telegraph wires at the end of the field.

"Nobody spoke to me for days," Dalziel writes in his notebook.

In a chapter called "Missing Trappers," Dalziel addresses the question of Eppler and Mulholland, conscious of the fact that, as he puts it, "the police and others have concluded that I abandoned the men."

As Dalziel tells it, on 12 February 1936 he was at Nahanni Butte. Jack and Joe Mulholland and Bill Eppler had, as Turner says, been trapping along the Liard, but not doing well. They wanted to try for marten. Dalziel suggested Glacier Lake, near Rabbitkettle. He had left a line there and knew of a cabin, built by someone else, at the outlet. Dalziel, when he had been there, hadn't stayed in the cabin, so he didn't know if it contained a stove. He never did like cabins, he says, and often in the manuscript he complains of trapping partners who thought they needed cabins.

To this point, Dalziel's story coincides with the police report, though the RCMP did depend to a large extent on information given to them by Dalziel. The men went in, in mid-February, to Glacier Lake. They did not, as Turner has it, go to Rabbitkettle Lake, about ten miles south of Glacier, in January.

Joe Mulholland and Bill Eppler decided to go, leaving Jack and Daisy to run the trading post. They would come out in May in a skinboat – a pole frame wrapped in hides or canvas. A roll of canvas was loaded onto the plane.

Here Dalziel's account varies from the one he gave police in June 1936. In that account, Eppler and Mulholland were to come out overland, down the upper Nahanni, over to Irvine Creek, and down to Faille's cabin.

Eppler and Mulholland figured they would take a chance on the stove, since there was really no room for one in the plane. They threw in some empty kerosene tins, planning to use them to patch together a stove and some stovepipe should they have to.

They had to. There was no stove in the cabin. While Dalziel showed Mulholland the trapline, Eppler improvised a stove and proceeded to make tea. Sparks from Eppler's stove ignited some of the moss chinking in the wall, and the men had some trouble dousing the ensuing fire. Then they had tea, and Dalziel left.

The cabin could have burned not long after. It would be hard to put out a fire in the wall of a log cabin at a time of year when copious quantities of water were not available. The fire could smoulder in the wall for a day or two and explode at a time when the two men were out on the trapline.

When Bill and Joe failed to appear in May, folks in Fort Simpson wanted Dalziel to fly in to check. He explained he couldn't due to "legal troubles." These "legal troubles" are not really specified; they seem to involve some marten that Dalziel had trapped live for breeding purposes. There were no rules about this kind of trapping, and Dalziel thought he had an agreement with the RCMP that would allow him to proceed. In his view, the police broke this agreement and laid charges. Dalziel was found guilty, and his plane was grounded. Turner talks about this. There's no mention of it in the RCMP report.

The trappers called what Dalziel calls a "miner's meeting" – a term that dates back to the Klondike, when isolated groups of prospectors often had to handle justice without benefit of police or magistrates – and the plane was released.

Dalziel says he flew a number of trips in. One was with Bill Clark and one with someone he doesn't remember. The RCMP and Turner don't mention Bill Clark. The RCMP say Dalziel's partner was William Cormack. Turner says it was Harry Vandaele. Turner mentions only one flight in. The police mention three at least.

Dalziel and his partner, whoever it was, flew low over the Nahanni and dropped into the lake, finding the cabin burned and no tracks leading anywhere.

The police also went in by boat, Dalziel says, but never made it to the lake. The RCMP report doesn't mention this.

Dalziel writes that he was partly to blame for the deaths of Eppler and Mulholland. "I thought they were woodsmen," he writes. "I learned they'd never slept out, never killed a moose. I made the mistake."

But Turner refers to Eppler as an experienced woodsman and tells us that Eppler had been around for a number of years before 1930, when Turner himself arrived in Fort Simpson.

Dalziel describes how he continued for many months after to check for signs of the fate of Eppler and Mulholland. One clipping from the *Edmonton Journal*, which can be dated by internal evidence at November 1936, reads:

NEW TRACE IS SEEN OF LOST TWO TRAPPERS / George Dalziel Finds Last Camp of Mulholland and Epler / Fort Simpson, NWT, Nov 11.—Further evidence of the fate of the two trappers, Joe Mulholland and Bill Epler, missing since they disappeared in the mountains last March, was brought to this post Tuesday by George Dalziel, well known "flying trapper" of the Nahanni river country.... The trapper said he found an encampment below the canyons on the Nahanni river, where cuttings of trees showed that Mulholland and Epler had made a log raft. It is believed that they lost their lives in the spring torrents which surge down this mountain stream and in which no man could navigate a boat, to say nothing of a raft.

But even this news item is questionable, and Dalziel may have been reported incorrectly. The Nahanni poses little risk, even during runoff, "below the canyons." If Eppler and Mulholland had made it that far, there's little chance they would have foundered before making it to Nahanni Butte.

And two years later, Dalziel reports in his manuscript, Zenchuk found traces of what must have been Mulholland and Eppler's last camp, at a point above Virginia Falls. Pieces of the roll of canvas were found at this site. But Kraus, Zenchuk, and the others found evidence of camps at the mouth of the Flat and at the "Gate," both locations well below Virginia Falls.

Dalziel speculates that the men might have gone through an overflow. If he came to the conclusion that they did come down the Nahanni, this would make sense. Overflows are caused by the flowing water freezing, backing up, flowing on top of the ice, then freezing again, creating layers of ice and water like puff pastry. You go through and slide between layers of ice and drown, or you get wet, can't warm up fast enough, and freeze to death. Overflows are hard to see and are the main reason that experienced stick men don't walk river or creek ice in winter, even though it seems like the natural thing to do to avoid bushwhacking and keep on course.

So the "mystery" remains unresolved. But there are still the notebooks, which even Sherry found mostly unreadable. Perhaps a handwriting expert can decipher them. There's Shebbach's diary, or maybe some family members who remember the circumstances of his journey. There's Zenchuk's interview at the Territorial Archives, waiting for 2010.

And there's Harry Vandaele, who was with Zenchuk, Kraus, and Faille when they found those signs of Eppler and Mulholland on the lower Nahanni and who, according to Turner, flew in with Dalziel on one of the searches. But who was Vandaele?

Over the winter, however, we had other things to occupy us – including our plans for the next summer's trip, a two- or three-week hike on the road north, past the Flat Lakes and into Howard's Pass.

It was a concept that Dalziel would have loved. I could hear him as I pored over the maps, the snow brushing against my window and a stack of grammar exercises sitting unmarked on the floor beside me.

"You won't have any trouble," he seemed to be saying.

6

Howard's Pass

"DAMN IT," said Vivien. "We broke a major rule."

"It wasn't exactly sex in a tent. It was sex in a tent that was pitched in a cabin."

"It was sex in a tent. And the cabin has no door."

Vivien and I were luxuriating on benches at a picnic table, in front of coffee and fresh cinnamon buns made from Vivien's biscuit mix, fat, brown sugar, and cinnamon. More coffee and buns were keeping warm on an oversized wood heater that murmured softly behind Vivien.

"That's the last time we go off alone in the middle of a trip," she said.

"Remember that your theory about fishy sex smells and bears is only a theory, as the wardens in Kluane, and that expert...."

"Herraro."

"Herraro told you when you met him at the Eco-Challenge in Whistler."

"Male cover-up. You guys can joke about sex, but when it comes to being candid, like warning hikers about sex and bears, you're embarrassed. And who gets it? The woman."

"For you, I'd fight to the death."

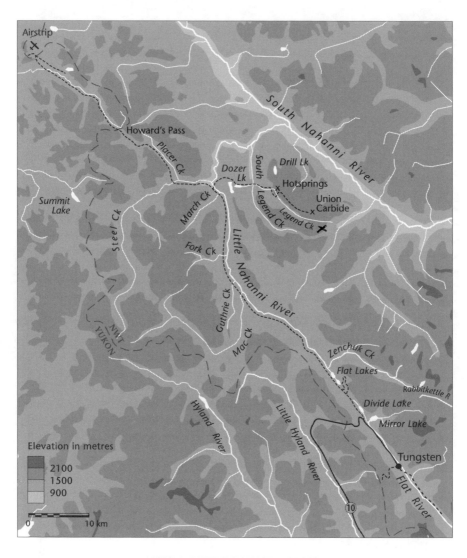

MAP 5: LITTLE NAHANNI RIVER

*Should be "Lened" Creek
    – There's rough emeralds There

"Ohh. I'll bet if the local grizzlies heard that they'd just be scared all to hell."

A fish jumped, close to shore, surprisingly loud in the morning silence.

"It was a monster!" Vivien exclaimed. She was facing the window, while I had my back to it.

I turned and saw the ripples circling from the spot. "I thought there might not be any fish in this lake," I said. "It's thick with glacial silt."

"We'll ask the Flat Lakes warden if the silt has any effect."

"I wonder if Elsebeth has already met him."

"I hope he cheers her up."

"Like you cheer me up?"

"In her case, whatever it takes."

Elsebeth was our hiking partner on this, our third summer in the Tungsten area. Vivien had met and travelled with her a couple of years earlier, in Nepal. Elsebeth was in her early forties (over a decade younger than us, I kept telling myself) and strong – the strongest hiker we had ever encountered. She was also strong on her bicycle, easily a match for my son Wes or for Birch, our two much younger companions on previous trips into Tungsten. And she had patience with machinery and equipment, a kind of healing touch.

She was also a leader, like Vivien, which meant problems.

Elsebeth was aware of this, fortunately, and was quickly learning how to avoid the problems. She felt obligated to Vivien for inviting her and flattered by Vivien's attention. In Elsebeth's world, the world of travel and adventure, Vivien was a name.

I was between them, trying to smooth things out, but often casting my vote less on the merits of the arguments from either side or on the basis of my own inclinations, and more on political grounds. Particularly, I didn't want Elsebeth to get the idea that Vivien and I were a unit and would automatically outvote her.

It was tiring. So I had proposed the side-trip to Mirror Lake, and Elsebeth had eagerly, and perhaps perceptively, expressed her desire to continue resting at the cabin on the Flat Lakes, so Vivien and I had gone off on our own.

Not that we'd had sex on our minds, or not that we had not rejected the idea of having the sex that was on our minds. I knew the rules about bears – rules that Vivien had been championing in newspaper articles and her Kluane guidebook for years. But we had wanted to be together, to return for awhile to our private dialogue on books and people.

And it was already dawning on both of us (I could tell) that our tryst at Mirror Lake could be a good story. I call this the Hemingway approach to writing. You do something stupid, and you write it up. Or you do something stupid because you want to do it, knowing at the same time that if you survive, you could have a good story to tell.

When you look at it closely, it's disgusting.

But it *was* a good story. At about midnight, a giant porcupine had walked through the empty doorframe of the cabin. A light sleeper due to a moderately inflamed prostate, I had heard the porky's asthmatic singsong approaching the cabin. I looked up and saw him, silhouetted in the spectral light reflected off the lake. He stopped, and his singsong turned into an inquiring whine. It dawned on me that if he decided to walk over to investigate, we would be helpless before his quills. So I pounded the flat of my hand on the floor of the tent/cabin.

The porky wheeled and scuttled away. Vivien sat up and tried to claw her way out of the tent.

I calmed her. "It's okay. Just a porky coming through the door. He's gone now."

She flopped back down, on her back, breathed deeply, and then told me she had been dreaming about bears.

"Guilt feelings?"

"Naked fear."

She had already this morning, I'd noticed while I was stoking up the stove and making coffee, scribbled some notes on this event for the bear section of the second edition of her Kluane guidebook: *In bear country, when accosted in tent by perverted male partner demanding sex, activate pepper spray.*

"Maybe the silt is good for the fish," Vivien said, turning away from the lake to grab the coffeepot. "That was one of the biggest grayling I've ever seen."

"So what do we do today?" I asked. "I hope it's something easy. For some reason I feel lazy, relaxed, unmotivated. Also, it's drizzling again."

"I'd like to get close to the glacier that feeds this lake. Maybe we can also get farther up the valley. My theory is that it leads over to the top of Zenchuk."

So we set out about an hour later, leaving our packs, tent, and bags hanging in the rafters of the cabin. I carried some food in the lid of my pack, which converts into a daypack. Vivien carried her camera.

Mirror Lake is bog on all sides. We had pitched tent in the cabin because that was the only flat and dry space we could find. At the east end of the lake a substantial creek flows in through a marsh. The creek comes from the glacier. Mirror Lake and its glacier are the main features of the impressive spectacle that confronts you on Highway 10 as you reach the summit of the pass that leads from the Yukon into the NWT.

Our climb to the glacier started right at the end of the lake, proceeding across a mossy rock glacier and up, on a maze of game trails, through a thick spruce forest. Rain drizzled on us all the way from the cabin to the toe of the glacier.

"Let's go back for more sex in the tent," I finally said as we munched on our cheese and cracker lunch.

"Don't you want to bushwhack through this forest for a better look up the valley?"

"I'd rather bushwhack up your...."

"Tell me. How you can go for *months* without it when we're at home, and as soon as we're in the bush you get randy?"

"I don't get randy. I get more in love because I'm with you more. Also, I don't have my job to think about, and my job is much scarier than any bear."

"For you. Not for me."

"A theory. Unsubstantiated."

"You want me to be the first proven victim?"

"No. The guilt would be terrible."

"In that case, I'll agree to go back. This drizzle is getting to me too."

We were back at the cabin by late afternoon, damp and tired. I napped while Vivien read. Then I examined the cabin in detail, something I hadn't yet had time to do. We had arrived late the day before and spent the evening tidying up the cabin for occupancy. It was full of porcupine shit and shredded insulation. The chimney was on the ground outside. The door was missing.

The cabin floor and walls had been built in the usual manner, a two-by-four frame sheeted with plywood. The roof, however, was supported by logs about eight inches in diameter that were laid along the tops of each of the two long walls, with one log laid parallel in the middle and supported by the end walls. Short logs standing upright on this middle log supported the ridgepole log. The rafters were two by twelve and were sheeted with plywood, caulked, which was the only roofing. From the outside the cabin looked top-heavy, but the log beams looked attractive on the inside, and the roof was high enough to be well beyond the porky's reach.

There was a large window in the front of the cabin, beside the door, facing the lake. There was another large window in the front end of the east wall, making for a bright corner in which the builders placed the table and benches, all securely nailed to the walls and floor. Messages were penned on the walls. *Shannon Joyce was here/May 2 '86. Doris and Willy Weh/4 may '86.*

I hoped that the Wehs enjoyed bear-free sex. There would have been a door then.

The broom handle said Christina.

"What do you think these people were doing here?"

"Racing snowmobiles on the lake is my guess," said Vivien. "Ice-fishing. You couldn't swim in this lake. You couldn't get a boat up in summer to fish."

"That might explain why we found no road or path cut in to here. They came only in winter."

The matter of a path had been significant. There was no sign of one when we looked across the valley from Highway 10 on the approach to Tungsten, so we had simply lined ourselves up with the creek flowing out of the west end of the lake, and bushwhacked. On reaching the Flat River after about a half hour, we cut poles and crossed. Even this close to the source, the river was substantial, and the rocks along the shore were slippery with moss. Then we bushwhacked up, angling north towards the creek that ran out of the lake. We dropped to the creek, but could make no headway there and so bushwhacked up onto the hill again until we finally saw the lake and found the cabin. It added up to a sweaty, two-hour scramble from Highway 10, made worse by a steady drizzle that soaked the bush, which soaked us.

But it was worth it.

We spent a second night in the cabin – no sex, no porcupines, and no bears – and were greeted (deservedly, in my view) by a clear morning sky that turned the grey waters of the lake into a sparkling green. Vivien got the pictures of the lake that she had been coveting. We returned, in some comfort and downhill, to Highway 10, where we picked up our waiting bicycles.

We decided to go into Tungsten for the hot springs and coasted down towards the town, enjoying the warm sun. Some distance before the Tungsten gates, however, at a narrow spot in the road, we found Gerald's grader parked sideways across the road with orange NO ACCESS signs braced against the front and back wheels.

"What's going on?" I wondered out loud.

"Hard to say, but it looks like visitors aren't welcome today. Let's just go back to the Flat Lakes. We can have sponge baths this afternoon."

So we turned our bicycles north, arriving at the Flat Lakes cabin just after noon.

Elsebeth had met the warden, Stefan. He had come over the previous morning and introduced himself. He was originally from Switzerland, so he and Elsebeth had been able to practise their German. Learning that she hadn't slept much due to the activities of a porcupine chewing out the floor from underneath the cabin, Stefan had gone back to his cabin and returned with a .22 that was now propped in the corner.

The gun made Vivien nervous and made me wonder out loud what kind of a game warden Stefan was supposed to be.

"The gun was to scare the porcupine, not to kill it," said Elsebeth. "It worked, too. He went away and never came back."

"Makes sense. But the word in Tungsten is that Stefan's a bit trigger-happy."

"There's also the matter of some Indians who've been hanging around the area," said Elsebeth. "Stefan spotted them, but they ran into the bush. Stefan radioed Gerald, who blocked the road into town."

Vivien and I looked at one another. The idea of a nervous Elsebeth cutting down a local, or one of us, with Stefan's .22 was unsettling.

"Spooked" was the word that Dwayne had used to describe Stefan during our first visit to Tungsten. Now it seemed like Stefan had also been reading up on the history of the area, especially the part about headhunting Indians.

"Don't ever surprise him," Dwayne had said.

"I've invited Stefan for dinner tonight," Elsebeth added.

"Good idea!" said Vivien. "Maybe he knows something about the road north."

I figured it was better to have him sitting across the table than wandering through the nearby bush where we couldn't see him.

We rested that afternoon, bathed, and sorted our stuff for the trip to what Gerald had called Howard's Pass, an abandoned exploration site on the NWT-Yukon border, approximately seventy-five kilometres north of the Flat Lakes. We would ride the road as far as possible with full panniers, and carry our mostly empty hiking packs on our backs. When riding became impossible, as it probably eventually would, we would ditch our bikes and walk.

Elsebeth, meanwhile, went off to Stefan's. She returned with a bag of shaggy-mane mushrooms, picked from along the road, and another bag of blueberries, picked from the hillside above Stefan's cabin. She rolled the blueberries into Vivien's biscuit mix.

Later, getting water for tea, I saw a man in gumboots down at the end of the lake, fishing. He wore a felt hat with a feather in the brim and had a short-muzzled rifle slung over his shoulder. He waved.

"He's bringing fish for dinner," Elsebeth explained. "He says it's legal to give us fish so long as he's invited for dinner."

"In that case he's invited any time we're here," said Vivien. "We love grayling and we've never tried any from this lake, have we John?"

Saying this, she gave me a significant glance, informing me thereby that I should be careful not to blab about the contraband grayling that we had caught the year before.

"I hope he catches some," I said.

"He will," said Elsebeth. "He says they snap at anything."

Stefan was a short, husky, balding man, about thirty-five years old. He brought a grayling for each of us. He expertly gutted and scraped the fish on the pier, scattering the remains out on the water. The tiny seagulls that hang around the lake dove for these remains. Then he sat for tea at the picnic table, placing his "bazooka," as he called it, flat in the middle of the table. It was a sawed-off, double-barrelled shotgun.

He explained that most bear encounters were at close quarters. "This stops them dead," he said. "If I stick my head out the door to spit, I take it with me."

Vivien was bursting to protest that bears were peaceful animals, that this was their habitat and we were the guests, etc. But I frowned at her and she shrugged and held her tongue.

Stefan talked about his job, saying that he had taken wildlife courses in Switzerland just so he could come to Canada to work in the bush. "I have it made," he said. "I get paid to do things that a lot of Europeans can only dream of doing, and that some will pay to do."

Elsebeth nodded.

"Doesn't the isolation get to you?" asked Vivien.

"I love it."

Stefan's only problem, surprisingly, was Gerald. Their relationship was generally good, but was soured by the fact that Gerald would not let Stefan have his pick of items from the mine site, items that were not being used but instead were rusting or rotting, and which would make Stefan more comfortable. Gerald stuck with company policy. Nothing was to be removed from the site without permission from head office.

I sympathized with Gerald. Once Stefan started carting stuff out of Tungsten, where would it end? Our Flat Lakes cabin looked like it had been put together largely out of materials and furniture taken from the townsite. So I changed the subject. "What's the road north like?"

"I don't know. Gerald told me you went up there last summer and found a cabin by the first bridge. That was new to me, so I went up on my quad to check the cabin out. I stayed overnight."

"It wasn't locked?"

"I hammered the lock off and moved most of the box traps outside. The trapper's not coming back. The Northwest Territories cancelled his lease as well as any other leases in this area, including the ones on these cabins along the lake. People on the road or the river might as well be using that cabin too. I thought someone *was* using it. That's why I went up there."

"You saw someone?"

"Yeah. And plenty of footprints along the road. Two people, it looks like. What Gerald and I can't figure is that there are no vehicles around. Keep your eyes open as you go up to the cabin, if you go."

"We're going," said Vivien. "Any sign of them at the cabin?"

"No."

"What's the cabin like inside?" I asked.

"Comfortable. A couple of bunks, a table, a lounge chair like the ones in this cabin, a rocking chair, and a large stove. There's lots of wood stacked outside. There's kindling in a wooden box."

When we asked about the fish in Mirror Lake, Stefan agreed they were good ones. "The silt doesn't do them any harm, that's for sure. But the cabin there is in bad shape."

"It sure is."

"You were there?"

"Yesterday."

"You people get around. Gerald told me you'd also been up to Zenchuk Creek and over into Rabbitkettle Valley."

"Do you know that area?"

"I've flown into the alpines on top of Zenchuk a couple of times to do sheep counts. I've stayed in the campsite you told Gerald about, with the old saw and fry pan."

"It was a beautiful spot," said Viv. "Only a short walk from the falls, too."

"You people *really* get around."

"They are very curious," said Elsebeth.

"How far up the road are you going?"

"As far as it goes."

"Make sure you tell me about it when you get back," Stefan said. "I've flown into Summit Lake, due south of Howard's Pass. The cabin and dock there are good, and popular with outfitters, but you'd have to cross a marsh to get to it from the north."

"When we get back, we'll have another dinner," said Elsebeth.

"Maybe by then I'll have some caribou steak to add to the fish," said Stefan.

I shot a glance at Vivien, expecting her to tell Stefan not to shoot a caribou on her account. But she was silent. Probably she was thinking about how welcoming the platter of steak and fish would be on our arrival back at the Flat Lakes. On some matters, or in some circumstances, Vivien was willing to compromise.

The next day dawned sunny. I woke up early, fully rested, lit a fire in the pit in front of the cabin, and sauntered out onto the pier to get water for coffee. I stared for a long time at the mountains ranged beyond the north end of the lake. In a few days we would be in them.

We made good time on that first day, the road solid and fairly clear, though as we had noted when coming through with Birch, the bush thickened slowly as we pushed north. The Little Nahanni, flowing out of the north end of the Flat Lakes, meandered quietly below the road, making big, serpentine sweeps through the muskeg.

We saw the fresh tracks of Stefan's quad but no other tracks apart from some of our own. We were glad to see that the sweepers, spruce trees up to a foot in diameter hanging or fallen across the road, were gone, thanks to Stefan; fresh sawdust on the road marked their previous locations. Once past the cabin we would have to clear these ourselves to facilitate our return, and I had brought my collapsible Swede saw for this purpose.

Our main impediments, more noticeable now due to our heavy panniers and packs, were the washed-out culverts wherever the road gouged, as it often did, a steep hillside. The culvert would be deep in the bush below the road or even down as far as the river, and a big chunk of road would be spread around it. Or the culvert would be high and dry in the middle of a big gully across the road. Either way, we had to unhook our panniers, carry them across, dump them and our backpacks on the other side, and then return to carry our bikes across.

After a full day, in which we travelled twenty-eight kilometres, we made it to the cabin that we had visited with Birch the year before, by the first bridge, on Mac Creek according to the contour map. We found it pretty much as Stefan had described it. After dinner I set up my mattress on the floor of the cabin while Vivien and Elsebeth spread their sleeping bags out on the trapper's mattresses in the bunks. Then we went out to reconnoitre.

"It's lucky for us that Stefan broke the lock off this door," said Elsebeth.

Vivien and I agreed. The lock was large, and the latch had been bolted on, with pieces of steel plate reinforcing the door where the bolts went through. No wonder Birch had broken his knife blade on it. We couldn't have broken in ourselves without smashing the window, and this way the cabin was sound and would be useful on our way back and on any subsequent trips.

We showed Elsebeth the trail that led from the clearing in front of the cabin to a slow bend on the Little Nahanni, just upstream from a small cutbank and across from a gravel bar.

"You wouldn't see the cabin from the river," said Vivien.

"Or any other sign of habitation," added Elsebeth.

We walked back to the road and turned north, walking a few metres to the first of the bridges. It was no longer intact as it had been the previous year when we stood on it with Birch. Now it was washed out on the far end and buckled up in the middle. Downstream we found a heavy plank, which we hauled up to the bridge and positioned so it reached from the end of the bridge to the opposite shore. Then we went back to the cabin to sleep.

There were four more such bridges ahead of us. We hoped they would be in better shape than this one.

Overall, they were. We encountered the second bridge, on Guthrie Creek, the following morning, only two or three kilometres up the road. It was complete. The third bridge, however, on Fork Creek, which we encountered around noon, was washed out at the south end.

That was where we decided to abandon the bikes. The vegetation on the road had been getting thicker, the washouts and sweepers more numerous, and the road softer. The vegetation on the road on the other side of the bridge was thick.

Below us, the Little Nahanni had been changing too. Where we could see it, it proceeded in big sweeping curves, its surface dotted by large boulders. Often it was invisible, roaring loudly below us through a canyon.

We emptied our panniers into our backpacks, stashed our bikes under some spruce trees that grew close to the bridge, and hung our panniers as high in the trees as we could get them. Then we roped our packs up onto the bridge, loaded them on our backs, and walked across.

In only a few hours we knew we had made a mistake and that we should have gone to the trouble of passing our bikes up onto the bridge and down off the other end. The road continued, no worse than usual, from the other side of the third bridge.

But the walking was pleasant. From high points on the road we gained panoramic views of the Little Nahanni.

The fourth bridge, on March Creek, was in good shape and we camped there, right on the deck.

By noon the next day we were looking down at Steel Creek. Near its confluence with the Little Nahanni, it looked more like a river than a creek. The contour map showed a winter road running off our road and crossing the Little Nahanni just above Steel Creek. We looked carefully for this winter road, hoping to mark it for a future hike to what Gerald had identified on the map as the Union Carbide exploration site. This site was situated at the beginning of a pass that led, we hoped, to a view of the Nahanni. We made three trips up and down the kilometre-long stretch before Steel Creek, but saw no sign of the winter road and decided to move on. We would try again on the way back.

The road up Steel Creek, heading west now towards the Yukon border, was in excellent shape, making us absolutely certain that we should have kept our bicycles. We camped on the road about five kilometres above the junction of Steel Creek and the Little Nahanni. Our site was close to a small creek that flowed through a culvert beneath the road. We had a good view up Steel towards the mountains that awaited us between Howard's Pass and Summit Lake.

At noon the next day we descended to Steel Creek and found the bridge intact. This was fortunate, as Steel Creek is large enough to make for a difficult and dangerous crossing. Elsebeth, ahead of us as usual, hollered in triumph.

Not only was the bridge in good shape, but in the centre of the bridge, sunk solidly into the planking, was an axe. The axe was new, or rather, unused, sporting the manufacturer's sticker on its head, even though the handle was bleached white. Obviously it had been on the bridge for some time. Since the bridge looked shaky, with a substantial amount of driftwood piled against the upstream supports, I took the axe and drove it into a solid stump in the middle of a hunter's camp in a spruce grove on the other side of, and upstream from, the bridge.

The road then rose steeply along Placer Creek. If we had taken our bikes as far as the Steel Creek bridge, this is where we would have left them. The road was now thickly vegetated and soft.

FORK CREEK BRIDGE

We camped halfway up Placer Creek. Over dinner, all three of us were full of speculation about the pass ahead. We spread out the 1:50,000 contour map, which showed a square dot indicating a cabin. Would it be liveable? Would it even be *there?* Only a few days outside make most thoroughly civilized people long for enclosure and pre-breathed air. Vivien, Elsebeth, and I were no exception to this rule.

We woke to light rain. By noon, the road was winding into alpine. Somewhere in the vicinity a winter road branched south and ran all the way to Highway 10 on the Yukon side of the pass over to Tungsten. We had found this winter road at *that* end – it started at the back of a gravel pit just off Highway 10. But at this end we couldn't find it.

Our hopes for Union Carbide were fading. If the winter roads were all so completely closed in, that hike could be impractical.

We spent little time on our search, though. The alpines beckoned, snow-streaked cirques in all directions. We could see that the nearby hills were gouged by exploration roads, and we passed claim posts and a set of moose antlers propped formally against a large rock. Then I noticed that the area to our left and slightly above us was abnormally level, had in fact been bull-dozed flat. I ran off the road, through what I could now identify as a ditch, across some hardened snow, and up onto the flat area. It was an airstrip, similar to the one in Tungsten. Orange fuel barrels marked the far side. Farther north were more barrels, obviously a fuelling area. Farther still were core-sample racks and the building we had been wondering about.

Home!

It was a machine shop, large, roofed with aluminum (though some sheets had blown off), populated by noisy marmots and birds, circled inside by shelves and benches that held old bearings, brake linings, engine parts, and broken tools. The shop was open at one end, but that entrance was blocked by a large pile of junk that might have been dropped in there by a front-end loader. The pile consisted mainly of oil heaters, but also included sinks, pieces of a radio tower, a giant gas range, and numerous auto batteries and fire extinguishers.

The back end of the shop was accessible through an ordinary door. Someone – hunters probably – had made this area liveable by arranging pallet boards on the floor and placing four metal beds and four chairs on the boards. They had even had a fire, lit in a tin washtub that sat on top of an oil heater. Before leaving (doubtless they came and went by plane), they had bagged their excess food in three bright orange garbage bags and suspended the bags from the ceiling using yellow nylon rope. They were obviously thoughtful hunters.

While Vivien and Elsebeth explored the area behind the machine shop, I lowered these bags and rooted through them, hoping for powdered cappuccino. No luck. But there were some bags of commercially packaged dried dinners. We selected one each, and I made a fire outside at the base of the hill and cooked them up for a snack. My water supply was a patch of compacted snow in a nearby gully.

As we ate, Vivien and Elsebeth told of how, on the hill above the machine shop, they had located the source of the great pile of junk in the shop. The miners had burnt a row of bunkhouses. First they had removed the heaters and other metal objects and dumped them in the shop. Then they had lined up a couple of dozen folding bedframes, on their sides, along the path leading to the bunkhouses.

"It was a bit surreal," said Vivien. "From a distance, the bedframes looked like a fence."

After our snack I set about to see if the shop could be made habitable. Vivien and Elsebeth, turning their noses up at the mess and the smell of engine oil, explored farther along the road, which continued north past the core samples and a field of compacted, forty-five-gallon fuel barrels. They left their packs and said they would be back in two hours at most.

"Take your time," I told them.

They were back in an hour. I had washed our dishes, placed the hunters' food into a couple of clean, five-gallon drums with lids, and suspended the drums from the ceiling; the plastic bags were being pecked through by the birds. I was busy rooting through the junk pile. Already I had gathered some useable items – a broom, a galvanized bucket, an aluminum coffee percolator, a box of nails, a pipe wrench and screwdriver, and a pair of worn but functional pliers.

Vivien and Elsebeth had discovered a cabin, but were arguing about whether it was useable.

"It's a beautiful little place!" said Vivien. "Obviously it was the office for the engineers who ran the mine."

Elsebeth wrinkled her nose. "It's full of porcupine shit and cobwebs," she said. "I think this is better."

Trusting to Viv's greater experience, I voted to pack up our stuff and move to the cabin. We carried as much of my scavenging as possible, figuring we could come back for the rest as needed. Vivien made sure we took the broom. We also carried a chair each.

"We can pitch our tents in the cabin," said Vivien. "Then we can do day-trips to explore the alpines around here."

"I'm not putting my tent on that floor," said Elsebeth.

But I could immediately see that the cabin was fine. It was painted a bright green and had a roof made of rolled aluminum that was solidly tacked down. Two radio towers were connected to it, one attached to a front corner. The windows, on the front and back walls, were unbroken. It was fully insulated inside, though in places the only covering on the insulation was plastic sheeting. The marmots had played havoc with some of the insulation, but most was in place. There was a bench all along the back wall on which the mining engineers had worked with their maps and core-bags, and there was a stand-up desk by the front window near the door.

A porcupine had eaten off the entire bottom of the door to get at the plywood on the bench. He was also eating his way in from the four corners of the building.

There were building materials galore around the site. Beside the cabin was a small shack that housed a stone cutter sans electric engine and, more usefully, a shovel. The road went around the cabin and down to a busy creek, past a dry sewage lagoon and the ruins of a washhouse. An ore-car track ran along the road. It ended at the edge of the creek beside a small workshed, started again on the other side, and disappeared into a tunnel, a gaping hole in the bluff opposite. The orange plastic tarp that had covered the entrance was shredded and flapping in the wind.

The creek had removed all trace of the bridge across which the ore-car track must originally have run. We found planks piled behind the workshop and laid them across the creek to gain access to the mineshaft. But it was not inviting. Just inside the entrance, the tunnel narrowed and was boarded over, though not completely.

We decided that we did not want to go into the shaft, even though we had flashlights. "There are often gases in mines like this," said Elsebeth.

A row of helmets and rubber outfits hung from the tunnel cribbing, and on our way out we found an axe.

By evening the cabin was spotless. Elsebeth was amazed. "The floor is new under all that shit," she exclaimed as she used the axe to pound nails into the floor to hold her tent.

"Too bad there's no stove," I said, watching Vivien, who had climbed into her sleeping bag and settled on a chair by the window to write her daily journal. Rain had started while we cooked dinner, so we were confined to the cabin – and were very pleased to be there.

"There must've been some heat originally," murmured Vivien.

"Propane or oil," I said. "There's a hole for a four-inch pipe in the gable above the door."

"Could you put a pipe through there?"

"I could. And there's an airtight heater up at the airport. The trick would be to put together an eight-inch pipe tapering down to four-inch. Only small fires would be possible."

"That's all we need to take the edge off," said Vivien. "And keep our coffee warm."

Elsebeth giggled. "You're actually going to install a heater?" she asked.

"John loves doing that sort of thing," said Vivien. "I call him 'the junkman.' You should see his homestead outside Prince George. An acre of cars, all rusting in neat rows. Another acre of old lumber, windows, doors, and tin roofing, all neatly stacked and rotting."

"He is talented," said Elsebeth. "His covered fire ring out in the parking lot worked well."

Elsebeth's compliment pleased me. I had made the fire ring out of a tractor wheel-rim and used some sawhorses, timbers, and plywood to shelter it and the cook (myself, usually) from wind and rain. Our fuel was a bundle of cedar wedges, found on top of one of the timber piles. It was lucky these wedges were there, because the surrounding alpines were bare of trees, and the timbers were too large to saw through. These twelve-by-twelve timbers were probably the cribbing for the mine, as well as material for repairing the bridges.

"I could spend weeks here," I said to Vivien later when we tucked into our bags.

"With your little saw and your little axe?"

"Those mountains of timbers out there, laid together like logs, would make lovely cabins. And there's roofing everywhere. I could make a motel."

"John'stown."

"I could rent the cabins to sheep hunters."

"No way. I was sick enough talking to Stefan about hunting."

"Think of those caribou steaks we might be eating if he has luck. What do we do tomorrow?"

"The road goes north for another fifteen or so kilometres to another airstrip, the one marked on the map. I wonder, though, if they didn't confuse that area with this area when they marked the maps. We want to go to the end of the road. Then we want to explore these alpines. We'll be here for a couple of days."

"Great!"

The next day dawned clear. We took our chairs outside and had our coffee and porridge on the sunny side of the cabin as we decided we would hike to the end of the road and the other airstrip the next day. First we would explore the immediate area, laze around in the sun, drink lots of coffee, and read our books.

In the course of lazing I noticed a radio licence and a Yukon Government building permit, #981, pinned above the front window just below the cabin's ceiling. These identified the location as Potato Hill and the company as Placer Development Ltd. Under the bench I found a Ritchie Brothers' Auction calendar dated 1981.

Later in the morning I started nailing pieces of galvanized steel and ¾-inch plywood (the sides of the ore cars) around the outside of the cabin. I intended to slow down the porcupine's work. I wanted the cabin to last another dozen years at least.

"John wants us to get out of his way," said Vivien, watching me from her chair.

"I'm wondering about that silver thing up on the hill across from the airstrip," said Elsebeth. She was leaning back in her chair, scanning the vicinity with the binoculars.

"Let's go find out," said Vivien.

I dropped my hammer. "I'm coming too."

The silver thing was a radio or microwave tower. Two hours later we were at it. On the ground beneath the tower was a wooden box full of batteries, and an aluminum stepladder. We posed on the ladder, an ideal prop

THE MINESHAFT AT POTATO HILL

for photos, and then noticed a pyramid-shaped mountain far to the north.

"Mount Wilson, maybe," Vivien said with awe.

"Mount Wilson is at the headwaters of the Nahanni," I explained to Elsebeth. "You can get there via the Canol Road and an old pipeline trail. That airstrip at the end of our road, if it's there, is about halfway between Tungsten and the Canol Road."

We returned to the cabin. Vivien and Elsebeth made tea and went back to their books. I went back to exploring the immediate area once again.

Inside the machine shop were messages penned on the plywood wall: *Meet you in the Cecil in two months. Darcy Delaney/Kenora Ont/July – Nov '81.*

The following morning quickly turned wet. Our trip to the end of the road and the mysterious airstrip took us across the creek, just below the mineshaft, and down into the valley on a road that quickly became a trail. It was another winter road, we figured, used only when the ground was frozen. The bottom of the valley was a bog, and we wasted a lot of time at first trying to jump from dry spot to dry spot. Eventually we gave up and just slogged on through, aiming for what looked like eskers to the north at the bottom of the valley. The map made it look like a left turn there would take us up onto some dry land, possibly to the remains of a good road.

Elsebeth quickly got tired of it. "I hate this wet all the time," she said. "Going through this bush is more like swimming."

I agreed, and so did Vivien. We were disappointed, though; still curious about what could be at the end of the road. Five hours after leaving the cabin, we were back. I continued my construction work. That night we fell asleep to yet another thunderstorm booming up the valley towards us.

But there was sun the next morning, so Elsebeth and Vivien decided to take advantage and start early into the alpines south of the cabin. Their idea was to scout a route to Summit Lake, due south of us. A large black ridge facing the cabin cut us off from any direct route, so they planned to go back towards the airstrip, behind which the ridge tapered down and became a mere hill. They hoped to find their way around or over the hill to a valley that turned south.

They took snacks and rain gear in one pack. I walked as far as the airstrip with them and returned with the airtight heater and some pipes. I figured that the pipe clamps I had noticed on the fixtures in the washing shed near the mine could be used to strap together my pipes and taper them to four inches. I would have a fire crackling in the cabin by the time Vivien and Elsebeth returned.

I was just conducting a final test, late in the afternoon, when I heard Vivien and Elsebeth yodelling. I went to the creek, got a bucket of wash water, and put it on the heater. If the heater or pipe got too hot, the water would be handy. Then I started our outdoor cooking fire and put water on for tea. In a few minutes they appeared, walking down past the rows of sample ore, arranged like long graves in neat, parallel lines on the slope below the ridge.

They had found an alpine valley, heading south.

"We should be able to walk right down to Summit Lake," said Vivien.

"Remember Stefan," I said. "To the swamp on this side of Summit Lake."

"And look at the stove!" said Vivien. "I'm going to wash a few dainties and hang them to dry."

"Good idea," said Elsebeth.

I rigged a string clothesline across the ceiling above the stove and explained to Vivien and Elsebeth that they had to feed the stove slowly, a small amount of wood at a time. "I'm worried about what could happen if some hunters got in here and decided to cook a steak on this heater."

"Would serve them right," said Vivien. "But look. The miners left a daybook here. It's got a lot of blank pages. Let's turn it into the cabin logbook. People can leave a record of their stay, and we can put in a warning at the very beginning about the stove."

Early the next morning we ate, packed our backpacks, braced the cabin door with heavy plywood, covered the chimney with a plastic ore bag, and left. I looked back often, but wasn't reluctant to leave. The day was absolutely clear, and Summit Lake was on the route back to civilization.

I wished the cabin good luck with its visitors.

That night we camped in the alpine overlooking Summit Lake. We had decided, over dinner, not to go down. Our side of the lake did look like jungle, as Stefan had warned. Instead we planned to turn left and proceed down to a creek, along which the northern section of the winter road that started from Highway 10 on the Yukon side of the pass should be in evidence. We figured it ran all the way to the entrance to Howard's Pass. If this road was useable, we would follow it back to Howard's Pass. If it wasn't, we would continue due east, up into the next range of hills, and then down to intersect our road just above Steel Creek. We hoped.

The next night we camped, uncomfortably, in the bush beside the winter road. We were disillusioned. The road was visible where it crowned any ridge or gouged out the side of a hill, but generally it wound back and forth right up the creek. Mostly it was invisible. So the next morning we selected a promising slope to the east and went over. It was tough going, but the weather was sticking with us. And we had further luck. Once we caught sight of the road below, winding up Placer Creek from Steel Creek, we also saw where a recent slide had cleared a path down through the heavy bush to the road.

We arrived late at Steel Creek and camped just above the bridge. I used the axe to build a roaring blaze on a gravel bar where the creek turned, and we bathed in the freezing water, dried off by the fire, and collapsed into our sleeping bags feeling wonderfully fresh and clean.

Three days later we arrived at the Flat Lakes. On the way back, Elsebeth sniffed out the winter road that turned off and dropped to the confluence of Steel Creek and the Little Nahanni and then, somewhere across the river, continued through the bush and up to the Union Carbide exploration site in the alpines above the Nahanni River. We marked it with a stone arrow and small cairn, and followed it down, and Vivien negotiated a crossing of the Little Nahanni just above the mouth of Steel Creek.

On the way back, too, we found our bicycles untouched, but our panniers, which we had hung in the trees above the bicycles, scattered on the ground and torn and bitten. Two, the newest ones, which I had bought especially for this trip, were gone. Fortunately our toolkit, stored in one of the older panniers, had been left intact.

It had to be a bear, we decided. "A bear with good taste," I added, thinking of my new, bright red, front panniers and of the weight I was now going to have to carry in my backpack.

JOHN'S STOVE

We searched for awhile, noisily but without conviction. We all felt that we should move on as quickly as possible. If the bear wanted panniers it was a small price to pay for our passing through.

Then, a half day away from the little trapper's cabin on the Flat Lakes, a big helicopter came thundering down the valley, over the river and level with the road. After days of absolute peace, except for the roaring of creeks and rivers, the sound was frightening. The chopper hovered over us, but, because of the trees, could not get close. We waved. The chopper turned and sped back the way it had come.

At the Flat Lakes, things had changed. There was no Stefan. No caribou steaks.

Elsebeth visited his cabin the morning after we arrived. She came back worried. "The door was open and a porcupine has been messing things up. His personal things are gone."

"His quad?"

"In its shed as usual. His propane fridge is still working."

"His radiophone?"

"Gone. All of his rifles too."

"He can't just be hurt somewhere in the vicinity. He wouldn't have all that stuff with him."

"We'd better move on to Tungsten right away, just in case. Maybe they know what happened. If not, they can report to Stefan's superiors."

"I wonder if it has some connection to that chopper."

We loaded everything and flung ourselves down the road, impelled by curiosity and the possibility that Stefan could be in trouble somewhere. We stopped only once, at Stefan's shack, to confirm what Elsebeth had seen. The shack was a mess.

The gates to Tungsten were open.

As we idled towards the recreation centre, regrouping after cranking up the hill from the gates, four armed figures in berets and baggy blue jumpsuits stepped out of the centre's entrance and blocked the road.

"We want you to get off your cycles, now, and stand quietly with your arms up," said the lead figure.

It's not easy to get off a bike and put your hands on your head. My bike, its back end heavily loaded, slid away from me and crashed to the ground. I bent over to save it.

"Do not pick up your bicycle!" the same voice ordered. "Stand quietly with your arms up."

"Just get that gun out of his face!" shouted Vivien.

"There's been a shooting in the area. We're checking everyone for weapons. Just keep your arms up until we finish."

The one-handed frisking didn't take long.

"Lower your arms and move away from your bicycles," said one of the officers. I glanced at her and noticed her blonde hair in a tight roll behind her beret. She approached me. "What is your name, sir?"

"John."

"Surname?"

"Harris."

"Do you have any identification?"

"In the wallet in the end pocket of my back pannier. I don't carry a wallet when I'm riding because it hurts my ass."

Vivien giggled.

"I'll retrieve the wallet," the female officer said. "Which pannier?"

"The back. The one on top."

She unzipped the pocket and groped inside.

"There's no wallet here."

I was starting to sweat. "Sorry. Must be the one underneath."

She kneeled on one knee, holding her rifle upright with one hand, reached under my rear wheel, unzipped the pocket, reached in, and, to my relief, pulled out my wallet. She stood up, went through the wallet, pulled out my driver's licence, and passed it to the officer who had spoken first.

He studied the photo and studied me. "When were you born?"

"Nineteenth September, nineteen forty-two."

"What kind of vehicle do you drive?"

"Mazda pickup, grey, white canopy on the back. It's at the washout."

"Where were you going?"

"To visit the Pitts."

He gave the licence to the woman, who put it back into the wallet and handed the wallet to me.

"You can proceed," he said. "Officer Burney will follow behind you. Go straight to the house. We'll have to check your bikes and your backpacks, so leave everything here. We'll reload it and bring it up to the house."

Viv and Elsebeth laid their bikes down on the pavement and we all removed our backpacks. We started to walk. I looked back to see Officer Burney following us and the other three beginning their search through our things.

"Have we got a story for you," said Terri, meeting us at her door when we arrived. Officer Burney stepped aside as we filed in. "Any messages?" she asked Terri.

"No."

"I've been manning the radio for them," she explained as she closed the door and ushered us upstairs into the living room.

"What happened?"

"It's all about Stefan. He's okay, sort of, but that's the story. Get yourself some coffee and wait in the living room. I'll get Gerald. He's just down at the generator."

"Where are the kids?"

"In Watson Lake, but that's also part of the story."

"She seems more amused than anything," I said as we waited, cradling our coffees, looking out the picture window. We could see Terri emerge from beneath the slope on the next terrace down. She entered the generator shack. In a minute, she and Gerald emerged, heading for the path up to the house.

"God that Flat River valley is beautiful," said Vivien, standing at the big living room window that looked south down the valley.

"The McLeod Mine's just down there. Zenchuk's cabin where Shebbach died. Faille's cabin. We've got to go down there some day."

Gerald and Terri came stomping up the stairs. Gerald got himself a coffee. "You tell them," he said to Terri once they had settled on the sofa.

"You," said Terri. "I'll register any omissions."

"I don't know where to start. Stefan's okay, sort of."

"I told them that already."

"You told *me* to tell the story!"

"They were *worried*. You can tell the rest of the story."

Gerald took a long swallow of his coffee. "Wednesday night – that's three days back in case you've lost track – Stefan radioed to tell us he'd been shot."

"*What!*"

Gerald waved his hand as if to restrain us. "It was only a flesh wound," he said. He wanted us to contact the RCMP in Watson Lake. He said that someone had bushwhacked him as he was fishing at his usual spot, near the cabin you stayed in. He'd returned the fire, in the direction of the cabin, two shots out of his shotgun, but that was more to cover his retreat. He saw no one, but knew roughly where the shot had come from. He ran back to his cabin and phoned us. He told us to get the RCMP to block off Highway 10 and to send a chopper in to his cabin. He said he'd go out and secure the area around his cabin. He said his arm would be okay. Then he got off to wrap up his wound."

"Why didn't he phone the RCMP himself?"

"He didn't say. I assumed he was shocked."

"The police got here fast," said Terri, "some in a chopper and some in a plane. The plane came from Whitehorse and the police in it are some kind of emergency response team. As soon as they were all set up down at the terminal, they sent the chopper to Stefan's cabin and picked him up. Then they put him on the plane and took him to the hospital in Whitehorse. They took the kids as far as Watson Lake – figured they'd be safer there, so I called some friends of ours in town to look after them. But really the police were thinking about themselves. Natasha and Alex wouldn't leave them alone."

"Another bunch blocked Highway 10 just up from the Robert Campbell Highway," Gerald added, "and turned back any vehicles that tried to get in. No one tried to get out. They cruised Highway 10 and saw nothing but your vehicle at the washout. They got very interested in you. You were the only real suspects. We told them who you were, that you'd been here before. Stefan evidently told them too. This seemed to disappoint them, but still they wanted to talk to you or see you, or at least see that you were safe. So they loaded me into the chopper and north we went."

"And there we were."

"All red and green and yellow, right on the road, and still quite a distance from the Flat Lakes."

"You don't think anything really happened to Stefan, do you?" said Viv.

"No, but we haven't said a thing about that to the police."

"Will they let us go to the hot spring?" asked Elsebeth.

"Oh yeah," said Terri. "We've been there, and the guy in charge of the

police is having trouble keeping the others out of it. I think they all figure that Stefan's given them a story. I'll get you some towels."

"I sort of hope we're all wrong and he *didn't* make the story up,"
mused Gerald. "For his own sake."

Gerald drove us to the spring. As we passed along the airstrip we saw
the chopper sitting at the trailer that served as a terminal, police standing on the porch with coffees in their hands.

"They're getting quite comfortable," said Gerald. "I overheard some
of them planning a sheep-hunting trip into here for September."

As we got out of the truck at the spring, he added, "I'm going over to
see what's up."

In an hour he was back, with Terri. "It's all over," he said to us from
the changeroom as he and Terri slipped into the bathing suits that they
kept there.

"You were right, then," said Elsebeth.

"Yeah." Terri and Gerald stepped down into the pool and eased into
the water, their heads and shoulders, like ours, up on the rocks, so it was
like we were all talking to the ceiling. "The doctor who checked Stefan's
wound was convinced it was administered at close range – in other
words that it was self-inflicted, and by a shotgun. They started asking
Stefan a lot of questions, and finally he admitted that he'd shot himself.
Accidentally. Still, he holds that there was someone at the Flat Lakes
cabin. A tall man. Stefan now says he saw this man. He dropped his fishing rod, reached for the gun, and slipped. The gun went off."

There was a long pause.

"Maybe someone was there," Gerald continued, "but there was no sign of
anything in the cabin except your neat pile of food. The place was spotless."

"I blame the Wildlife Service," said Terri. "They knew about Stefan,
but still they let him come out here, year after year, all by himself."

"Stefan could be in a lot of trouble," said Vivien.

Gerald and Terri nodded. "Public mischief or something like that,"
said Terri.

"So," said Gerald, easing the back of his head down into the water.
"We're going out. We have to pick up the kids, and in light of all the
excitement, we get a day of rest and recreation, at company expense, in
the Watson Lake Hotel. Would you like a ride out to your truck? Or let's

put it this way: would you like a ride all the way to your truck instead of just to the gates, which is where I have to take you before we can leave?"

"Hallelujah!" I said. I got up, dizzy from the heat, and made my way to the door. As I dried off and dressed, I heard a growing commotion from the airstrip – the chopper was starting up. I walked the road around the outdoor pool with its sundeck and diving board and stood on the edge of the airstrip. The police were loading the chopper. Eventually they piled in and took off. As they turned over my head, one of them waved. Then the chopper made its way down the Flat River Valley until it was a tiny speck in the sky.

On our way out, our bikes and packs piled into the back of the truck, Viv said, "We've got one more area we need to look into before we head over to Kluane Park."

"Oh yeah," I said. "The mining road just north of the campsite."

"We'll make it a day hike or bike, an experimental probe. If the area has potential, we'll go back in next summer."

"What does she mean by 'potential'?" asked Elsebeth.

"Alpines," I replied.

Gerald drove the crew-cab four-by-four right through the washout. At one point, when the truck was having trouble making headway, we opened the truck doors to let the water flow through, just as Will had speculated when we were here with him on our first trip in.

Gerald and Terri waited until our truck started. Then we said goodbye.

"You be sure to stay with us in the fall, on your way out to Red Deer," Vivien said to Terri.

"We will."

We drove to our unnamed creek, found the mining road that led up it, and made camp on a wide space a few metres up the road. There was an old firepit there, a metal grill, and some log benches.

The next morning we decided to leave our bicycles and proceed on foot. The road looked unmaintained, in places thick with willow. We made a late start. The first thing we came upon was a log cabin, its rooftree split and its roof collapsed onto a beautiful cookstove and the remains of some wooden furniture. In the vicinity of the cabin were numerous fire rings, and on the opposite side of the road was a comfortable wooden bench.

"Strange place to build, or even to camp," I commented. "No convenient drinking water in evidence."

"This could be a trapper's cabin," said Vivien. "In other words, he was in only in winter and melted snow for water. As for the hunters, they'd have their trucks and jerry cans right here."

About half an hour later we came across a flow of sweet, clear water springing from beneath some willow on the left side of the road. We soon crossed a small creek and then started on a steep uphill grunt through a pine forest.

"Someone's been here recently," said Elsebeth, stopping and pointing at the road.

Vivien and I panted up to her. She was right. In the damp bottom of a pothole was a footprint and a bicycle track.

"Running shoes," said Vivien.

"I've seen smaller prints too, just as fresh," said Elsebeth. "There were two people at least."

"Oh, oh," I said. "Isn't that what Stefan saw on the road around the Flat Lakes?"

"He didn't see bicycle tracks."

"He didn't *mention* bicycle tracks. Anyway, *our* tracks are still there from last year, and he knew we were on bikes. I don't like this. I think we should go back."

"No way!" said Vivien. "This is getting exciting. Maybe we can figure out what really happened to Stefan."

"He *told* the police what happened to him, Nancy Drew. There is no mystery."

"Who is this 'Nancy Drew'?" asked Elsebeth.

Vivien explained.

"I think we should go on," said Elsebeth.

"Yeah," said Vivien. "Remember that nobody shot *at* Stefan. He shot himself."

I sighed and moved on. We quickly passed the treeline and moved through shrub willow into the open alpines. On shaded sections of the road, the snow was still up to a metre deep. Here and there on the soft clay adjacent to the edges of the snow, the bicycle tracks appeared. Two bicycles.

"The bicycles are heavily loaded," said Elsebeth.

"Look at the cirques!" said Vivien.

We took our eyes off the road and saw the snow-streaked cirques extending in a half circle to the west of us. We passed a small lake with a large rock protruding from its surface. There seemed to be some graffiti painted on the rock, but we couldn't make out any message.

Then the road forked, the bicycle tracks going off onto the right-hand fork. There were pieces of lumber and plywood scattered around, and right at the fork was an outhouse, lying on its back.

We stood the outhouse up. I fancied I would use it, but it looked too conspicuous standing in that barren spot. I grabbed my bag of toilet paper and scouted out a depression off the side of the road, among some low willows.

"What's the matter?" asked Vivien, laughing. "Do you want us to dig a hole, too? Maybe we can find the door somewhere and put it back on."

"Well I'm going to use it," said Elsebeth. "It has a nice, smooth plastic toilet seat."

"I'm using it too," said Vivien.

We continued to follow the tracks. The road went up. From the top of a small hill we looked down on a creek, weaving its way out of the alpines and across the road. The creek was fringed with stunted pine. From a spot in the pine, close to the road, rose a column of smoke.

"This is it," I murmured. "Maybe we should go back now. We can notify the police and let *them* investigate."

"They've already seen us," said Elsebeth.

A tall man emerged from the trees onto the road. He waved.

"It's Birch!" said Vivien. She waved.

"Really?" I said, squinting. The man *was* wearing a safari hat, Birch's preferred headgear. "Somehow he looks older."

Vivien started down the hill.

"Who is Birch?" Elsebeth asked.

"The kid who came in with us last summer. We told you, I think."

"Yes. The one who lost things."

Vivien and Birch collided in an enthusiastic embrace. Then Birch extended his hand to me. He did look older, his face tanned and clear of pimples, his movements slower and more deliberate.

"You look great," I told him, shaking his hand. "Who's with you?"

"You'll see," said Birch. "Got any coffee?"

Birch's campsite in the stunted pine by the creek featured a barrel stove and some benches made of tree rounds and planks. On the stove was a kettle. Tending the stove was a hairy little man who looked at us with great, brown eyes. We knew right away who it was.

"Felix, I presume," said Vivien, extending her hand.

"I've heard so much about you," said Felix, taking her hand and kissing it. Vivien turned and waggled her eyebrows at me.

"And you are John," said Felix, extending his hand to me. "Birch has told me so much about you both."

"This is Elsebeth," I said as I shook his hand.

"Are you German?" asked Felix as he pressed the back of Elsebeth's hand to his lips.

"Danish."

"Ganz gut."

"Danke."

"The water's boiling," said Birch eagerly. "Where's that coffee?"

"Poor Birch," said Felix. "We didn't take enough when we left Conglomerate Creek."

Vivien produced our bag of coffee and we settled around the fire.

As Birch was scooping coffee into the pot, I asked, "So what happened with Stefan?"

Part of a scoop of coffee spilled onto the stove, sending up a pleasant aroma. Birch turned to look at me, then added a final scoop. "The silly bugger pulled his gun on me," said Birch, settling back on his heels and watching the pot intently. "We'd just gotten to the cabin and I grabbed the kettle to get water from off the dock. I saw him over at the end of the lake, standing in the mist, fishing. He dropped his rod and whipped his shotgun around and I dropped the kettle and dashed for the bush before he could point the gun at me. But it went off right away, both barrels, and when I looked from behind the willows he was feet up in the water. I thought for a minute he was dead, but in a second he was up and running for the opposite shore. So we got the hell out of there fast."

Felix nodded. "Is Stefan badly hurt?"

"No," said Vivien. "It was only a flesh wound. But he lied to the police, telling them that someone had shot him."

"He would do that," said Felix sadly. "I wanted to go to his cabin, but Birch wouldn't hear of it."

"No way I'm going to get my head blown off. He could've just stepped into the bush to reload and then come at us."

"We didn't really want to see him anyway," said Felix.

"No wonder they were all over here with that chopper," said Birch. "Anyway, we got our stuff together and ran our bikes up the path to the road. Then we strapped our bikes onto our packs and took off straight west over the hills to the winter road. We were a night out there and then a half day getting back to the Tungsten road. It took us awhile to get back down the road. We spent a lot of time keeping out of sight."

"Stefan finally had to tell the truth," Vivien explained. "But he stuck to his story about seeing someone."

"What were you doing there?" I asked.

"Heading for that cabin on the Little Nahanni," said Birch, moving the swirling coffee away from the centre of the heat. "But we never made it. Boy, does that smell good! Do you have any sugar?"

Vivien hauled the sugar out of her pack and handed it to Birch.

"There's not enough bush around the Conglomerate Creek cabin," Birch continued. "That's a place for hunting caribou, but we don't want to get into hunting, at least yet. I'm into snaring rabbits and ptarmigan, and I figure I'll get into trapping. I can use the boxes we saw in that cabin."

"Also, we ran out of firewood," said Felix.

"You mean you've been in here all winter?" asked Vivien. "You promised me you wouldn't do that."

"I met Felix and had to change my plans. Hand me your cups."

Birch poured coffee for everyone and then shoved some large pieces of wood into the barrel stove. It was an ingenious affair, a shortened forty-five-gallon fuel drum with a door welded on the side and a stovepipe welded on the top.

"I see you like the stove," said Felix.

"I'm always amazed at what those miners could do."

"So am I. I'm an engineer, but I have none of those abilities."

"Felix is a klutz, like me," said Birch. "If I ever went to Germany, I'd want to know who'd built any bridges that I had to cross. But we're learning. I've stopped losing things, even. See, I still have that Swiss

Army knife that you gave me." Birch lifted the velcro lid of one of the lower pockets on his pants and hauled out his knife. "Have I ever been putting it to use. Especially the scissors. I miss the blade I broke off it, but I had to get a bigger knife anyway for skinning and scraping."

"I heard you were around the museum looking into Dalziel," I said.

"Who told you that?"

"Rhea, at the museum."

"Oh yeah. She told me where the house was. I saw the trophy collection. That guy was some nimrod."

A classical allusion from Birch? I would have to revise my estimation of the quality of street English.

"How did you get to see the collection? They told me the place was boarded up."

"Me and a buddy pried some boards off."

"We learned a lot about Dalziel too," I said.

"Later," said Vivien. "We can get into all that on the way out, and we have to be heading back soon. I want to know how you two met up."

"One evening at the end of last summer a few of the kids at the residence were talking about this guy who bought all sorts of supplies, including a plastic wagon, loaded the supplies into the wagon, and headed out onto the highway. I figured from what you'd told me who it was, and I rode my bike out the Robert Campbell. There he was, about ten kilometres out of town."

"We agreed to work together," said Felix. "For me, it was very lucky. He got me using a bicycle, for example, which is much more efficient than a wagon."

"It's like Patterson's canoe," said Birch, winking at me. "You can load it and push it up the road, and if you have to get back to town you can get there in a couple of days instead of a couple of weeks."

Felix nodded. "I didn't want to go near Gerald, so I had no place in mind to live. Birch took me up Conglomerate, where you had been."

"For me it was a choice of wintering in here or going back home," said Birch.

"You needn't worry about Gerald," said Vivien. "He can't keep you out of the Flat Lakes cabin, only out of Tungsten. And I understood that Stefan was friendly."

"It's more complicated than that," said Birch, looking at Felix, who shrugged.

"I'm on the lam, as Birch puts it," said Felix. "I flew into Seattle, hitch-hiked to the border, and then stole across the border through a park. I want to stay here for a couple of years. Then my investments in Germany should be enough to buy entry. I should've been patient and continued working in Germany, but I couldn't face it."

"Felix is crazy like me," said Birch. "His friends call him 'the mad trapper'."

"So that's why you disappeared so quickly after Stefan shot himself."

"The fewer people know that Felix is in here," said Birch, "the better. We figured we might have to face Stefan, and we were glad when he was-n't around his shack when we passed. I do all of Felix's business for him. I go to town for stuff. In fact, I was about to head for town today. Felix was going to wait here, away from the cabin, just in case, but I guess he could go back now. Are you going out soon?"

"We're off to Kluane today," said Vivien. "You can have a ride out. If you do your business quickly, you can have a ride back to Miner's Junction too. We're going to Dawson City on the way to Kluane; Elsebeth's never seen it."

"It might be good for Stefan if you went to the police and confirmed that you were at the Flat Lakes when he shot himself," said Elsebeth. "I feel sorry for him. You don't have to tell them about Felix."

"I don't think so," said Birch. "Too complicated. They'd probably come in and check me out. And anyway, I'd have to tell them that he pulled a gun on me for no reason. That's against the law."

So we said goodbye to Felix, who was going to strike across the alpines to the cabin at Conglomerate Creek. Vivien stuffed our emergency dried dinner into his pack and gave him the rest of our coffee.

"If you get into the cabin on the Little Nahanni," she told him, "we'll be coming through next summer."

Felix stood on the road watching us until we disappeared over the hill.

We decided to spend the night at the government campsite on the Hyland. Once we got there, we set up our tents in the picnic shed as usual. Birch immediately went down to the Hyland and came back with trout.

"We can cook it in some of the canned bacon we left in the truck," said Vivien.

Birch and I were dancing in delight. "You were gone only fifteen minutes," I said to him. "I wish I could do that."

"I'm getting good," said Birch. "If we were in the alpines and I had my snares, I'd have a marmot just as fast. That's Felix's favourite."

Vivien grimaced. "Do you think Felix is going to make it in the bush?"

"Once it becomes routine, and that's pretty much what it is, he'll be okay. Right now he'd starve to death in a couple of weeks if it wasn't for me. But it's a fair trade. He arranged for money to be sent to me at my postal box in Watson Lake. I buy what we need. Without Felix, no coffee. No warm clothes. No snowshoes."

"So you get along?"

"Sort of like Faille and Patterson," said Birch. "Partners."

TRAIL INFORMATION

Howard's Pass from Flat Lakes

IN THE EARLY 1980S, Howard's Pass was a major exploration site for copper, lead, zinc, silver, nickel, molybdenum, and gold. For a time it was believed that a mine would develop there, and a committee of officials from Placer Mining Company and the Yukon government planned a permanent access road to the site. Their choice was either to improve the road and bridges from Tungsten or to build a new road from MacMillan Pass on the Canol Road. The MacMillan Pass choice was favoured, as the deposit of tungsten in that area is huge.

The Yukon government has studied the possibility of cleaning up Howard's Pass. If a cleanup happens, the comfortable cabin there would likely be burned to the ground, along with the hangar or workshop at the airstrip, so don't depend on anything being there. This pains John whenever he thinks about it.

You can take a bicycle as far as Steel Creek. Walking that far with packs full of food would take far longer and far more energy than cycling. Once at Potato Hill, the scenery is spectacular and it is fun to explore the surroundings. The area through the alpines to Summit Lake is something few people will ever see, and that walk is highly recommended. The animal life is abundant and wild, afraid of humans except for the herd of caribou living above Summit Lake. They are curious.

Most of the camping between Flat Lakes and Howard's Pass is along the road. There are many small creeks flowing across the road, some of which have caused substantial washouts. There is a creek at Howard's Pass, but no wood except for some timber and boards left by the miners – and by the time you arrive, these may have been burned.

TOPOGRAPHICAL MAPS: Shelf Lake 105 I-1 (1:50,000), Upper Hyland Lake 105 I-2 (1:50,000), Dozer Lake 105 I-7 (1:50,000), Placer Creek 105 I-6 (1:50,000)

EQUIPMENT NEEDED: You must be totally self-sufficient and pre-pared for the worst. You will be a minimum of 100 kilometres from the nearest radiophone, which means that, in the event of an accident, it will be days before you can reach help – or before help can reach you. You will need food for two weeks at least and warm camping gear even if it is July when you go. Snow can fall at any time of year in this area. Larry Whitesitt in *Flight of the Red Beaver* describes his regular flights into Howard's Pass as chancy due to the changeable weather at the site.

THE ROUTE

0.0K FLAT LAKES CABIN. Proceed from the Flat Lakes cabin to the road and cycle north. The road is in excellent condition above the Flat Lakes, and once above the second lake you may spot the yellow cabin protected from porcupines by tin sheeting. The cabin is in livable condition and should the other cabins at the south end of the lake be occupied, you might want to use this one, though the trail from the road is difficult to find. There are some washouts along the road but nothing that presents a serious obstacle.

Approximately three hours from the Flat Lakes cabin is a huge pile of culverts stacked on a flat plateau between a couple of washouts. They offer a comfortable place for lunch or camping. Some of the culverts are big enough to sleep in if temporary shelter is needed.

The next landmark is a swampy lake to your left, followed by a section of road that also becomes swampy, making cycling with a heavy load impossible. You will also have to struggle along an animal trail through some dense bush growing on the road. Resign yourself to pushing your bike. But think of the weight it is carrying; weight that could be on your back. The road will improve in a short while.

26.0K TRAPPER'S CABIN ON THE LITTLE NAHANNI RIVER. Partway across a flat plateau, above the river and shrouded in willows, is a trail that goes off to the right. A tree blocks the road, beyond which is a bright blue outhouse. This trail leads to the trapper's cabin, perched about 100 metres from the Little Nahanni River. It is an excellent place to camp, but having this as your destination makes the first day of travel from the Flat Lakes a bit long. You can store some of your return trip's food supply in the cabin. Be certain that the door is tightly closed before leaving.

28.0K MAC CREEK BRIDGE. The north end of the first bridge over Mac Creek has been washed away, and the centre is buckling, so it is not advisable to go onto the structure. However, in low water this is not a difficult crossing, and even in high water it shouldn't be too hard.

30.0K GUTHRIE CREEK BRIDGE. Less than two kilometres past Mac Creek, after passing through scrub birch, you arrive at Guthrie Creek, with an intact wooden bridge. This is a beautiful place to stop, as the creek offers clean water and there are many comfortable campsites along the road.

35.0K FORK CREEK BRIDGE. The next section of road, which leads to the bridge over Fork Creek, is long and dry, with water available at only one creek. Fork Creek Bridge is washed out at the south end. To get onto the bridge you must crawl along the support beam that goes from the side of the bridge across to the hill – this can be intimidating. One person should climb onto the bridge and the others should pass the gear up before they, too, climb onto the bridge.

The camping in this area is excellent, but watch out for a curious animal with expensive tastes that lives in the area. It ate John's panniers when we stored them here during our first trip in. We decided to leave our bikes at this point rather than hoist them onto the bridge. It was a mistake.

47.0K MARCH CREEK BRIDGE. Two more creeks cross the road before the next bridge. There are many campsites and good views of the Little Nahanni from this stretch. There is a waterless flat plateau with a tent frame lying on the ground beside the trail. At the far end of this plateau and just down the hill is March Creek.

March Creek Bridge is in good shape, but one of the support pillars on the south side is cracked, so this end of the bridge will soon wash away. If the bridge is washed away when you arrive, the creek would be crossable in low water.

48.5K TRAIL TO LITTLE NAHANNI RIVER CROSSING. The winter road leading to the Little Nahanni River crossing is only 1.5 kilometres past the March Creek Bridge. There is a small cairn, and an arrow made of stones points across the road towards the river to mark the spot where the winter road begins. If you are past March Creek and you come to a creek with a non-functioning culvert, you have gone too far. The winter road, which goes downhill all the way to the river, is padded with cladina lichen and shrouded by willow. It is possible to camp on gravel bars at the confluence of Steel Creek and Little Nahanni River, a few hundred metres downriver from the winter road.

56.5K STEEL CREEK BRIDGE. As you continue along the road towards Howard's Pass the way is open and clear, and the scenery is inviting. The road skirts the mountains above Steel Creek and carries on around the valley, past a slide area, and then down to the Steel Creek Bridge. There are many tiny creeks with fresh water to drink along the way. I would recommend camping on Steel Creek, on a gravel bar west (upstream) of the bridge. However, if the weather is bad, there is a hunter's camp on the north side of the creek where the trees will give some shelter. There should be a new axe driven into a stump in these trees. Use it and leave it for others.

If you are biking, this is probably the best place to stash your bikes.

The next hour's walk is a steep uphill climb above Placer Creek. The road then levels out and becomes a gentle uphill walk to Howard's Pass. Although the road is quite overgrown, there are many campsites between the last bridge and the pass, as there are creeks where you can obtain water. During the spring, when there is still stagnant water along this stretch, the bugs become herculean.

69.0K HOWARD'S PASS. Once on Howard's Pass, other passes beckon from every direction. You will see an airstrip, an airplane-hangar full of rubbish, oil barrels, metal beds, plastic pipes, and batteries, and a plethora of junk (or artifacts) just waiting to be put to a useful purpose. This is assuming that the place has not been cleaned up.

70.5K POTATO HILL. Continue past the airfield and hangar in a westerly direction to a cabin with a good roof and a stove that works – though I wouldn't trust going to sleep with a blazing fire in the stove. This is Potato Hill. Behind the cabin is a creek. There is never a moment without wind on Potato Hill, so bugs will not be a problem. But stoking a hot fire may be!

There is a mine shaft behind the cabin down by the creek. There are also numerous buildings and some great timber piles in the vicinity, so it is not hard to make yourself comfortable. You can catch some great views from the bald hill (70 degrees east of the cabin) to the north of the airstrip and above the road that led to the pass. Triangular Mount Wilson is visible from this mountain on a clear day. To summit Bald Mountain takes two hours up and one hour down.

90.5K AIRPORT. The abandoned airport west of Potato Hill is about 25 kilometres farther along a winter road, which actually means no road. However, in most places there is a path or rut to follow. To get there, cross the creek behind the cabin and pass the next knoll. Then go down and across the valley to the road on the side of the hill. This road eventually changes into a trail and then a game trail that passes through many bogs and swamps. I have never gone to the second airstrip.

For a pleasant day hike, go to the set of lakes (as opposed to the little lake) over the south ridge into the next valley. The views are spectacular. If you are not taking the alpine trip towards Summit Lake, this day trip is a must.

To get to the lakes from the cabin, walk back along the road towards the hangar till you get to the piles of black rock (mine tailings). Go south onto the side of the hill from there and continue around the hill, staying high until you can see the second set of lakes, with an orange oil drum floating at the east end. This takes about two hours without a pack. Return by going over the ridge and back down to the cabin. The climb over the ridge takes about one hour and the ascent is just above the east end of the lakes. For a descent, do not take the hill that is made of brown shale; take the ridge just before it. Heavy boots are essential, as the scree is unstable on the north side of this hill. It is possible to camp near the lakes.

If you are not going to Summit Lake, return to the Flat Lakes cabin by the same route you came.

Potato Hill to Summit Lake and Placer Creek

THE ROUTE

0.0K POTATO HILL CABIN. From the cabin, walk back along the road towards the hangar to the piles of black rock (mine tailings). Go south onto the side of the hill and from there continue around the hill, staying high, until the tiny lake can be seen. This takes about an hour.

2.0K LAKE NEAR POTATO HILL. From this lake, cross the valley and walk towards the obvious pass going south. It takes about three hours to reach the pass from Potato Hill.

6.0K SET OF LAKES OVER RIDGE. It is possible to camp at the set of lakes north of the pass (the lakes with the oil barrel at the east end). Continue south from there over the pass. It is an easy walk with no bushwhacking.

9.5K FIRST PASS. Continue over the pass and down a scree slope, staying on the left. Cross over an alluvial fan where vegetation has started to grow, and then continue to veer towards the left of the valley. There is a steep canyon and heavy vegetation down the valley, so cut across (to the east) and head for the top of the treeline. It will take about two hours to reach treeline from the pass.

Hike around the hill. There is lots of water, but flat tent spots are at a premium. The Placer Creek topographical map shows a flat arm on the north side of the large creek. This is a decent campsite that will hold two tents for sure; with a lot of manoeuvring you might be able to squeeze in three.

17.25K ALPINE ABOVE SUMMIT LAKE. Walk down the gully and ascend the other side. It takes about half an hour to get back up to the alpine and level walking. Continue in a southwest direction until you see Summit Lake.

If you decide to go to Summit Lake, drop to the northwest end of it. The southeast side, where the cabins are located, is swamp. You should beat your way around the west end of the lake to the cabins, but if you are going out to the road on Placer Creek, between Howard's Pass and Steel Creek, you will have to come back to the ridge above Summit.

If you want to travel the Steel Creek winter road, go east over the mountains from the Summit Lake cabins. The Steel Creek winter road is the one that ends on Highway 10 just before the traveller turns and starts up the hill towards the Yukon/Northwest Territories border. Remember that winter roads are usually horrid going – an average of one kilometre (or less) per hour.

18.25K LAKE EAST. To get to Placer Creek road from the alpines above Summit Lake, make a sharp left turn and proceed down the valley, past the tiny lake that can be seen from above. This little lake is a perfect camping spot, with lots of flat spaces, wood, water, and shelter from the wind.

There are two possible passes ahead, with a ridge between. Stay on the small ridge to the left of the creek and walk towards the lower spot on the two passes. Both passes lead to the same spot on the opposite side, so it really doesn't matter which one you choose. There is a herd of about twenty caribou hanging around this area. The animals are unaccustomed to humans and they are very curious.

26.0K WINTER ROAD. Continue down the valley, bushwhacking all the way. It is moderately difficult. You will come to the winter road that runs from Highway 10 towards Howard's Pass. It can be difficult crossing the creek where the winter road crosses, as it is swift and cold. When we tried to follow the winter road towards Howard's Pass, we found the road about 10 percent of the time – the rest was straight bushwhacking through very thick brush.

29.5K PASS CROSSING TO PLACER CREEK – 34.2K JUNCTION OF WINTER ROAD – HOWARD'S PASS – 34.0K PLACER CREEK (GOING OVER MOUNTAIN). Before you can get onto the hill clear of vegetation east of the winter road, you must bushwhack up the valley along the trail of the winter road for at least four kilometres. The hill is far too steep to ascend before that. Once you have spent four or five hours fighting the brush, head upward.

From the top looking back you will see the alpines between Howard's Pass and Summit Lake. Looking in the opposite direction, the view is of Placer Creek and the road. Go down to Placer and the road, and follow the road back out to the Flat Lakes the same way you came in.

7

Vandaele and Lewis

"The guys who were in here before were tough," said Vivien to me one November evening in 1997. We were reading, prostrate on the sofas in our living room, our heads elevated by pillows and our bodies covered by Viv's hand-stitched wool blankets, brown for her and grey for me. Surrounding us were the relics of journeys to all the corners of the world – a wooden bucket from the Sudan; ceramics from Peru, Greece, and the Ukraine; prayer wheels from Tibet; a wood carving from Beijing. The light from the room illuminated snow falling heavily outside the window, the first big storm of winter.

Lazily trying to guess the context of Viv's comment, I looked over and noticed that she was rereading *Dangerous River,* a first edition, signed by Patterson. It had been a gift from Wes on my fifty-fifth birthday, a rare find he had made in one of the used bookstores in Sidney.

"No nylon tents," I said. "All of their equipment must've been heavy, and they carried rifles and ammunition."

On the other hand, I mused, they didn't carry as much food as us, since they hunted. They used pack dogs and they built cabins everywhere, an activity that I would really enjoy.

They also used airplanes. The first such use may have been in August 1929. Kraus says that he traced some of the old claim-stakes on Bennett Creek to "Doc" Oaks. Oaks is in the Aviation Hall of Fame. He was a decorated Canadian RAF vet who had, after the war, acquired a degree as a mining engineer and become Canada's foremost "flying prospector."

Kraus wrote to Oaks to inquire about a skeleton and a .44-.40 rifle that, according to local legend, Oaks's party had found and buried about a mile down the creek from their claims. Kraus had a theory that the rifle and skeleton belonged to a certain "Yukon" Fisher, who hid out on Bennett Creek years before, on the lam from the RCMP. Apparently the police had nothing on Fisher, and people passing through the area had tried to tell him that, but Fisher was evidently bushed. The RCMP *Quarterly* mentions that he died on Bennett Creek in the mid-1920s.

Kraus wanted to know more exactly where Oaks had buried the bones. Oaks replied that he had to check his records in Montreal, but Kraus received no further correspondence from him.

Kraus says nothing more about Oaks's exploration of Bennett Creek, but *National Geographic* adds to the story. A casual glance at an index to that magazine in an Abbotsford antiquarian bookstore turned up a reference to the Flat River. A half-hour search through boxes of back issues turned up the article. Dated 1929, it described some prospecting done by a team flown in by Doc Oaks. The article contained this sentence: "According to Oaks' logbook, August 1929, he was at the headwaters of the Nahanni, on the divide between the Yukon and the NWT, following up the story of a rich placer strike and murder mystery which has been a lure for miners for years."

The McLeod legend had struck again.

The photo accompanying the story was of Oaks's plane at "Landing Lake, NWT." Kraus says this was the original name of Seaplane Lake on the Flat River.

Planes were used, too, during the 1934–36 Flat River Gold Rush. Patterson mentions, in his caustic way, that the only people to find gold during the rush were the operators of riverboats and "a certain airline company." Undoubtedly he meant Mackenzie Air Services, run by Leigh Brintnell (pilot-owner, another Hall-of-Famer who got his name on a creek and a lake north of Rabbitkettle) and Stan McMillan (chief pilot). Brintnell flew Kraus in to MacMillan Lake in 1933–34, and Kraus says that MacMillan Lake is named after Stan McMillan – though someone got the spelling wrong – because of the number of times McMillan flew in there.

And Wop May, too, in possession of the LeGuen treasure map, flew in early in 1934 with Bill Clark, getting the jump on the overland parties that included Turner, Faille, and Eppler.

After the rush, George Dalziel dominated airplane activity in the Nahanni watershed.

"They used planes, though," I said to Vivien. "Remember Gus Kraus's story? Kraus and Clark got supplies through Dalziel in March 1936. That's when Dal told them he'd just put Mulholland and Eppler in to Glacier Lake. And the two guys who were with Kraus and Clark had been expecting a food drop, probably from Dalziel."

"Harry Vandaele and Milt Campbell."

"Right."

"What's your point?"

"Both of them disappear from the ongoing story, unfortunately."

"So?"

"*Not* tough, maybe."

"Or not in love with the country, like Albert Faille."

"Or not well-heeled, like R.M. Patterson."

"I'd had a run of luck lately," said Vivien in her best English accent, quoting Patterson on how he could afford to spend a year or two exploring the Nahanni.

"He's my favourite," I said. "I'm glad you're rereading him. He's a real stylist, an excellent model. And what élan. He mapped the river. Faille and the others used that map when they made their first rush up the Flat River. Patterson made money as a trapper, too. No dreams of McLeod gold for him."

"A talented prig," said Vivien, placing *Dangerous River* on the floor. "A twit. Satisfied only with what he saw, including himself, unfortunately. A single, scientific vision. Willing to spend two pages telling you how he got his canoe into some eddy. Faille's my guy. He was a better trapper. He didn't *need* any map, and he got there before Patterson."

"Using a motor," I said, working on Viv's prejudice for the more traditional modes of transportation.

"That was practical. Doesn't Kraus say in his interview that after Faille and Patterson met, Faille towed Patterson most of the way up the Nahanni? Kraus says that Patterson chose to leave that out of his book, which has led a lot of people to think that it's fairly easy to line a canoe up the Nahanni."

"Kraus does say that. It might be sour grapes. Anyway, it seems as though the trapping was vital. Patterson, Faille, Turner, Kraus, Zenchuk, and Dalziel were expert trappers. If you weren't, you were doomed, since no one ever found any gold. Vandaele and Campbell were prospectors, not trappers, according to Kraus. Maybe that's why they disappear from the story."

"But what were they doing prospecting in the winter?"

"Digging holes, probably. Remember the old photos in Dawson City? The prospectors dug all winter along the creeks, lighting fires in the holes to melt the frost. The smoke from the fires was all over Bonanza Creek, a major occupational hazard. The men wanted to get down to bedrock, where most of the gold was. They hauled the diggings up and piled them for sluicing in spring once the creek thawed."

"But Vandaele and Campbell left before the thaw."

"They ran out of food, because of Dalziel it seems."

"And then they disappear."

"Poof. No interviews, nothing. Gone, with whatever they knew about the Mulholland-Eppler search along with other things."

I was wrong. A few days later, wandering off from our table in the bistro section of our favourite bookstore, I noticed, on the spine of a paperback in the "New Arrivals" section, the word "Nahanni." I grabbed the book.

Nahanni Remembered by A.C. Lewis of Sooke, B.C.

The name wasn't familiar, but on the first page of his prologue Lewis says that his book is about his sojourn in 1937 up the Nahanni, "with one of the finest men I have ever known. His name was Harry Vandaele."

"Holy shit," said Viv, who by now had caught up to me and was looking over my shoulder.

"This is amazing."

We bought two copies and read nonstop for over two hours.

"This guy could still be alive," said Viv after we had finished.

"We should meet him."

"We *have* to meet him. He tells a good story, but he knows a lot more than he tells. Why did Vandaele die so young? He was only forty-eight, Lewis says. What kind of a scam was Dalziel pulling off, flying Vandaele in to look for Eppler and Mulholland and then not taking him all the way to see their camp?"

"Dropping him in for a winter's trapping instead. *And* spending two weeks training him. How did Dalziel explain *that* to the RCMP when he got back to Fort Simpson?"

"Maybe he didn't have to. He and Vandaele were searching in the fall. The RCMP *Quarterly* makes it clear that the investigation ended in August, after four searches, two of which involved Dalziel."

"Vandaele confirms the skinboat part of the story."

"But he has them at Rabbitkettle Lake, like Turner, when it seems they really were at Glacier Lake."

"That's at least ten miles farther up the Nahanni."

"At least."

"I'd trust Lewis as a reporter."

"Me too. But what about Vandaele?"

"Lewis worshipped Vandaele. And Vandaele comes across as a really attractive person. There doesn't seem to be any reason why he would lie to his best friend. It all comes back to Dalziel. He didn't take Vandaele to the burnt cabin."

A few months later, with concerns like these burning holes in our patience, we made a trip to Vancouver Island to visit Wes, and to try to find Lewis. I was on an unpaid leave for the spring semester, a situation that was becoming a habit despite a growing anxiety about the state of my pension. We were on the way to Venezuela, sun and cheap tickets to Caracas (through Houston) being our main motivation. We also had our hearts set on a walk up Mount Roraima, a tepuy or giant mesa near Venezuela's southern border, a contender for the setting of Arthur Conan Doyle's *Lost World*. And we wanted to cross the Amazon region of Brazil by boat up the Madeira River, if possible, to get into the Andes on the Bolivian side of Lake Titicaca.

Lewis was in the Sooke section of the Victoria phonebook. I called from Wes's place. On the other end, a cracking but lively voice said, "Hello?"

"Is this A.C. Lewis," I asked, "author of a recent book on the Nahanni?"

"It is indeed."

"My name is John Harris. I enjoyed your book very much. I bought three copies, one for my son, one for my wife, and one for myself. Would you be willing to autograph the books for us?"

"Glad to," he said. "Afraid I don't get to town much, though. Half blind now. When Fran died I moved from Victoria to Sooke because I missed the bush, and now I can't see it."

"We'll come to you, if that's alright."

"I'm past Sooke, but I take a mini-bus to the seniors' centre on Tuesday and Thursday, and I'm in the public library from one till three. You never know what you'll find in a public library, and I get tired of talking to the walls."

"Tomorrow's Tuesday. Tomorrow at the Sooke public library, then."

"Tomorrow."

So on a sunny winter afternoon in Sooke, we walked into the public library, holding *Nahanni Remembered* in our hands. We recognized Lewis immediately, even though the photo of him on the back cover of his book was taken in 1984, eleven years earlier. He was aging with grace, slight (about 160 pounds), and five foot seven. He was moving briskly from what turned out to be the northern history section to a table near the entrance. On the table were some books and papers and a large magnifying glass.

We introduced ourselves and sat down across from him. He immediately explained that his wife was dead but he had two loving stepdaughters, of whom he was very fond. They took care of him; otherwise he would be back in Victoria, in a seniors residence. Then he said, "Look at this book."

It was *Denison's Ice Road* by Edith Iglauer. Lewis put his finger down on one of the photos. "See that white shack there, on the right side of the photo of the Con mine? My first job when I got to Yellowknife was to build that shack. That was just after Dal took me out of Simpson. I lived in that shack for a year."

Starting with that, Lewis settled back and let us ask questions. We had a long list of them, mostly concerning Harry Vandaele's role in and comments on the search for Mulholland and Eppler. Some of our information was new to Lewis and surprised him, but he quickly recognized and pointed out any impossibilities. Mainly, he questioned Kraus's account of his April-to-May 1936 trip out with the other Flat River trappers and prospectors. Vandaele and Campbell, Lewis pointed out, couldn't have been there. He also doubted that Dalziel could have forgotten Harry's presence on the search.

IT TOOK US A FEW WEEKS after we returned home from South America, settling into a spring dedicated to writing and preparing for what we referred to as a "final assault" on the Nahanni via what Gerald had told us was the Union Carbide exploration site, to fit Lewis's story into what we knew from Patterson's *Dangerous River,* Turner's *Nahanni,* Dalziel's manuscript, the RCMP *Quarterly,* and Kraus's interview. It's not a good fit, as Lewis had already pointed out in the course of our afternoon in the library.

In his book, Lewis doesn't bother with background, apart from saying that Turner's brief account of him and Vandaele (two pages I had completely forgotten, but which I reread immediately after reading Lewis's book) is "somewhat inexact." He tells his story straight.

To put it briefly, in mid to late January 1937, Dalziel contacted Lewis in Edmonton and told him that his friend Harry Vandaele was stuck up the Nahanni at Rabbitkettle. Vandaele would need help coming out, Dal explained, because Dal's plane would be "out of commission" for some time. No further explanation was offered. Vandaele was expecting to be picked up in May. "You can build a raft," Dalziel suggested. "Better still, you can put a platform on my set of pontoons."

Dal arranged for Lewis to fly in with Stan McMillan of Mackenzie Air. Lewis spent the winter trapping with his friend. In June Vandaele and Lewis rafted down the swollen Nahanni – not on the pontoons, since they wouldn't have been able to get them around the falls or any other portage. They drowned their raft regularly, flipped it once, lost almost all their cargo, but became the first (and only?) people to successfully raft the lower Nahanni at high water. (Vandaele's trip the previous May with Kraus, Faille, Zenchuk, etc. had been accomplished between breakup and high water, and in a scow rather than on a raft.) Both men ended up in Yellowknife due to the recent discovery there of large gold deposits. Lewis learned carpentry and plumbing and left after three years. Vandaele left after a few months to have an operation on his back. He eventually acquired a mink farm in Calgary. He died in 1956.

"Of leukemia," Lewis told us when we asked how Vandaele died. "One morning he simply couldn't get out of bed. He died shortly after. Too young," Lewis added, sadly.

In conversation with us, Lewis expressed two specific complaints about Turner's account of him and Vandaele and their winter of trapping up the Nahanni. "He says we didn't have dogs," said Lewis. "That's why, on the book's front cover, there's a picture of me with the dogs. They look like dogs to you, don't they?"

"Sure do. How did you happen to have a camera, by the way?"

"My school friends bought it for me as a farewell gift when I headed north. It was a fold-out that held a roll of film with twelve exposures. As you can see by the pictures, I didn't really know how to use it, and I never thought to buy more film."

"How'd you get the camera and film down the river without getting it wet?"

Lewis smiled. "Put it in a tobacco tin, turned the tin upside down, and melted spruce gum into the lid to seal it.

"Turner," Lewis continued, "also says we didn't stay overnight at Daisy Mulholland's when we got out. He says this was because she was alone at the trading post and afraid of some impropriety. I can tell you that no one in the north, then or now, would act like that, least of all Daisy Mulholland."

"Turner attributes that whole story to Vandaele," I pointed out. "He says that Harry told the story of your raft trip to an 'appreciative audience' in the Turner cabin. This happened shortly after you and Harry returned to Simpson. For some reason, you weren't present."

"Harry would've laughed at the whole idea," Lewis told us. "He just would've laughed. As I said in the book, Daisy gave us fresh bread with butter and jam. I can still taste that bread. And the next morning, pancakes with coffee. I can still taste that coffee, too. Then she loaned us a canoe, so we could go up the Liard to meet Milt Campbell. She said that he'd been asking after us, that he was worried.

"As for me not being at Turner's cabin that time," Lewis pursued, "there was no problem with that. God knows what I was doing at the time, but as soon as I got to Fort Simpson I got work clearing land. Probably I was at work or sound asleep. Turner could've walked a few feet over to the river to ask me, though. I was camped right there for the next few weeks. Even much later, when he wrote his book, he could've contacted me."

"He knew where you were?"

"Yes. Not only that, but I wrote him shortly after his book came out. I pointed out the inaccuracies in the story. There's been a few printings, but no corrections. And still later, in 1984, when I made that nostalgic trip mentioned in the Epilogue to my book, I sent him a letter by way of two lovely ladies who we met on the Nahanni. Their trip was in memory of a friend who'd lost her life in an accident on the Liard and who'd always wanted to do the Nahanni. They were going out through Blackstone, where Turner was at the time. I know they would've delivered the letter."

Lewis did explain how Vandaele got to Rabbitkettle. Surprisingly, it had to do with the disappearance of Eppler and Mulholland. But what Lewis was telling us seemed to contradict most of what Dalziel, Kraus, and the RCMP say, and some of what Turner says. Here's how Vandaele explained it in conversation with Lewis on 9 February 1937, a week after Lewis's arrival at Dalziel's camp near Rabbitkettle:

"Dal flew [Mulholland and Eppler] in to Rabbitkettle Lake early in January of last year. They had gone to trap marten and lynx. Apparently they were staying in a cabin that was already there… They were supposed to come out to the mouth of the Nahanni in the spring, after open water. They never showed."

"Did they have a boat?"

"Jack Mulholland told me that the boys took several yards of canvas with them to build a canvas canoe. Down at Fort Simpson it was arranged that Dal fly into the Nahanni to see if he could locate the boys. I went with him on that flight, and that's how I came to be here at Dal's camp. Their cabin had burnt down sometime during the winter, because there were two rounds of logs still showing, which meant the fire must have occurred when there was a couple of feet of snow on the ground. I was busy making a new cache here and cutting wood. I never went with Dal on the search, so I didn't see the remains of the cabin."

HARRY VANDAELE AS A YOUNG MAN IN 1928

Turner elaborates on how Vandaele got involved in the search for Mulholland and Eppler. Since his own brother, Stan, was also involved, it is likely that Turner was well informed.

In the spring of 1936, Turner says, when it was clear that something was amiss with Eppler and Mulholland, Vandaele and Stan Turner (at loose ends in Fort Simpson because he had put an axe into his foot the previous winter) composed and circulated a petition. It asked the authorities to release Dalziel's plane for the sole purpose of flying to Rabbitkettle Lake to look for Eppler and Mulholland.

Dalziel, in his manuscript, mentions this "miners meeting" that got his plane released for the search. But in his account it all seems to have taken place in June, including the resulting flights in. And Lewis specifies that the search involving Vandaele took place "in the fall of 1936." If Turner is right about the date of the petition, a lot of time went by before Dalziel and Vandaele flew on their search.

Everyone is clear that it was trapping violations that had grounded Dal's plane. But the incident with the martens, which Dalziel described in his manuscript, may not be the specific reason for his plane being grounded in spring 1936. Lewis had another theory. He said he thought it was wolves. Apparently the newspapers told of Dalziel's run-ins with the law over the shooting of wolves. "Dal hated wolves with a vengeance," Lewis said to us, quoting a line that Harry Vandaele utters in Lewis's book.

Turner merely leaves his readers with the implication that Dalziel had a bad attitude to officialdom and so was often in trouble. Turner sympathized. He and his wife Vera ended up caring for Dalziel's martens when the animals were taken as evidence and started to die in the care of the RCMP. Dalziel mentions this in his manuscript and says how much he appreciated what the Turners did for him. The animals were worth $500 each.

Turner states that most whites in the area objected to the different trapping rules applied to whites and Indians. The whites all felt that the federal government wanted to keep the Northwest Territories as a kind of gigantic Indian reservation wherein the bureaucrats could regulate and patronize the Indians to death. Indians were defined as minors, for example, and so couldn't easily get alcohol. They were required to send their children out to residential schools run by various churches. The kids were "kidnapped," as the *Yellowknife Blade* put it at the time.

The white trappers believed that in order to keep the Indians in, the authorities had to keep whites out. A white might be inclined to share a drink with an Indian friend, for example. Whites would mean business for Indian guides and outfitters; business would mean money and the independence that money buys. Whites would spread stories about the patronizing attitudes and policies of government and church officials.

But Canada was a free country, for the whites anyway. At that time, the only way authorities could really keep whites out was to make it hard for them to survive economically. This was why a white man had to wait four years for a trapping permit – or pay an exorbitant sum for a non-residential one – whereas in the Yukon you could get one for the asking. This was also why whites weren't allowed, most years, to take beaver, whereas Indian trappers were allowed to.

Turner positively raves about the stupidity of these trapping rules. He even tells a story about how he and his brother spent some time in

AL LEWIS ABOUT TEN YEARS AFTER HIS
NAHANNI ADVENTURE

jail, unjustly convicted of trapping violations and unwilling to pay the fine. They wanted to register a protest. Turner even volunteered to fight the officer who had turned him in – providing, of course, that the officer was man enough to face him out of uniform.

Lewis, in conversation with us, approved of the trapping rules. Time might have softened his views, but I don't think that is the explanation. It is clear, in *Nahanni Remembered,* that Lewis hated trapping and hunting. He loved animals. When he and Vandaele finally got out of the Nahanni and went their separate ways in the summer of 1937, Harry took his two dogs with him, and Lewis seems to have missed them almost as much as he did Harry. Lewis was surprised and upset that Turner said, in *Nahanni,* that Vandaele had no dogs. And Lewis thought the most impressive thing about Dalziel was that, according to Vandaele's retelling of his famous trek from Lower Post to Fort Norman, he had lost none of his dogs, and one of the dogs had even given birth to a pup, which had survived the journey.

We did tell Lewis what Dalziel had actually said about his long walk through the Mackenzie Mountains. We even quoted him: "had to kill the bitch … lost three of the weaker dogs."

Lewis was skeptical. "You'd be crazy to do a trip like that in summer," he said. "You'd do it in winter. We must be talking about different trips."

But if Lewis thought Dalziel was a good man with dogs, he had major reservations about his trapping activities. "Dal was a prime example of why they needed rules," Lewis explained to us, "and why they had to keep adapting them to new situations. Dal was no fool. He realized, way ahead of anyone else, that he could make an absolute fortune if only he had a pilot's licence and a plane. Fur was worth a lot of money back then. Originally Dal was just an ordinary trapper. When he got his pilot's licence he ran lines everywhere he could land. He'd find a good lake for landing and set lines radiating out from it, like the spokes of a wheel. Usually he'd plant a partner there to walk the lines, as he did with Harry. But sometimes he'd just go back and forth himself. The police couldn't check all those lines; the RCMP didn't get planes until the late thirties. But they guessed what was happening, and every once in awhile they managed to catch Dal up on one infraction or another. Dal would set his traps at one lake, go to the next line near another lake, and set more. More often than not, something would happen and he wouldn't get back for weeks to check those lines. Imagine the suffering of those animals."

Lewis paused, made anxious, it seemed, by his line of thought. Then he continued. "I believe Dal also took big game hunters in, which he wasn't licensed to do. You folks know the north, so I don't have to explain to you what that means. Those are men who will pay anything to get the trophy they want. Do you think they're going to wait for the right season or go home empty-handed if they see what they want?"

Whatever the reasons for the grounding of Dalziel's plane, the Fort Simpson trappers thought it important that it be released so that a search (or yet *another* search) be made. They were willing to "take all responsibility if there is a question of Dalziel breaking the seizure of his airplane for the purpose of the search."

Everyone signed the petition – even the RCMP themselves. Vandaele and Stan Turner then presented the petition to the RCMP. Turner continues the story:

> Dal took off with Harry, I believe, as an observer and flew the river to Nahanni Butte, up the Nahanni through the canyons, past the falls right to Rabbitkettle. He flew just over the water, following every turn in the river so as not to miss the boys in case they were stranded on a sandbar. They returned to Simpson without seeing a sign of the lost men. Dal is an expert bush pilot and we all thought it extremely unlikely he would have missed the boys if they were anywhere to be seen.

Turner doesn't seem to know that Vandaele didn't return with Dalziel from that trip.

What puzzled Vivien and me the most was the fact that Dalziel never took Vandaele in on the last and conceivably most important stage in the search – up to Rabbitkettle Lake – instead leaving him at the trapping camp. What was Dalziel doing? Was he afraid of having a witness along, or was he just being his usual efficient self? Dal had, after all, been up to the cabin twice already in June. He might have felt there was little possibility of learning anything new by digging around in the rubble.

We told Lewis Dal's version and produced the article from the *RCMP Quarterly*, which Lewis read carefully. Finally he said, "I never heard about Glacier Lake until about July of 1984, when I was arranging to revisit the Nahanni. But in 1937 Harry, Dalziel, Stan McMillan, Leigh Brintnell, and others knew where Glacier Lake was. Where did Dalziel fly Mulholland and Eppler? It could've been either one. All I know is that Dalziel led Harry to believe that he flew Mulholland and Eppler to Rabbitkettle Lake or somewhere not too far up the Rabbitkettle River. As for the RCMP report, in those early days, members of the RCMP were green men. They knew nothing of the north. They did their jobs as best they knew how. I know that Corporal Regis Newton could easily have been mistaken as to which lake the cabin was on."

Then Lewis added, "Nobody at Simpson to my knowledge ever mentioned Bill Clark flying in with Dal. As for Dal not remembering Harry, I find that strange considering the amount of time they spent together. Dal spent two weeks up there with Harry, laying out the line and showing Harry how to trap. But what Dal and Harry did was a bit of a conspiracy against the police. Dal might not have wanted to remind anyone of it."

Vandaele's theory about what did happen to Eppler and Mulholland is reasonable. He believed they drowned trying to come down the river on a raft. He had learned from Dalziel that the men had not died in the fire. No human remains were found in the rubble, and a cabin fire would not normally have the heat to entirely consume a human skeleton. Also, no rifles or axes were found in the rubble or the cache, which suggests that the men survived the fire and tried to walk or float out.

Vandaele rejected the idea that Eppler, the experienced one, would have opted to walk out. According to Lewis he said, "It's about 200 miles from here to the Liard River. It's an impossibility without a good dog team and plenty of supplies. To try it would be like signing your own death warrant."

The better choice would be to dig in and wait for the thaw in May. Almost certainly Eppler would have known this, though Dalziel in his manuscript questions Eppler's experience. But Eppler's real problem, according to Turner, was not inexperience, but a lack of both patience and fear. And if one or both of the men had been burned, there would be an urgency to their actions.

Vandaele also rejected the idea that Eppler would have tried to leave in a skinboat. In late summer maybe, but not in spring. The previous summer, when Fort Simpson was rife with speculation about the missing trappers, Vandaele had asked Faille about such boats.

"It would be a sure way of committing suicide," said Faille, and Vandaele knew that when Faille gave advice about the river, you listened.

So it comes back to the question of Eppler's experience. Would an experienced woodsman chance his life and that of his partner in a skinboat? A skinboat loaded with a winter's accumulation of fur? It didn't seem reasonable to anyone.

When we told Lewis Dalziel's opinion of Eppler, Lewis uttered an emphatic "NO! Eppler was considered one of the best, according to Harry. Joe Mulholland was inexperienced, but Eppler was an experienced trapper. A canvas skinboat? No way would Eppler have done that. He would've built a log raft."

And would Dalziel, probably the most experienced of the trappers apart from Faille, have gone along with the skinboat idea, as he seems to have done? Wouldn't he have expressed some concern as they were loading the canvas into his plane? Especially if he regarded them as inexperienced?

Apart from muddying the Mulholland-Eppler story, making the ground even more fertile for legend, Lewis's book and conversation indicate that Vandaele was one of the losers, a victim of the Nahanni legend. He started as a believer, like Turner and Faille, but unlike them he lost his faith. He felt that he had been cheated, by Fate perhaps (and character, they say, *is* Fate). His winter near the Rabbitkettle was an act of desperation, and it was also his last adventure on the Nahanni.

What Vandaele did say to Lewis about the gold rush, what Lewis recorded in his book, was poignant. "Perhaps we were too determined to find it, too reluctant to admit defeat," said Vandaele. "I've thought since that we were looking for something that wasn't there in the first place." Of McLeod Creek, the focal point of the gold rush, he said, "That's where all the BS began." Vandaele told Lewis that the McLeod brothers had almost certainly died of starvation and that there was no such person as Weir.

A sad fall from grace. Vandaele and his partner Campbell were among the most energetic of the prospectors involved in the Flat River rush. Vandaele told Lewis the story over a few quiet evenings in their tent – and there were only a few such evenings since the two were usually camped out on their respective sections of the trapline.

In the spring of 1934, Vandaele and Campbell left jobs in a Calgary service station to join the rush. The newspaper stories that had drawn them were the notorious ones in the *Edmonton Journal*. In addition to colourful speculation on the so-called murders, the headhunting Indians, and the lost mine, the articles explicitly stated that gold had been found in the area. "You can kick the gravel heaps and see gold gleaming like butter," said one article. "The Nahanni gold fields are yielding good pay," said another.

Lewis told us the articles were "garbage." They influenced Harry, who was a bit of a dreamer. "That's one of the things I liked about Harry," said Lewis. "But it sometimes brought him bad luck." Vandaele said to Lewis that he and Campbell "had bought all those tall stories, the newspaper stories."

Vandaele and Campbell arrived in Fort Simpson in the spring of 1934. Lewis doesn't explain in his book how they financed their trip, but in conversation he told us that Vandaele paid. Campbell was broke. "The Vandaeles had money," Lewis explained. "Hard-earned money. They were all hard workers. Harry's parents, as I say in the book, worked themselves to death. They were also frugal. Each of the kids, on their twenty-first birthday, got $1,000. Harry received his in 1928. He bought wheat futures and parlayed his thousand up to $4,000. Harry was smarter than most. He lost his earnings [in the crash of '29], but kept his original $1,000. That money disappeared entirely when he went prospecting up the Flat."

From Fort Simpson, Vandaele and Campbell took a twenty-eight-foot canoe with two five-horsepower outboards up the Liard, the Nahanni, and then the Flat. They staked near Kraus and Clark, on Bennett creek, about seventy miles up the Flat and only five miles away from McLeod Creek, which was heavily populated by other prospectors including the Turner brothers, Faille, and Eppler.

Vandaele and Campbell went in again the following spring, the spring of 1935, by the same means, and came out again in the fall. And then, according to Kraus, they flew in during the winter of 1935–36, this time to McLeod Creek, and came out in May. Kraus explicitly states that they had been expecting supplies by plane and that the plane had not arrived. Consequently, they had come down to join Kraus and Clark to get something to eat and arrange a way out.

Lewis told us that Kraus must have been mistaken. "Harry and Milt could not possibly have been up the Flat River in 1936. They went in to Bennett Creek in the spring of 1934 and came back to Calgary and the farm in the fall of that year. They repeated the procedure in 1935. It was likely in 1934 or '35 when they met Kraus on the Flat tributaries. In the spring of 1936, Harry, Milt, Joe Vandaele, and Dick Turner's younger brother went to Fort St. John to buy equipment, which they transported to Fort Nelson and thus to the Liard and down to Lodema and Art George's place. You can see the photo for yourself in Turner's book. Harry bought an expensive force pump and they spent all summer washing flour gold out of the banks of the Liard. This operation was a complete failure."

The photo in Turner is dated May 1936, and Turner says that on 10 May he went up to Art George's cabin to meet his brother Fred, who was coming in by scow from Fort Nelson with a placer-washing outfit.

The *RCMP Quarterly* has Kraus and his party, which Kraus says included Vandaele and Campbell, still up on the Flat, leaving Irvine Creek on May 8.

It seems that Lewis is correct. Yet Kraus is so sure that Vandaele and Campbell were with him, and the historians are clear that Kraus came out only in 1936, not in 1934 or 1935.

At any rate, everyone agrees that the gold-washing experiment was a disaster.

So after three years of hard work, Vandaele and Campbell were broke and at loose ends in Fort Simpson. Neither of the two partners knew how to trap. And as Vandaele tells Lewis in *Nahanni Remembered,* a non-resident's permit cost seventy-five dollars, a big sum at the time, and an absolutely impossible one for a couple of broke prospectors.

They could, however, work for an established trapper. Campbell finally landed a job working a trapline up the Liard on the Netla River. Vandaele ended up on Dalziel's line at Rabbitkettle. Lewis puts it succinctly in his book: "Like so many others, Harry had resorted to trapping when he failed to find gold."

If Vandaele worked with his gold machine until freeze-up, it was likely November before he flew up the Nahanni with Dalziel. Dalziel dropped him off at the camp two miles south of the mouth of the Rabbitkettle, told him to build a cache, and flew on to the burned-out cabin. He returned and spent two weeks showing Vandaele how to run the line.

During these two weeks, the two did go up to the hot springs at the mouth of the Rabbitkettle to search for signs of Eppler and Mulholland. The northern part of the line ran around the base of the springs. They found nothing, but probably didn't expect much. The hot springs would not be a refuge for men in trouble. Unlike the hospitable springs at Tungsten, which pour from a dozen small springs at the base of a hill, forming into a pool and then emptying down a small creek into the Flat, the Rabbitkettle springs are surrounded by tufa deposits. Because there is no sulphur in the water, the dissolved calcium carbonate in the springs precipitates as a solid, forming these deposits. Over the centuries, they have formed into hills or mounds, one of them seventy feet high. From the air, these tufa mounds look like giant cow paddies. They look solid, but the tufa breaks off or collapses when you step on it, making for uncertain footing. The water inside the tufa is merely lukewarm. The pools appear bottomless. Because of their crumbling edges, it would be extremely difficult to get out once you were in them.

After his two weeks with Vandaele, Dalziel presumably flew to Fort Simpson and made his report. Then he flew to Edmonton and turned his plane over to the authorities. Lewis figures that Dalziel either convinced the Fort Simpson police to let him turn over the plane in Edmonton so that he could see his family or that the authorities ordered him to take the plane to Edmonton. It's obvious that by this point (December 1936, January 1937) Dal was more than just a nuisance to the authorities due to real or imagined violations of trapping regulations. He was also political trouble. In Ottawa, Parliament was debating the end of airplane trapping in the Territories. According to the *Edmonton Journal*, this law was passed in February 1937. The *Journal* described the debate:

> One white trapper had obtained a pilot's licence and bought an air-
> plane with which he was able to cover traps over an area of 125
> miles. Discouraged Indians in that district had given up trying to
> compete with him.

Dalziel isn't directly mentioned here, but in another article, placed adjacently under the same headline, he is mentioned, so the reader can make the obvious connection:

Canada's one "flying trapper," George Dalziel, who spent the early part of this trapping season up the headwaters of the Nahanni river, in a country little frequented even by Indians, may find his present enterprise ended by the government's new ruling. Use of the plane in trapping was less for the purpose of covering a trapline than of scouting out new trapping territory. It was Dalziel's practice to seek out virgin areas, from which furs were not being drawn by other trappers, white or native, friends state.

When did Dalziel arrive in Edmonton? The 11 November 1936 *Journal* article, "New Trace Is Seen of Lost Two Trappers," states that Dalziel had just arrived at Fort Simpson with this message, probably returning from his "search" with Vandaele. If this is the case, a couple of months went by before, sometime in late January, Dalziel contacted Vandaele's brother Joe. Perhaps Dalziel spent that time trying to get his plane out of hock and lobbying parliament not to pass the law prohibiting airplane trapping. And perhaps, when that law was passed, Dalziel realized that even if he could get his plane out of custody, it would be illegal to pick up the pelts – and Vandaele – in May.

Whatever his motivation, Dalziel told Joe that he had dumped Harry up the Nahanni, where he would trap until May. Joe had already heard about this arrangement from Harry and was worried. His brother was not an experienced trapper. He also suffered from back pain; sometimes, especially in cold weather, he was incapacitated by it.

But when Dalziel went on to say that he was not going to be able to pick Harry up in May, even though Harry was expecting to be picked up, Joe must have felt the hair rise on the back of his neck. How was this supposed to work? Harry had no canoe, and how could one man manage a cumbersome raft, loaded with a winter's take of furs, on the Nahanni in spring?

Joe Vandaele immediately contacted a neighbour, Bill Lewis, a good friend and hunting partner of Harry's. Joe knew that Bill had a younger brother, Alfred, who was eager to seek his fortune in the north. Joe discovered that Al, as he was called, had already left, planning to find work on the Mackenzie River, but was still en route, in regular contact with his family.

Al had soaked up the stories that Harry and Joe, on various trips back to the family farm, told of their experiences up the Liard and Nahanni. Even better, he admired Harry, six years his senior. Turner tells how Harry had returned to town in a Peerless car and a pinstripe suit. He had taken Al to a dance, where Al was further impressed to see his hero cutting a fine figure on the dance floor. And later, in 1929, Al was impressed by Harry's devil-may-care attitude. "Come easy go easy," Harry had told Al when the Peerless was turned over to creditors.

Turner portrays Lewis as Vandaele's admiring, wide-eyed sidekick. Lewis expressed no objections to this. In his book, he refers to Vandaele as "my idol." In conversation, he simply said, "Harry was my best friend."

But probably the best thing about Al at the time, so far as Joe was concerned, was that he had saved up $240 to finance his adventure. Joe well knew that the only way up the Nahanni in mid-winter was by dog-team or plane. Neither Joe nor anyone Joe knew had any experience with dogsledding, and no one had run a team that far up the Nahanni itself. The familiar route was from the Butte directly over to one of the (supposedly) gold-bearing creeks up the Flat River.

There was only one way. Someone would have to fly in, and that flight would cost. Only Al had the wherewithal to rescue Harry.

Bill Lewis contacted Al, who had already headed north, hitching a ride to Edmonton and then hopping a freight to Dawson Creek, most of his money stitched into a hidden pocket in his wool longjohns. Bill's wire intercepted Al in Dawson Creek, just as Al was arranging a ride on one of the horse-drawn freight sleighs that moved between Dawson Creek and Fort St. John. Al immediately wired back that he would return to Edmonton and join Harry at Rabbitkettle.

Al met Dalziel and Bill at the Leland Hotel in Edmonton. He was impressed by Dalziel, thirty years old at the time, medium built but with boundless energy. "A man," Lewis later wrote, "who knew where he was going – and how to get there. A man of action and little talk."

Besides being a little less than candid about the difficulties of rafting down the Nahanni, Dalziel was evasive about his plane. He told Bill and Al that it was "out of commission." Al, when he arrived at Rabbitkettle a few days later, tried to explain this situation to an obviously puzzled Vandaele.

"Do you mean that Dal won't be in after open water? It doesn't take that long to repair a plane," [Vandaele said to Lewis.]

"I distinctly asked him if he would be coming to fly us out. He said it wouldn't be possible. He spoke of repairs and mentioned that there were other matters to be taken care of."

"Other matters – now I think I understand," Harry commented.

Lewis remarks, "I was waiting for him to explain but he didn't, and I didn't ask him to. I did have the feeling that something was amiss, somewhere."

Vandaele probably knew something about Dalziel's legal and political problems.

In other ways, however, Dalziel was more than helpful. He gave Al a list of essentials (mosquito bar, etc.) to pick up in Edmonton. The list included a .303 rifle. Dalziel checked the rifle out after Al bought it and made a point of telling him never to take it inside the tent. When it was later taken *outside* the tent, Dalziel explained, water would condense inside the barrel, then freeze, causing the gun to blow up when fired.

There was also a list of groceries to pick up, on Dalziel's own account, at the Hudson's Bay Company store in Fort Simpson. He gave Al a bottle of rum to share with Harry. Then he arranged for the flight in with Mackenzie Air. The flight cost just over two hundred dollars, using up Al's entire savings.

The winter of trapping was, overall, a disaster, though Stan McMillan, as instructed by Dalziel, did fly out Harry's small accumulation of pelts after he dropped Lewis off. But the two friends hit it off exceptionally well and, for the most part, enjoyed themselves. They immediately fell into the pattern of referring to one another as characters in their favourite book, *Robinson Crusoe:* Al was Friday and Harry was Crusoe. For a young man like Lewis, the difficulties were mostly just part of the adventure, and he tackled them with élan. The hunting and trapping bothered him, and in the end he felt guilty – it was all for nothing, the entire catch (predictably) destroyed on the way out. On the raft, running at high speed through endless standing waves, they could not keep the furs dry and free of mold. In the second canyon, just past Pulpit Rock, they flipped and spent the next few hours in ice-cold water, trying to get the overturned raft ashore and unload the tied-down cargo. Finally they ended up burning all their fur except for a couple of more recently acquired beaver pelts.

As for the hunting, Lewis noted that he and Vandaele probably ate only about half of the meat they killed. In the spring they tried to stop the spoilage by building an icebox out of poplar, packing the meat with ice from shady spots in the bush. No luck. Then they tried to smoke the meat as Vandaele had seen the Indians doing on the Flat. With this they were more successful, but some of their bagged meat got wet on the way out and had to be burned.

The particular image of four rams, shot mostly on impulse when the men knew they could keep only one, stayed in Lewis's head for years. In his book he captioned his photo of these rams: "It could and should have been a different picture." He also remembered the moose, shot downriver after their raft flipped and soaked their dried meat. They were desperately in need of this meat, but were able to use and pack off only fifty pounds of it.

Lewis also suffered considerable anxiety for Vandaele, who was often in pain from his back. Lewis had to pack in any meat they shot, and he did his best to take on any other chores involving lifting. Vandaele's refusal to complain or saddle Lewis with an unfair share of the work was endearing, but made things difficult, and Vandaele's back pain slowed him down. Lewis told us that one of his most painful memories is from the difficult portage around Lafferty's Riffle in the First Canyon.

"I turned around and told Harry to speed it up. I'll never forget the look on his face."

"What did he say?"

"Nothing. He wouldn't have. He just kept walking. The bugs were driving me nuts, you understand. We all wore these berets with netting over them. But the berets weren't effective in keeping the netting away from your face. Plastered on your face, the netting was useless. I believe that when you lose blood at the rate we were, you get weak. When I looked back to see if Harry was still with me, I could see that he wasn't even trying to swat the bugs off his face. I got angry, more at our situation than at Harry. Poor Harry!"

And Lewis also agonized over his own errors like, to start things off, his failure to keep track of his baggage at Nahanni Butte, the result being that he arrived at Vandaele's camp with some of Daisy Mulholland's luggage (cosmetics and lingerie) instead of a big and badly needed sack of flour. Vandaele, in an attempt to cheer Lewis up, went through the contents of Daisy's bag, commenting on every item and who would get to wear or apply it should they need entertainment later on. Lewis also convinced Vandaele that they should do their beaver trapping by chopping into the lodges. After a wasted half day, they realized that they might just as well have tried to chop into Fort Knox. The beaver glued their dams and lodges together with clay, which in winter froze to the consistency of stone.

And yet Lewis's errors were nothing compared to Vandaele's. In fact, if Lewis had not arrived, Vandaele could well have died even before he made an attempt to get down the river. Between the time that Dalziel left and Lewis arrived, Vandaele made the classic mistake of taking his Ross .280 hunting rifle inside the tent, the very thing that Dalziel was careful to warn Lewis about. The Ross blew up on Vandaele the next day as he attempted to shoot a wolf caught in one of the traps. Vandaele was knocked unconscious for a short time. All he had left to hunt with was his .22 Hornet, in which (Lewis told us) he used long-rifle shells that could bring down moose at close range. It would be near useless against a bear, and before they left Rabbitkettle, Lewis and Vandaele had a few disputes with the bears over a nearby patch of cranberries. Lewis's new .303 was a godsend, and Vandaele was very happy to see it there in Lewis's pile of equipment.

Also, Vandaele had failed in the fall to take the opportunity of milder weather and shorter time on the trapline to build a cabin. He took the blame for this, though it is obvious from Dalziel's manuscript that Dalziel would have given him no help or encouragement and might have prohibited him from building a cabin. Dalziel had no use for cabins on a trapline. But as Lewis noted, living in a tent doubled the work and the discomfort. Frozen animals brought in from the line had to be thawed out before they could be skinned. In a cabin there was lots of solid ceiling for hanging the animals to thaw. In a tent, that was impossible.

The ride out was also a disaster, except for the fact that they made it out alive.

That summer, Vandaele and Campbell headed for the Yukon to trap. Lewis, broke, hung around Fort Simpson, doing odd jobs.

In September, Dalziel turned up, his plane reclaimed and back in service. Lewis was surprised to see him. Dalziel said that he had already encountered Harry up at Nahanni Village and that he knew the story of their raft trip out. Then he said, "They've struck it rich in Yellowknife. The real thing. Big investors. Big company. You can make five dollars per day as a miner. I'll take you there."

The price was a mere sixty dollars.

Dalziel was his usual self. When he landed near Latham Island in Yellowknife Bay and got a local girl to row them ashore, Lewis asked what was wrong with the floatplane dock and got the usual cryptic response: "That dock belongs to Canadian Airways and they can go to hell! I don't need any help from them."

Lewis found work as a carpenter. It was a trade he knew nothing about, but the demand was there. Months later, Harry turned up alone in Yellowknife after an unsuccessful winter trapping in the Yukon. The two friends had dinner together at the Wildcat Cafe and Al found out that Vandaele was working on a rig drilling core samples.

"I've seen more gold in the past week than all that time I spent in the Nahanni or the Liard," Vandaele said.

It was in the cafe that they found out they were famous. The owner recognized them. "Are you the two guys who came down the South Nahanni on a raft? The next time you come in, your dinner will be on me."

Three months later, Harry told Al that his back was giving him trouble. "I need an operation, and it may have to be done in the States."

So once more the two friends said goodbye, addressing one another as they had done through their winter on the Nahanni:

"Goodbye Crusoe."

"Take care, Friday."

Three years later, in 1942, Lewis left Yellowknife, and the north, for good. There was nothing in the north or its legends that attracted him. His approach was practical. He was a young man starting out, and he needed a career. But he loved Vandaele, and on his way out to Vancouver went to Calgary to visit him. The back operation had taken place in Rochester and been a success. "Not a total success," Lewis told us, "but a big improvement. Harry had to wear a special belt."

Vandaele now owned and operated a mink ranch south of Calgary. "The farm was *quite* a success," Lewis said.

THE DISAPPEARANCES of Eppler and Mulholland were soon woven into the fabric of legend. Two years after their disappearance, Eppler was sighted, by Fort Simpson hotel owner Andy Whittington, in downtown Vancouver. Whittington was certain he had seen Eppler, stating to Dick Turner that "with that one eye and pug nose of his I could never mistake him."

One eye? One eye missing or one funny eye? Is that why Eppler wore sunglasses for the photo in Turner's book? Or was it because Eppler, as he had once explained to his Fort Simpson friends, was a refugee from American justice? In 1918, when Eppler was only eighteen, unemployed and riding the rails through the U.S., he had stood trial for the murder of the Greek owner of a cafe. He and the owner had gotten into a fight over the bill for a meal, but no harm was done and Eppler had wandered away, watched a baseball game, and then found a place to sleep. The police arrested him the next day after finding the Greek shot to death. Eppler spent some days in jail, and on one of those days his cellmate, who had already been tried for murder, was taken out, protesting his innocence, and hung. Eppler was brought to trial, but the testimony of some of the boys who had been playing baseball saved him. It seemed that, during the game, the baseball had rolled into the grass in Eppler's vicinity. The boys couldn't find it and accused the stranger of taking it. Eppler allowed them to search him – no ball and, most significantly, no gun. A few minutes later, the boys found their ball.

Eppler was acquitted. He made straight for Canada, believing it to be a place where justice was more phlegmatic, and then he made his way to the far north. Maybe he was worried that American justice could change its mind about him as quickly and erratically as it had charged, tried, and acquitted him.

Turner speculates that if something had happened to Joe Mulholland, Eppler, because of his earlier brush with the law, might have lit out rather than take a chance on being blamed for Joe's death. Or the two might have found gold, had a disagreement on what to do, and fought. If Eppler had a fault, Turner says, it was a tendency to argue. Joe might have been killed.

Turner says Eppler flew to Vancouver and then Australia.

Lewis, when we mentioned this story, laughed. "Turner's got a wild imagination," he said. "It seems obvious to me that the river took Eppler and Mulholland."

"But on 11 November 1936, Dalziel told the *Journal* that Eppler and Mulholland seem to have made it all the way down past the canyons. The RCMP accepted Faille's word that there were signs of camps as far down as the Gate. That far down, there's less chance of accident. Maybe only one man was going out. Turner might've been thinking about that."

"I still wonder about Dalziel's part in the story," Vivien put in.

"When I paid that visit to Harry in 1942," said Lewis, "we spent most of our time digging a well together. In the course of it, I asked him if he thought that Dal could've had anything to do with the deaths of Eppler and Mulholland. 'Funny you should say that,' Harry replied. 'My brother Joe's been putting that question to me. There have been stories of Dal dropping men into faraway places – men who are never heard from again. But he did send you in to get me, didn't he?' 'True,' I said. 'I've given it a lot of thought,' Harry continued, 'but I don't think Dal is guilty. Maybe I pride myself too much on my judgment of men, but I liked Dal. In a big hurry, yes. Impulsive, yes. And, consequently, insensitive. Oh yes. But not a man to deliberately do harm.'"

"Dalziel dropped Eppler and Mulholland in there," Vivien continued.

"But they were to come out in a skinboat or raft," objected Lewis. "We have to admit that Jack and Daisy Mulholland understood that and reported it to everyone concerned."

"What if there was a last minute change as they flew up the river?" Vivien persisted. "They *must* have known that the skinboat was a stupid idea."

"Yes," admitted Lewis. "And the fact that Dal alludes to it in his book makes me suspicious. Dal was even more experienced than Eppler. There's no way he would have taken the idea seriously. But I still don't think Dal actually intended to strand the two men, and neither did Harry Vandaele think that."

"There must have been some reasons for concern among the Fort Simpson trappers and prospectors," Vivien continued, "or why would they have been so insistent on a search months after the RCMP had closed the case?"

"If there was a change in plans on the flight in," I added, "that would explain why Dalziel never took Harry up to examine the cabin. He would want to remove any incriminating evidence with no witnesses present."

"Evidence," Vivien agreed, "like a note saying 'No more food. No sign of Dal. We're out of here.' In fact, Dal could've burned the cabin himself, just to make *sure* there was no evidence."

"Or he burned the Rabbitkettle cabin down after he found the one at Glacier Lake," I added. "He took the RCMP to the Rabbitkettle one, where he'd be sure there was no evidence."

"I can see now how you two got into writing books," said Lewis.

8

Chestnut Bear

WHAT LED TO VIVIEN's defeat in the alpines above Union Carbide was
not the rain nor the inhospitable condition of the site nor the chestnut bear,
big and implacably planted on our route as he was, but Elsebeth and me.

Elsebeth hikes for pleasure. The vision of the legendary South Nahanni
River promised by the cliffs above the abandoned Union Carbide site was
less to her than the hike up to those cliffs, and that hike had been plagued
by rain, which meant mud and wet bush, which meant slimy feet and long
hours spent drying out tents, sleeping bags, boots and clothing. The
vision was less to her, too, than the fact that the contour map indicated
cabins on the site, seven cabins to be exact, a veritable city. Cleared of marmot shit and patched with pieces from the other cabins, one of these cabins was to serve as a base camp for our exploration of the cliffs above.

We talked yearningly of these cabins as we slogged through the rain.
We even looked for other cabins in the bush along the trail, though no cabins were indicated on the map. On all of our other bicycle trips and hikes
in the area west of Nahanni – Conglomerate Creek, Dolly Varden Creek,
Howard's Pass, and of course the route into the area itself, Highway 10
leading to Tungsten – there had been cabins. And more! The mining

industry had been most generous in its castoffs. There had been trucks, bulldozers, outhouses, barrel heaters, drilling platforms, buckets, axes, lumber, shafts drilled into rock faces, and other items of immense value and interest to the long-distance cyclist-hiker.

Elsebeth also hikes for wildlife. She *likes* bears and other animals and the idea of their being around. In fact, they are a major reason why she is around, so far away from her home in Copenhagen. Canada is, she reminds us from time to time, one of the last of the great wildernesses, and the grizzly is its main attraction.

In this way only, Elsebeth was happy with our trip to Union Carbide. On our first day out, cycling Highway 10 after abandoning our truck at the washout, we saw a pair of timber wolves. We had just camped near a cabin and corral, and erected our tents under our tarp, which we had spread over an old pole frame built there by some hunting guide or out-fitter. Our fire was burning heartily, despite the rain, in a heater made out of a forty-five-gallon drum, and we were waiting for hot water for instant cappuccino.

The wolves came along the highway, relaxed as if they owned it – which, for almost all of the year, they do. At a distance of a hundred metres they saw us or sniffed our smoke and then stopped and subjected us to a long, thoughtful look. Elsebeth snapped some photos and I reached for my bear spray. Then the wolves disappeared into bush on the opposite side of the road to us. Hours later we still felt that long look, as if it were being continued from some hidden spot. Elsebeth expressed her pleasure at seeing the wolves, marvelling at their size and hoping out loud that her photos turned out well.

"They are talking in Sweden of wolves appearing near the outskirts of Stockholm," she said, "but I have not seen signs of them myself and I doubt it. We Scandinavians want back all those beings that fill our history with adventure and mystery. We are so hopeful that we invent stories. Here, wild animals are taken for granted. I understand that some people even regard wolves as a nuisance."

We also saw, and heard, a pair of loons. On our fourth day out (we had left our bicycles and were now hiking) the loons announced our arrival on the bluffs along Dozer Lake. Their wavering cry, with its mournful falling notes at the end, fascinated Elsebeth. It was the first time she had heard loons.

"Marvellous," she whispered.

And it was. On that day, at that time, the rain had stopped, though it was only for an hour, and the faint trail to Union Carbide opened wide, unvegetated and dry, on a bluff, an hospitable patch of gravel that we could rest on and gain a view from. We could see the lake almost end-to-end, with its rocky island directly below and the loons swimming side-by-side for the opposite shore, crying.

And on our ninth day, when we were rushing away from Union Carbide, a gigantic and fully racked bull moose suddenly sprang from cover and surged along beside and then in front of us, head and back visible above the high willow.

This was an animal that, like the chestnut bear, Elsebeth would rather not have seen so closely. Moose, surprised and springing in the wrong direction, can turn into writhing bundles of flashing, cleaver-like hooves. This one, fortunately, sprang away from us, and Elsebeth had the presence of mind to get another photo.

Along with a love of comfort and a love of animals, Elsebeth has great respect for bears. A couple of years earlier, on Elsebeth's first hike in Kluane Park in the Yukon, she and Vivien had confronted the wilderness's main attraction face to muzzle. The bear, it turned out, was a young male, not particularly hungry, but curious. He snuck up on Vivien and Elsebeth, who had just made morning coffee in their creekside campsite. His approach was covered by the sound of the creek. He was breathing down Vivien's neck when she turned, screamed, and ran through the creek and up the opposite bank, coffee cup still full and poised. Elsebeth watched this performance curiously (Vivien is given to dramatic gestures), wondered what might have instigated it, then turned and saw the bear. She dropped her cup and joined Vivien. The bear examined the camp, leisurely, and then turned around and shambled back from where he had come, evidently happy with the information gained.

Vivien and Elsebeth rushed to break camp. But what to do with the bubbling pot of porridge? It could not be left, or even dumped into the stream, lest the bear get a good smell or taste and connect that smell and taste with them. Vivien fixed the lid onto the pot and stuffed it in the top of her pack. Down out of the alpine they went at a half run, into the possible safety of trees and a popular hiking trail winding through them.

They chattered nervously about how lucky they were to be near the end of their hike and near the trail. But they were two days up that trail. Should the trail happen to be deserted, and the bear happen to be persistent, they could still be in trouble.

They arrived on the trail after an hour and decided to eat the porridge, straight out of the pot. The porridge was now cold, but they were hungry. Just as they finished eating, the bear appeared again, ahead of them on the trail, blocking their path to safety. He crisscrossed in front of them, coming, at each crossing, a little bit closer.

Vivien got angry. The obvious option of spending a day or two up a tree watching the bear explore their packs was unthinkable, especially near the end of a ten-day hike. She broke all the rules (of which she is chief exponent in Kluane) and began to yell and lob rocks at the bear. Elsebeth reluctantly joined her, realizing that this could anger the bear, but also realizing that unanimity was of the essence in this situation. If you opt to intimidate a grizzly, you had best be serious about it.

The bear moved off the trail, but as soon as Vivien and Elsebeth rushed past him, he moved back onto it, browsing among the soapberries along the edge as if to suggest his total lack of interest in Vivien and Elsebeth. "Who, *me?*" he seemed to say in response to their evident concern. So they continued down the trail, looking often over their shoulders, and within an hour they ran into the arms of a trail-clearing crew.

The bear immediately reappeared, now obviously in hot pursuit of Vivien and Elsebeth. The trail crew clustered and cocked their canisters of pepper spray. The bear stopped. One of the trail crew found the radio. A half hour later, during which time the bear simply paced back and forth across the road, his eyes never off them, a helicopter arrived and took everyone away. As they lifted over the trees, they noted the bear moving down the road towards the trail crew's camp.

A persistent bear, the kind likely to make an impression. Elsebeth was, thereafter, assiduous in carrying out her bear-duty, yodelling her way through the bush. She carried her pepper spray on her backpack belt. She watched for signs.

As for me, I am, everyone says, the perfect companion for Vivien. Everyone means by this that my somewhat anxious nature complements her somewhat impulsive one. But there are rare occasions in which this ideal combination is the wrong one, and the Union Carbide hike was one of these.

As with Elsebeth, the goal of a hike is not my primary objective. My objective is peace of mind. Safety and security. I hike only to be with Vivien. Without her I would stay on my rural acreage, chopping wood and watching the stars. And yet I had come to enjoy hiking and, almost as much as Vivien, I wanted to see the Nahanni, carried to the view by my own legs. It would have been something to bore my children and grandchildren with. "Hey guys, *slides!*" It would have been a bright memory to carry into my imminent old age.

Some of the anxieties that I carried on this trip are routine baggage. It was at my insistence, for example, that Vivien and I had begun carrying pepper spray. Also, the day before we had picked Elsebeth up at the Vancouver airport and started our long trip north to Watson Lake and Highway 10, Vivien and I had argued in a downtown hiking supply store over the purchase of an electronic location finder and emergency beacon. Activated, such a beacon instantly alerts a satellite, which alerts the nearest rescue unit, providing the location of the emergency.

I felt that, for such security, the price was nothing. Vivien thought I was being an idiot. I might have bought the beacon anyway, but was stopped by her argument that I was quite likely to set it off accidentally. I would have to cash in all my RRSPs and sell my acreage in order to pay the expenses of a helicopter and rescue crew thundering in from Watson Lake or beyond.

Besides bears and other accidents, and besides looking stupid and losing my kids' inheritance, I fear Vivien, her tendency to take big risks, especially when she is close to a goal. Captain Sir Richard Francis Burton, explorer of the Nile, is her hero; she has read all the biographies and even parts of some of his own books. I'm always aware that not-so-subtle comparisons are being made. Unfair comparisons, in my opinion. It seems clear to me that without the help of his Africans and his friend Speke, Burton would never have found his way to the outskirts of Cairo.

But Vivien disagrees. Just the previous summer, in Kluane, she had tried to make me make a third try at getting past a mother grizzly and two yearling cubs. She was trying for a ridge that would give the purchasers of the next edition of her guidebook a view of the Donjek Glacier from high up and only two or three days away from trailhead. I had declined, on the grounds that "third time lucky" could apply to the bears rather than me. Isn't it at a year old, I asked Vivien, that young bears get taught the rudiments of tracking, wounding, and burying alive a large mammal?

Vivien wouldn't speak to me for the entire day's trip out to trailhead.

I also fear *for* Vivien. She's susceptible to cold and has a weak ankle on which she regularly "goes over." The ankle then swells up over the top of her boot. This results in at least two days of painful walking and two sleepless nights. Vivien "solves" this problem by getting cortisone shots before hikes and gobbling painkillers and anti-inflammatory drugs during hikes. My fear is that she could easily sprain or break this ankle – especially since the drugs she takes make her groggy.

Vivien's one gesture in the direction of safety (and it is a very casual and irregular gesture) is to try for a minimum of three people on any long hike: one to get hurt, one to stay with the one hurt, and one to go out for help. She had done this in the case of the Union Carbide hike; we had even agreed to postpone it if Elsebeth couldn't make it, though I wondered if Vivien would stick to this agreement. But this safety measure, whenever I contemplate its implications, merely compounds my anxiety. What if I had to leave Vivien and go out for help? Possibly worse, what if I had to stay to nurse her?

Also, Vivien hates rain. It is not just that rain increases the possibility of getting cold or of making tactical mistakes due to impatience and discomfort. Rain can prolong a hike, almost doubling the time needed. Hours must be spent under a tarp and around a fire, drying out tents, clothing and sleeping bags. To move on without doing this, to pack wet tents, sleeping bags and clothing, is to court hypothermia.

For Vivien, rain is more than just an obstruction and a danger. It is a psychological problem. Rain is a sign to her that the world is not, after all, concerned about her, but has its own agenda. At the start of the twenty-minute CBC-TV program on Vivien's hiking and travel career, she says, "I hate rain." Rain puts her into a state of absolute depression. Communication with her becomes near impossible. This depresses the people hiking with her. It especially depresses me. Vivien and I work together by means of unending dialogue. Without that dialogue, I'm lost.

But rain does not stop Vivien. It makes her even more (if grimly) determined.

Vivien went over on her ankle on our fifth day into Union Carbide. She slipped on a wet root that stuck like an arthritic elbow out of the side of the trail. She didn't go down, or even stop, but I could see that her face was rigid with pain. When I talked about taking some of the weight from her pack, she said, "Never mind!"

And so my calculations began – mainly in terms of: how long would it take me (or Elsebeth) to get out for help should Vivien immobilize herself?

These calculations were complicated. We were already three days walking and two days by bicycle from any possible assistance. That assistance could be found at a cabin and floatplane depot on the Flat Lakes north of Tungsten. Should that cabin be deserted, Tungsten was another half day away by bicycle.

And trailhead, where our bicycles were stashed, was at our crossing-place on the Little Nahanni River. When Vivien had originally tried this crossing out the previous August, Elsebeth and I watching sleepily from a sunny knoll, it had gone easily. Vivien picked her way upstream and then downstream on various gravel bars until suddenly she was shouting and waving to us from the other shore. But that had been in the middle of a dry summer. Our Union Carbide hike was in early July of what turned out to be a very wet summer. The crossing was one of the most difficult we had ever experienced.

The tallest of our party, I had made my way over first, in the prescribed manner, pack fully loaded but unbuckled, and body facing upstream and leaning forward, supported by a heavy stick. The water was, in places, boiling against my abdomen. I had to keep my eye on the bottom, searching out the lay of Vivien's gravel bars, and I had to patiently resist the numbing cold and stop regularly to force my gaze upstream and away from the dizzying rush of water immediately around me. The pack provided enough weight to keep my feet on the bottom, but because it was unbuckled, it put me off balance when I moved. I thought of going back. Even if I made it, what about Elsebeth? And Vivien, a scant five feet tall? Impossible! Why tempt her with my presence on the opposite shore?

But I can't lie to her, so I inched my way on and on and, finally, over. Once there I threw down my pack and paced the shore in my underpants and creek-crossing sandals, rubbing warmth into my legs, for there was no sun though the rain had mercifully stopped. I could see that Elsebeth and Vivien were conferring on the opposite shore, gesturing in my direction. Obviously Vivien had conceived some sort of plan, possibly involving me. This made me nervous.

Then Elsebeth moved into the stream, pack belts unclipped, pole extended. It was a harder fight for her; while she is stronger than me, she is also a couple of inches shorter. It took her longer (Vivien timed us both). For up to ten seconds at a time she was unmoving, leaning at a ninety-degree angle to her pole, water churning at her chest, her foot searching for solid lodging on the bottom so she could shift a few inches sideways. I grabbed my pole and moved towards her, but this was mere show, for encouragement. What could I do for her? If she lost her footing she would be gone in a second, and if I grabbed at her I would be gone too.

She made it. Dumping her pack and jumping around as I had done, she told me to go back over to Vivien. "She thinks she can cross in your wake."

I hadn't thought of that. "Do you think she can?" I asked.

"I don't know. It's dangerous."

So I went back, first taking about ten pounds off my pack for better stability. As I crossed, I became angry. Crossing in my wake could work, but Elsebeth was correct: it was a desperate move. Vivien would have to be immediately behind me, with no pole to lean on should I slip. She would have to stabilize herself by holding the back of my pack. We would have to move in coordination. It would be a dance of death. I decided to refuse. We would get Elsebeth back across, cycle back to the cabin, dry out, and then go elsewhere. Somewhere far away, where the sun was shining. Kluane maybe.

But back on the other shore, I said nothing. I could see that look on Vivien's face. Maybe the freezing water and the force of the current would turn her back.

They didn't. In fact, she seemed to find the crossing easy. I did too. I knew the route now and was more stable with my slightly lighter pack. The only real impediment this time was a cramp that started to form in my right leg. I had been too long in the water.

Vivien and Elsebeth were ecstatic. I pretended to be. We talked in the nervous, rushed manner of people spooked by their own adrenaline. But now we were across a river that we had to cross again and that was certainly rising. I added this item to my bag of anxieties.

And there was the trail itself to worry about, a winter road. Unlike the all-season one that we had cycled to the crossing, carrying our bikes and packs around washed-out culverts and bridges, the winter road had been used only when the ground was frozen, meaning that it had reacquired its vegetation quickly. The road was fairly easy to follow from the crossing to Dozer Lake and the loon family, but after Dozer Lake, going over to South Lened Creek, it disappeared into a boggy, tangled jungle of willow. Finally we found it again in some heavy forest up the creek.

We followed it easily, too, from South Lened across a plateau to Lened Creek and up Lened to a point where it crossed the creek towards a white gash in the forest. The gash turned out to be hot springs, bubbling scalding hot from beneath a canopy of ferns at the top of the gash, and flowing in shallow channels through a layer of tufa into Lened Creek. We thought the road would reappear somewhere off the top of the springs, but it didn't, so we had to bushwhack up to a switchback that was visible in the alpines high above. Trail-finding took the three of us, one sitting with the packs on what we hoped was the road or close to it, and two others fanning out ahead, searching for clearer signs. We looked for two definite, parallel depressions in the ground or for sawed stumps.

And finally there was the rain, which never stopped for long, the clouds settling in thick and low, blocking our view of the mountains ahead. Such weather could hinder any rescue. It seemed to rain hardest in the jungles of spruce and willow around Dozer Lake and across Lened Creek. The rain was so bad there that, on the afternoon of our sixth day, it stopped us altogether. Elsebeth could stand it no longer. On a spacious if noisy gravel bar on Lened, just above where it flows into South Lened, she proposed that we settle in and wait it out.

I was reluctant. Our usual rule for rain is that you go as far as you can and then camp and wait. So long as you are walking, your stuff is dry and you are warm. But Vivien supported Elsebeth, and so I quickly agreed. Elsebeth was clearly finished, psychologically. Vivien, with her ankle sore and swollen, was tired. Also, I had noticed that good campsites were scarce. The hiker's platitude that nature abhors a flat spot was never truer

ELSEBETH CROSSING THE LITTLE NAHANNI RIVER ABOVE STEEL CREEK

than on the route to Union Carbide. It could have taken a couple more hours to find another good site.

So we were in our tents by 6 p.m., water from the inevitable tent leak slowly dripping onto our sleeping bags. Fortunately the leak was at the foot of the tent. We were warm and had our fire smouldering under the protection of our tarp, with a good stock of wood stacked and covered.

It was still raining on the morning of our seventh day, so we ate a quick breakfast and crawled back into our bags. All day long, during any likely pause in the rain, we were up, tossing our books aside, making coffee, tea, soup, or instant cappuccino, finding and cutting more wood.

But the rain never stopped for long. It stopped sometime during the night so that the bush was dry by breakfast on day eight. But after breakfast, while we were drying out and preparing to move, the rain started again, more seriously.

We were too restless at that point to wait, so we continued drying out and then packed and moved on, across Lened Creek, through wet forest up the creek, and then across it again, but not on the road because the creek there was too fast. We backtracked, crossed the creek, climbed a hillside of slimy cladina lichen (the primary food source for caribou, but no friend of the hiker), and intercepted the road on a bushy plateau. The clouds thinned and, looking up, Vivien saw the scars of switchback roads on the hills above Lened Creek. It was the Union Carbide site – our dreamed-of city of cabins – only one day away along the creek on our side, then a crossing, and then a half day or so up along the other side. We hauled out the binoculars. There should have been drilling platforms along those switchbacks, but we could see none. We failed, in our exhilaration at having our objective in sight, to catch the implication of this.

So on we went, through the rain, right up to two huge rows of rotting core-sample racks and five rectangles burnt into the tundra.

Elsebeth and I were immobilized by shock. We broke out a bag of trail mix and wandered around the core-sample racks. Elsebeth brooded while I worried. We were eight days from any source of rescue, across a rising river, up a faint trail. We were wet and we were cabinless.

Vivien set off to examine the area more closely and look up into the ridges that could lead over to the Nahanni.

After awhile, made nervous (as I always am) by Vivien's absence, I started picking up nails and scrap wood, including a half-dozen full-sized though soggy sheets of plywood. These, I deduced, had blown off the tops of the racks. I leaned the plywood against the racks, found some lengths of four-by-four and leaned them beside the plywood, and then located a dozen dry two-by-two claim-stakes that would provide us with a good fire for the night and maybe the next morning. I figured Vivien would want to stay at the site, though water was ten minutes away and fuel much farther. Also, the site was infested with marmots, famous for chewing through tent walls and food bags.

Elsebeth laughed at my efforts. "There's another squall coming," she said, nodding back down the panorama of Lened Valley. "We should go down to the creek for shelter. This is not a good place."

I nodded.

Vivien appeared a few minutes later. "Isn't this a beautiful spot?" she said.

"We should go back down to the creek," I said. "There's another storm coming."

"Aren't we staying here?" said Vivien, surprised.

"There's no wood or water," said Elsebeth.

"There are a dozen dry claim-stakes," I said. "They wouldn't last long, though. And if we tried to use the place as a base camp, the marmots would wreck our tents and bags."

While I talked, Elsebeth and I shouldered our bags. Vivien looked on and then silently followed suit. Her silence worried me.

Our move down was a disaster, a tactical error of the first order. I knew it even as we walked off. After all, there was *some* dry wood on the site. We *could* collect rain water. The plywood, leaned against the sample racks, would be *some* protection.

The thing was, I kept telling myself as we moved down, there were supposed to be buildings. Four walls and a roof, possibly a door and some windows, and maybe even a barrel heater between us and the weather and the marmots and the wolves and the bears. From a cabin we would do a series of excursions onto the cliffs that could lead, at only five or six kilometres distance, to a view of the Nahanni.

Not five minutes from the racks, the storm hit us. Then I realized that the creek was not at all hospitable. In fact, it turned out that I had misunderstood Elsebeth. She had meant the next creek, farther down, where we had noticed a good supply of dry wood and some flat spots on the road. But that creek was two kilometres away.

While we mulled this over we unfolded our tarp and stood under it to avoid a complete soaking. The rain had never been harder. I looked at Vivien. Her face was wet, and not just with the rain. She was crying. As if she already knew.

The rain eased and we set out. Halfway down, Vivien went over on her ankle again and down hard onto her knee. She was instantly up and moving, as always, but staggering, the rain washing the blood down her leg. And I was close to tears. I knew that, up at the Union Carbide site, I had simply panicked and let Elsebeth, who was at least decided, lead, and now Vivien was in danger. We should have been under the plywood sheets, the claim-stakes burning, making some cappuccino out of rain water, intimidating the marmots, reading our books, studying the core samples, or deciding our next move. Instead we were stumbling down, routed.

Once we arrived at the second creek, we struggled in our weariness to cut poles for the tarp and erect it, to cut firewood and light the fire, and to get the tents up. Keeping the fire going was especially difficult, as the alpine wood was dry but hard. We sawed coin-sized pieces of wood and fanned the flames steadily. Vivien stood dumbly under the tarp, dressed in every dry piece of clothing she had and still shivering. We cooked some dried soup, drank it in our cups, and crawled into our tents.

Vivien took her map bag with her.

"Why did we come down?" she whispered to me, Elsebeth's tent being a scant couple of metres away.

"I panicked," I said.

"You've both decided to go back, haven't you?"

"No," I said, truthfully, sort of. "But I think we should get out of here. There are no cabins. There were supposed to be cabins."

"We don't need cabins! This can be our base camp. See on the map. The switchbacks above this creek lead into the alpines above Union Carbide. We can get up onto the ridges. For God's sake, we carried in food for an extra week. We can't go back now!"

"I'm afraid."

"What of?"

"Everything. We're a long ways out. It hasn't stopped raining. Your ankle's swollen. There are no cabins."

"We can do this hike tomorrow. Say yes."

"Yes."

I had a restless sleep, dreaming of Vivien hurt, of Elsebeth nursing her while I tried to walk out, of me not making it, lost in the Little Nahanni, lost on the trail, eaten by bears or wolves. *"Where are you going, little boy?"*

Next morning I awakened early and got up immediately to work on the fire. It was raining again, lightly, but the night had obviously been dry. There were some dry, half-burned sticks left in the fire, and I had placed some silver-dollar-sized pieces of spruce into a dry place in my pack. I got enough fire to make coffee and porridge. I wanted to engineer a calm, civilized meeting.

It was evidently two votes to one, I pointed out to Vivien and Elsebeth as we stood under our tarp, sipping coffee. I asked if there were any compromises possible. Vivien produced the map and showed the route. Elsebeth argued. This was not a secure base camp. There was no cover from the wind. The wood was no good.

Vivien pointed out a grove of poplar below. "I was thinking about that last night," she said. "This wood is too hard. If we get enough dry stuff from down there and cover it up for when we come back, can we do a day hike into the alpines?"

Elsebeth looked up. The rain had stopped and there were some patches of blue sky. "Yes," she said, shrugging.

It turned out that down across the creek there was enough dead, dry, and porous standing poplar to last for days. We dragged it up to camp, sawed or broke it up, and stacked it under the tarp. We loaded a pack with snacks and rain gear, secured and covered the other packs, and headed back up the trail. The route was ten kilometres, but we would move fast. We decided to go back up to Union Carbide, then farther up and along the cliffs, and then down our creek to camp, thus doing the bushwhacking part of our trip on the downhill.

It was an unlucky decision, as it turned out. On the other route, we probably would have outflanked the bear.

But what a start! A bit of sun, a light load (Vivien and Elsebeth with only their cameras), and a dreamscape of snow-streaked alpine valleys leading easily (it seemed) up into the cliffs between us and Nahanni. Vivien was chirping like a bird about the fresh alpine flowers, about the view, about previous trips, about friendship. At one point she thanked us for relenting, for agreeing to do what we had originally planned to do. I pointed this out to her, momentarily secure in the feeling that our chances were good, that we would return late from a wonderful hike, eat a good meal, sleep hard, and wake up to a sunny morning and more interesting routes to follow. Or we would glimpse the Nahanni, take some slides, and then do what I still, at heart, perversely, wanted to do: get the hell out.

We scarcely glanced at the core racks as we passed, though we did stop to count the burnt rectangles nearby, as if to be sure that one of cabins had not maybe walked off somewhere. We noted that the site was impeccably clean – scarcely even a piece of plastic or rusted lid from a tin can remained.

"I've never seen such a complete clean-up," said Vivien.

"That's why there are no drilling platforms on the hills above," said Elsebeth. "They burned those also."

The bastards, I thought. But maybe now it didn't matter.

And then, a kilometre above the cleaned-up site, a chestnut-coloured grizzly, very big, browsing.

Vivien saw him first and whispered a warning. Elsebeth looked. I didn't want to look, turned around as soon as Vivien spoke, heading back down.

And then the rain resumed.

Back at camp I proposed a day of rest. I said I was tired. Elsebeth wanted to pack and move down, but said she would stay if we wanted to. I mused that moving down *would* have one advantage: we would easily get to our next campsite, on Lened Creek not far from where we crossed beneath the hot springs, where the poles for our tarp were already cut and the tent spots cleared. This would synchronize us with all the campsites that we had made on the way in.

Stupid! Why did I get into this? It led to a misunderstanding, Elsebeth and Vivien now assuming that I wanted, after all, to leave. Vivien half-heartedly proposed that we light the fire and cook lunch, but none of us were really hungry and we were each, for our own reasons, demoralized. The packing-up began.

I glanced at our stack of poplar firewood as we moved off, a pitiful testimony to our dream.

For two days, slightly clearer days (as a sort of reprimand) than those that had gone before, right up to the point that the passes above Union Carbide disappeared in the distance, Vivien followed behind, looking back regularly. At our camp on the gravel bar on Lened Creek I tried to talk to her, wishing now that something could happen to take us back, but she turned away or rushed off to do something, hiding tears. On the third day she talked again, but now it was of going to Kluane. Elsebeth seized upon the idea, and we proceeded to make our plans.

Hearing Vivien speak again was a relief for Elsebeth. "I can't stand this silent treatment!" she had said to me back at Lened Creek after Vivien had gone, early, into the tent.

"She's disappointed that we didn't finish the hike," I explained.

"We got to Union Carbide. There was nothing there but a grizzly!"

"We didn't see the Nahanni."

"So why did you want to leave?"

"Fear. You?"

"Not fear. Maybe the bear would move off, maybe not. It just wasn't worth it. There are no cabins. We're wet and tired. Vivien is exhausted. I've never seen her like this. You have the camera and the tent now. I have the extra food she was carrying. And still she's staggering by mid-afternoon. This is not hiking. It's torture!"

So I have to explain it all to Vivien, sometime when her disappointment has eased. I'm no partner for her when she's chasing a dream. Even when I share that dream.

I didn't even chance a look at the chestnut bear, which, now that I think of it, would have been a rare thing to see.

TRAIL INFORMATION

Union Carbide

This is not a route to be tried at the beginning of summer, as the water level on the Little Nahanni River is usually too deep at that time. Water levels usually crest by mid-June, so mid-July would be the earliest recommended time to do this hike. Once across the river there is a half-day slog through the swamps of yet another winter road. However, after you get past Dozer Lake and up Lened Creek, the trip is a thrill.

TOPOGRAPHICAL MAPS: Shelf Lake 105I-1 (1:50,000), Upper Hyland Lake 105I-2 (1:50,000), Dozer Lake 105I-7 (1:50,000), Mt. Appler #105I-8 (1:50,000)

EQUIPMENT NEEDED: You will be a long way from the closest radiophone, and if the water on the Little Nahanni comes up while you are on the other side, you will need food to wait for its drop. Because it takes almost four minutes to cross the river, you will need creek-crossing shoes. Durable rain gear is essential as it rains at least once a day and occasionally all day for many days in a row. This is a difficult trip, requiring total self-sufficiency.

THE ROUTE

0.0K WINTER ROAD TURNOFF. The winter road leading to the crossing of the Little Nahanni River is only 1.5 kilometres past the March Creek Bridge. There is a small cairn, and an arrow made of stone points across the road towards the river to mark the spot where the winter road begins. If you are on the main road past March Creek and come to a second creek with a non-functioning culvert, you have gone too far.

1.5K LITTLE NAHANNI RIVER (3- to 4-minute crossing). At the fork in the winter road, near the river, go to the right. It will lead to a bank over the river from which your river-crossing route is visible. The crossing place is at the elbow in the river with a gravel bar partway across. Walk to the south end of the elbow and look carefully into the water. There is a spit (an elevated strip of gravel) about twenty feet from the bend and two or three feet under the water. It leads across the water to the gravel bar. The crotch-deep water is not swift, so it is easy to reach the gravel bar.

Once on the gravel bar, cross at the widest point of the river. Although it looks like the opposite shore is the mainland, it is actually an island. Crossing from the island to the mainland presents no problems.

When you cross from the gravel bar to the shore of the island, there is one small strip of deep water that is also swift. I would suggest that if you have anyone in your hiking party who is less than 5 feet 6 inches, he or she should cross in the wake of a taller person. This crossing takes more than three minutes, which is a very long time to be in freezing water and fighting against a swift current. It is important that you are psychologically ready for this crossing. It is also important to have good creek-crossing shoes, as your foot and leg muscles will knot if they are not protected. Have your tallest person cross first to test the levels and then work from that bit of knowledge, even if the tallest person has to cross three times to get everyone in your party across. Water levels will go down during the night unless there is a heavy rainstorm.

Once across, you will find a good campsite along the shore where there is a log for drying clothes and/or sitting upon. Driftwood is available on the island.

2.0K WINTER ROAD TURNOFF. Go downriver (north) on the east side of the island until you find the double-tracked winter road. Cross a tiny strip of water to the mainland. The road passes a shale outcrop and then continues up a steep hill through forest. If you lose the trail, it is better to reconnoitre until you find it again than to bushwhack over the hill. Looking back, the Little Nahanni and the road leading to the Steel Creek Bridge are visible. You will pass a little lake nestled in the valley.

7.5K DOZER LAKE. There is a creek in the old-growth forest where you can camp. It is not advisable to camp near Dozer Lake as it is swampy and surrounded by deadfall. The road through the forest is easy to follow for most of the way, but near the far end it peters out. However it can be picked up again on the north shore of Dozer Lake, across from the island.

An overgrown trail continues to the end of the lake. There you can cross the inflowing creek on a log. Once across, carry on through a swamp and more forest before reaching South Lened Creek, where you will find an old snow-measuring stick. The road improves greatly from here.

14.5K LENED CREEK. Grunt up the steep hill and cross the plateau to Lened Creek. There is one good campsite at the creek with enough room for three small tents or two tents and a tarp. If needed, there is some room for a tent on the plateau. You may want to tent up there and have your kitchen by the creek.

16.5K HOT SPRINGS. Return to the plateau. Do not cross Lened yet, even though a branch of the winter road crosses here. We explored this road and it goes nowhere. You simply have to recross Lened Creek at a spot where it is far more difficult. Continue to the end of the plateau through willow that is about six feet high. This is easy walking through natural meadows along a winter road and on game trails. There are also tons of blueberries to eat. Across the valley above Lened Creek there are switchback roads snaking up the hill.

At the end of the plateau, cross Lened Creek to the hot springs, recognizable by the white rocks, the green vegetation, and a strip of hill that looks like an avalanche area. There are two very hot water sources coming from the mountain, but to date no one has dammed the water to form a pool. Calcium tufa mounds are starting to accumulate. Caribou and elk come to eat at the springs.

18.7K BASE CAMP ON ROAD. There are two roads from the springs to the switchbacks. Both are on the contour map. The road near the top of the springs goes north away from Union Carbide. Walk south, on the east side of Lened Creek, from the springs until you find a trail that swings left and up into the alpines.

The first road above the springs, the one that goes north, will lead to a ridge where Mount Wilson, Dozer Lake, and your route back come into view. If you have time for a sidetrip, leave your packs and continue on this road over the hills above the switchbacks until you reach some ridges that give you views of the cliffs along the east side of the Nahanni. It is a spectacular place to visit.

When you return from the sidetrip, continue on the road up Lened Creek Valley to the next side valley. This one will lead to an abandoned miner's cabin that has partially caved in. The cabin is a dot on the contour map. There is water and flat spots for a tent should you wish to camp here. The cabin could give some shelter if you got really wet and cold during bad weather, but the roof has collapsed onto the floor.

19.7K ROAD UP LENED CREEK VALLEY. The road continues south up Lened Creek Valley towards Union Carbide. Various switchbacks merge with this main road, so you may want to mark your way back. There is a small creek crossing where there is a branch road going east up that valley. It passes through a poplar grove. This is a good base camp from which to explore. There is no wood or water right at Union Carbide.

21.8K UNION CARBIDE. The road to Union Carbide will lead to a stack of core-sample racks. From here you can continue in numerous directions. If you follow Lened Creek up to the pass at the end of the valley, you will come to a little lake and then a valley that could go down to the Nahanni River. There is another lake near the headwaters of Lened Creek, in a valley to the left. This valley hooks up with the next valley, which eventually leads to the Nahanni, but this route is more difficult than following the pass east up from the Union Carbide site.

If you go up the valley from Union Carbide, you will traverse a lake on the pass and arrive at another site with core-sample racks. Going to the right will take you down the valley towards the Nahanni. We think this is probably the best way to go to reach the river.

25.9K LAKE PASS. Walk left (west) and hike up the scree slope to a pass that will lead back to your base camp or to another pass and ridge where you can see a huge lake and can almost see the Nahanni River. This area is littered with scree, but most of the walking is stable. The view over the pass towards the Nahanni is stunning and well worth the climb.

Returning to your camp, head down valley towards the rock glacier. You will soon be fighting your way through thick willows, but only for a short distance downhill.

28.4K BASE CAMP (FROM LAKE PASS) If you have made arrangements to be picked up at the Honeymoon Lakes or Rabbitkettle Lake, continue down to the Nahanni by following the valley south at the east end of Union Carbide Pass (as opposed to going west up the scree slope). This pass comes out above Bologna Ridge, across from the Honeymoon Lakes. If you did not arrange a pick-up, return by the same route as you came.

John believes that the Union Carbide hike is the easiest route to the Nahanni River, but I believe that going to the Cirque of the Unclimbables is the better route.

Epilogue

THE SUMMER FOLLOWING the events described in this book, Viv and I hiked out of Tungsten into Glacier Lake. We visited the Cirque of the Unclimbables, above the lake. A team of Austrian climbers was there, waiting for the weather to break so they could go onto the rock. They were playing cards and the harmonica, yodelling, and reading books. They were also searching high and low for their powdered cappuccino, part of a food drop they'd arranged that had hit a rock and exploded. We joined them for a couple of days, but the weather continued overcast and the powdered cappuccino remained lost, so we said *Auf Wiedersehen* and descended to Glacier Lake to make a permanent camp.

From there we were due to leave, in three or four days' time, by float-plane, back to the Flat Lakes and thence to the hot springs at Tungsten. But first we had to look for a cabin at the east end of Glacier Lake, a cabin that had burned down in 1936. The chance arrival of a guided tour off the Nahanni (two canoes, a guide, a cook, and four very happy trekkers) gave us our opportunity. We could use their old Grumman while they went up to the Cirque for two or three days.

The most likely spots at the lake's east end were on the south shore.

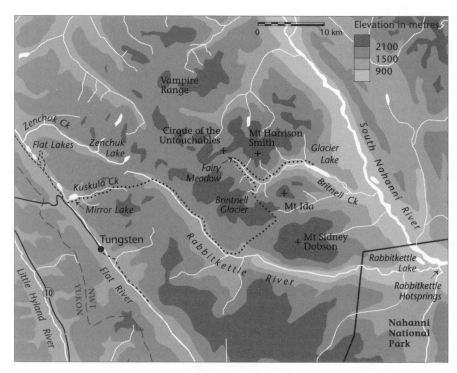

MAP 6: GLACIER LAKE

There we found some old iron, some notched and burnt logs, some old blazes on old trees. All very tantalizing, but not conclusive. What could we expect? Eppler's sunglasses? A fuel drum with DAL painted on it in red? Stuff like that would be long obscured by moss or hidden in bush or drowned as the lake rose and fell and changed its shoreline over the years. To do a serious job, you'd need to fly in with a metal detector, a shovel, and a trained archaeologist. You'd have to have a lot of time.

We contemplated a day's hike down to the Nahanni and back so I could dip my boot into the legendary river, but we were lazy after three weeks on the trail, and I rationalized that it was probably better for me if my arbitrary destinations, like the Nahanni or the location of Eppler's sunglasses, remain over the horizon and in my imagination.

The hike to Glacier Lake will be our last big hike from Tungsten to the Nahanni. We'll continue to haunt Tungsten, pedalling in from the washout and staying at the Flat Lakes cabin or Stefan's cabin, which we've saved (temporarily) from marauding porcupines. We'll ride the road to Howard's Pass one more time. But we're hanging up our boots. When you measure the extent and difficulty of a trip in terms of the number of Advil tablets consumed, it's time to call a halt.

We got to Glacier Lake because of the enthusiasm of former hiking companions who agreed to join us. I think they regarded it more as a rescue mission than a hike. Elsebeth Vinborg came from Denmark; we've lost track of the number of summers she's been with us in Kluane and Nahanni. Stephan Schiedermann and Mike King (with whom we'd done the Donjek in Kluane) came from Germany and Toronto respectively. Richard Lazenby and Carol Fairhurst, other Donjek veterans, came from Prince George.

Others took pity on us. Our next-door neighbors in Prince George, Len and Carol Johnson, helped in preparations for the trip. Harold and Virginia Lawrence, the new caretakers at Tungsten, came to get us through the washout on Highway 10 and fattened us up while we were relaxing in the hot springs prior to launching into the bush. There are some advantages to looking a little old, a little tired.

Viv is writing a book about the Glacier Lake hike, but she's letting me publish the trail description here. She says it's for our companions and others who might be interested in carrying on where we left off. Some of our companions were talking about going right down the Rabbitkettle to the hot springs, or about making a circle hooking up Kuskula and Zenchuk Creeks. There was talk, too, in the Tungsten hot springs and the Flat Lakes cabin, of finishing the hike through Union Carbide and of checking out Hole-in-the-Wall Lake and Valley.

This is the kind of talk Viv likes to encourage.

TRAIL INFORMATION

Cirque of the Unclimbables (Flat Lakes to Glacier Lake)

THIS ONE-WAY ROUTE could easily be completed in twelve to fourteen days. For those really gung ho, it could be done in ten. Estimate your likely time carefully and give yourself an extra few days. It would not be good to miss your return flight from Glacier Lake.

Your flight out must be arranged in advance. Piggy-back onto another flight that is going to Rabbitkettle Lake or the Honeymoon Lakes with canoers. That way the pilot can drop off the canoers, pick you up, and take you back to the Flat Lakes before making his return trip to Fort Simpson, Blackstone, or Watson Lake. It makes the cost less. We flew with Jacques Harvey of South Nahanni Airways, and the flight back to the Flat Lakes via a round-trip tour of the Cirque was worth the cost.

This hike should not be done with less than four people as there is no help along the way should an accident occur. We went in with six people and it turned out to be perfect. There were enough people to keep our humour up and the chores at a minimum for each person. This in turn kept us from getting too tired and having an accident. Also, weight is more efficient with two to a tent and with items like repair kit, first-aid kit, saw, stove, and pots serving everyone.

The route requires bushwhacking and route-finding abilities, advanced skills in river crossing, and the stamina to be in the bush for a long period of time. Once committed to this trip, there is no exit except possibly going all the way down the Rabbitkettle River to the lake, where there is a warden's cabin and a lot of river traffic, but that could be a tough hike.

The bushwhacking is difficult above Mirror Lake and moderate on the Rabbitkettle River. Some ascents are very steep and one descent is difficult. You will always be a long way from a rescue, so take care never to travel when tired, as that is when most injuries occur. Take your time and enjoy the sensational scenery. We averaged 8 kilometres per day.

TOPOGRAPHICAL MAPS: Shelf Lake 105-I/1 (1:50,000), Mount Sir James MacBrien 95-L/4, Mount Sidney Dobson 95-E/13, Dolf Mountain 95-L/3 (only for going to Rabbitkettle Lake)

EQUIPMENT NEEDED: You must carry enough food to last the two weeks of travel plus enough to hold you until your plane arrives. The flight could be delayed due to bad weather for up to a week, so plan for this possibility. Dehydrated soups are good for times when you are waiting, not working. Creek-crossing shoes are needed as the Flat River and Brintnell Creek are both long, difficult, cold crossings. The smaller unnamed creeks and the upper Rabbitkettle can be managed without shoes. Your tent must be leakproof and your sleeping bag must be warm. Expect snow on any one day and rain every day. On the other hand, you could have two weeks of blazing sun, in which case you will need lots of sunblock. The long days (about twenty hours of daylight) make sunny days extremely hot. The sun is directly overhead for many hours of the day. A location finder is nice but not necessary if your map-reading abilities are good. The landmarks are so extreme in this area that you should never be lost. Stove and fuel are necessary for at least three days of alpine travel where there is no wood. A nylon tarp makes rainy periods bearable. We spent a couple of rainy half-days under the tarp, and we waited two days for our plane to arrive. Part of that time was spent listening to the rain patter onto the tarp.

In this description I use map co-ordinates to give the exact location I am describing. Since this hike is not along a road, more exact locations are needed. The first number of the co-ordinates corresponds with the number of the horizontal line on the map; the second number corresponds with the vertical line. Their intersect is the bottom left-hand corner of the square on the map. The distances in this description are in kilometres and are approximate.

THE ROUTE

0.0K Leave your bikes in the cabin located at the Flat Lakes/Tungsten Road junction (Shelf Lake 79-35). Shut the door and close the back window so animals won't get at your gear. Walk almost two kilometres towards Tungsten to a curve in the road (Shelf Lake 76-36). From there go into the bush towards the cutbank on the other side of the Flat River. During the bushwhack you will encounter a couple of small creeks that will have to be jumped. If you go towards the river north of the cutbank you will have to slog through swamp. Once at the Flat River, walk upstream past the rapids and the curve to a wide section. The rocks are slippery and the water is swift. This difficult crossing will take time.

4.0K After crossing the Flat River, bushwhack your way up the hill. Veer slightly towards the lake but do not go down the slope onto the creek that drains the lake. Not far past that creek, and on the hill above the lake, is a cabin (Shelf Lake 77-37) partially eaten by porcupines. The cabin is a nice refuge if there is rain. There is a good stove and an axe. If you have started late in the day, the cabin is the best place to camp. When leaving the cabin, follow animal trails along the lake's south shore.

5.0K There are boulder-strewn slopes at the east end of the lake. These must be negotiated carefully, making it slow going. Stay low as much as possible. It is advisable not to go too high on the slope, as you must come down to get past some cliffs. Stay on the south side of the lake and creek. The bushwhacking starts in earnest between the hill above the lake and continues to the gravel bars on Kuskula Creek (Shelf Lake 78-41).

8.0K Before the gravel bars there is a waterfall and a small canyon that must be scrambled around. You must cross one skookum creek that comes down from the south. It is fed by the glacier above. Although there are some camping spots at the east end of the lake, the gravel bars on Kuskula Creek are recommended, as wood, flat spots, wildlife, water, and scenic vistas are abundant. Also, sleeping is better when bushwhacking is over. From the cabin on the lake to the gravel bars on Kuskula takes about six hours. Once on the bars we put on sandals and walked up the creek rather than in the adjacent bush.

13.0K At the upper end of Kuskula Creek are two glacier-fed lakes set in a moonscape (Shelf Lake 79-46). The glaciers are partly visible. The area is hospitable for a lunch break during sunny weather but bleak during rain. To reach the Rabbitkettle River, pass the two lakes and walk over the ridge directly to the north of the second lake. Once at the top, follow the creek, which you will see from the pass. There are camping possibilities along this creek. Stay on the north side of this creek; due to its water volume, you must cross the Rabbitkettle River above its confluence with this creek.

15.5k A deep canyon on this creek, with sheer cliff walls and a raging torrent of glacial water passing through, is your next landmark (Shelf Lake 80-49). Once close to the trees, pick your route and bushwhack down to the river. The Rabbitkettle Valley looks inhospitable and difficult, but in fact it is fairly easy when compared to the bushwhacking above Mirror Lake.

17.0k Cross the Rabbitkettle where the water is still clear and then cross the creek coming in from the north. (If you are walking this route from the Cirque, follow the Rabbitkettle River until its water becomes clear, as opposed to glaciated. Then go up and over to Mirror Lake.)

Once across the Rabbitkettle River, go directly up the gravel bank close to the edge of the creek and look for an animal trail. The one we found was so distinct I thought it must be an old horse trail used by prospectors (Shelf Lake 81-50). Follow this trail down the Rabbitkettle River, past numerous creeks, using the two large rock glaciers (Mt. Sir James MacBrien 80-53 and 76-56) that spew into the river as landmarks. The trail disappears near swamps, but it is well worth your time to drop your packs (with someone standing guard over them) and look for the trail again on the opposite side. The bushwhacking is horrid and slow without a trail. If unable to find it, go back to the river and cross into the bush in a diagonal direction until the trail crosses your line of walking.

29.0k This is the Rabbitkettle canyon (Mt. Sidney Dobson 73-58), which must be climbed around, but you need not go very high to get past. Once over the canyon, the river opens up and gravel bars become abundant.

30.0k Camping anywhere along these gravel bars is not only easy but delightful. Travelling downriver, continue in and out of the bush as necessary. Pass the curve on the Rabbitkettle and go down to the creek you will ascend to reach the plateau beside Mount Sidney Dobson (Mt.

Sidney Dobson 69-67). The valley across the way is wide and protected at its entrance by a distinctive pyramid-shaped mountain.

43.0K This creek is recognizable because of the two huge towers of sand-coloured stone with a passage in the centre that looks intimidating. The climb is steep and a few scree spots are slippery. Carry water. It will take from two to three hours to get up onto the plateau. Once out of the bush, the walking becomes much easier. From here to the descent to Brintnell Creek, you are in one of the most beautiful alpines I have ever seen.

48.0K There are camp spots on the plateau before the lake (Mt. Sidney Dobson 72-70), but if you can make it to the lake for camping, the scenery is spectacular. There is a hanging glacier at one end of the lake that occasionally drops ice cubes into the water. I have never been on such a stunning plateau. There is a grizzly who lives up here with her cubs, but she is wild and terrified of humans.

54.0K Skirt the second large lake (Mt. Sir James MacBrien 76-71) along its north shore and then cross diagonally over the hill beside the lake to the next creek. Do not go too high, because on that creek there are cliff walls that are not easily descended. This creek leads to Mount Ida and lies in a wide, open valley.

57.0K There is pleasant camping from the junction of the three creeks (Mt. Sir James MacBrien 78-71) all the way to the top of the main creek, which lies in the shadow of Mount Ida. Once on the large flat plateau beyond the headwaters of the creek, you will get your first view of the Cirque. It is from this plateau that Galen Rowell got his world-famous photo of Proboscis, one of the towers in the Cirque. You will also see Brintnell Glacier and Creek, including the wide gravel bars where the creek levels off. This is where you will cross Brintnell, unless you are a high-wire expert and want to try the famous log bridge (see **62.0K**)

58.0K Getting down off the plateau and onto Brintnell Creek is a challenge. The map is incorrect. The tiny rock glacier that is shown on the map (Mt. Sir James MacBrien 78-68) is not there. To get off this mountain, go to the vegetated arm at the northwest corner of the plateau.

Going down the creek bed on the west end of the plateau is intimidating and unsafe. The descent will take a few hours and in places packs may have to be lowered on a rope rather than carried. I lost the bum of my pants crawling down parts of this slope.

59.0k Once on the little valley below the hanging glacier, the walking becomes easier. Continue down the valley along the moraine beside the creek until you are in the bush. Then veer to the west until you hit a second moraine. This one is made of rusty brown boulders. Cross over that and descend to the braided washout of a tributary to Brintnell Creek. Once across the washout, go to the flats beside Brintnell. Camping is excellent anywhere along Brintnell.

62.0k Your trip is now just about over. Your last challenge is to cross Brintnell. If you go upstream you will come to a canyon with a log over the water. Some people are known to shimmy across, but the rushing torrent below is intimidating. We crossed downstream at the flats early in the morning, when the creek was at its lowest. You will need to navigate up and down the creek along gravel bars to get across, but it is possible.

67.5k The creek that runs down the huge granite face of Mount Harrison Smith (Mt. Sir James MacBrien 70-84) comes from the entrance to the Cirque of the Unclimbables and Fairy Meadows. Go up the talus slope along the edge of the grey perpendicular wall. It is a steep ascent among huge boulders that are often tippy, and it takes a few hours to reach the top. There are some cairns showing the best way to go. Coming down along this route is not recommended.

69.5k Fairy Meadows is exactly as its name suggests. It is a lush green meadow surrounded by huge pillars of rock and dotted with boulders the size of suburban houses. Walk through the meadow along a well-worn path towards the back of the Cirque, where there are two rock overhangs. Climbers have made these two places comfortable by placing rocks for chairs, hanging ropes for pack lines, and clearing flat spots for tents. The creek is close, but there are no toilet facilities, in spite of the area's large number of visitors. Be certain to hang your packs on the lines as the marmots and low-bush grizzlies will invade your gear, chew through your new $400 backpack, and eat your last chocolate bar.

Make this a base camp and explore the Cirque with daypacks. You may never be in a more spectacular place in your life.

75.0K To reach Glacier Lake campsite (and your flight out), leave Fairy Meadows by following the trail back to the upper creek crossing on the talus slope. From there, go into the bush and beat your way through the alder and willow to the spruce trees. It is a short (30 minute) bushwhack, but once in the forest there is no underbrush, the slope is gentle, and the vegetation underfoot makes walking easy. This route is much safer and quicker than descending by the boulders on the talus slope. Coming up this way would be difficult because fighting against the growth direction of alder is a nightmare. Going down this way means you never cross the creek flowing from Fairy Meadows.

Once down the steeper part of the mountain you will cross a trail or arrive back at the creek where there is a log to cross and a rope to hold on to. This is actually for those coming from Glacier Lake and going up to the Cirque. Follow the trail turning to your left towards Glacier Lake. At Glacier Lake there is a small cabin in which tents can be pitched. There is a large gravel bar in front of the cabin, with a clear water creek on each side of it. If you do not want to stay here, you may also cross the easterly creek and continue down the lake for a couple of hundred metres to a camping site tucked into the trees. The ground is flat and there are many flat spots. There is also an established firepit with rustic furniture around it. The planes like to unload here on the small beach.

Index